Dr. Gabrielle Morrissey formally began her career as a sexpert in 1990. She has worked as a sexuality educator and counselor in both Australia and the United States. She earned her Masters Degree in Human Sexuality Education from the University of Pennsylvania in 1995, and her Ph.D. in Sexology from Curtin University of Technology in Perth, Western Australia, where she now works as a lecturer and heads the Sexology program. Dr. Gabrielle also practices sex therapy in her private practice in Perth and conducts workshops across the country. As a sexpert, Dr. Gabrielle is often asked whether she ever gets tired of talking about sex. Her answer? Never!

Dr. Gabrielle has lived in Asia, America and Australia, and is half American and half Australian.

Also by Dr. Gabrielle Morrissey

Sex in the Time of Generation X

urge

Dr. Gabrielle Morrissey

Ultimate Bedtime Reading

Thorsons

Thorsons
An Imprint of HarperCollins*Publishers*
77–85 Fulham Palace Road,
Hammersmith, London W6 8JB

The Thorsons website address is: www.thorsons.com

and *Thorsons* are trademarks of
HarperCollins*Publishers* Ltd

First published in Australia by HarperCollins*Publishers* Pty Limited
This edition published by Thorsons 2002

10 9 8 7 6 5 4 3 2 1

A catalogue record of this book is
available from the British Library

ISBN 0 00 714932 8

Printed and bound in Great Britain by
Creative Print and Design (Wales), Ebbw Vale

Note from the publisher

The information contained in this book is not intended to recommend any illegal practice or the use of
any illegal controlled substances. Any application of the ideas and information contained in this book is
at the reader's sole discretion and risk. Equally, any prescribed medication should only be taken on the
advice of a qualified medical practitioner. Please remember that the legality of sexual practices varies
from state to state and country to country.

this book is dedicated to all the lovers
I have had the pleasure of,
for every urge felt, and every urge
exquisitely satisfied

"Foreplay"

My first real kiss was an exhilarating invitation into the world of sex.

I was not prepared for it, nor was I prepared for what it awakened in me. I was a pathetically naïve thirteen-year-old, with a massive crush on a fourteen-year-old boy, a "rebel without a cause" type who I was sure was the cutest human being created in the year 1970.

One afternoon, we were — gasp! — Alone In His Bedroom, so already I was dizzy with a sense of taboo. He leaned over and with what I thought at the time was absolutely no warning (remember, it was my first real kiss), he puckered up and planted his lips on mine. I went gooey and warm. Then he slipped his tongue in my mouth and I snapped my head backwards in a violent whiplash-style reaction. What the hell was that? His tongue?! Oh sure, I'd been told in graphic misinformed detail in girls' school toilets about French kissing, but let me tell you, at that point, with his tongue somewhere between sly and slick, halfway past my teeth, knowing something French and doing something French were two distinctly separate things. He smiled at me, realizing it was my first kiss and leaned in again. I silently vowed I would not be caught off-guard by this second attempt! As he began again his ooh-la-la moves on my lips, I became completely overwhelmed with the urge to explore his mouth with my tongue. I remember this first feeling, this urge. My body took over my mind. Or rather my body just took over, bringing to an immediate halt all logical thoughts and analytical observations. I was consumed with my sexual urge. I wanted to reciprocate pleasure, explore someone else's mouth and body, feel more, open more, experience more.

That first thrill of tongue awakened my sense of the sexual urge and I have been chasing it and catering to it ever since.

My approach to this book has been one much like that first kiss. I wanted to probe every corner of the sexual world, push the everyday ordinary buttons and boundaries of our understanding of sexual desire, and peel back our conceptions of sexual behavior to see what naughty secrets and neon passions lie under our masks and fancy dress. Peel, push and probe, peel, push, probe ... a kind of collective striptease sexposé of our carnal lives. I investigated the carnal lives of people around the world, conducting interviews with people mainly in Australia, but also in Europe and the US. Some of the language we use to talk about different things varies, especially with slang, but whether we shag, screw, have fannies or pussies, bums or butts, arses, willies or dicks, woodies or hard-ons, and whether we wank or jerk off, the issues are the same the world over. We are all sexy beasts and we all want, and deserve, to have satisfying sex lives.

In writing this book, I decided to stick out my tongue for another kiss, to take a titillating, twisted, flickering, salivating, piercing taste of our physical culture. I've kissed the girls, kissed the boys, and kissed the frogs. I've peeked through the keyhole into our collective bedrooms, and indulged my urge to then let that door just swing on open. I've peeped, I've kissed, and I've told.

Acknowledgments

One does not expect to write a book on sex, and do it alone. Certainly I didn't. The process of writing this book was an orgy of ideas, interviews, field research, favors asked for, and favors granted.

I sacrificed a lot of my Saturday nights writing about sex, rather than indulging in having it. I had to fit the writing of this book somewhere in my life and, sadly, Saturday nights it was. I never would have survived fifty-two-odd Saturday nights of celibacy, with a laptop as my only companion, if it hadn't been for my incredibly supportive and understanding friends and family.

I'd like to give sincere and grateful thanks to everyone at HarperCollins for backing me from the beginning, and sticking with me, every step of the way. Alison Urquhart, you are a star. Shona Martyn, Nicola O'Shea, Cheryl Rose, all the publicists, and everyone else on the team, thank you for all your enthusiasm and hard work.

My family members were the anchors that kept me grounded and sane through all the crazy times and strange places which the journey of this book took me to. I'm not altogether sure that I'm comfortable with the idea that my family is going to read some of the contents of this book. (Dad, please skip over the oral sex chapter, please, please.) My parents, Peter and Di Morrissey, I'd like to say you taught me everything I know, but we know that's not true (and thank goodness, given the contents of this book). You did teach me, though, about passion and the value of learning and listening with an open heart and an open mind, and I thank you and respect you for that. Nick, you're one amazingly patient brother to put up with a sexpert sister like me. We share a love of writing, and I want to thank you for always being supportive and proud. Aunt Rosemary and Uncle Jim, I am at a loss for words to describe my deep and profound gratitude for the enormous and selfless support you have shown me. I know of no one else who would have literally taken me in, and provided such a nurturing writing environment. You took care of me when I needed a quiet, focused space in which to write, and if it hadn't been for you, I'd still be writing this book.

To my friends, a huge, warm, appreciative thank you. You are sexy, beautiful, helpful and supportive creatures, every one of you. Tricia Duffield, Jeremy Bakker, Sasha Hayes, Cassie Hayes, Kate Irving, Sandra Macken, Peter Madden, Rebecca Agg, Tom Walker, Nick Jones, Kristin Little, and Jeff Hendricks. You gave me words of wisdom, listened when I was frustrated, urged me on when I was manning looming-deadline panic-stations, and some of you (I'm not telling who) gave me tell-all raunchy tales from below your belts for me to use and abuse. Smooches are deserved, and will be delivered.

A special thank you to David Haines for being my go-between into the world of pornography. Thank you for all the inside information, and for a most unforgettable and enlightening tour of brothels, sex shops and adult film industry locations.

A big thank you also to Professor John Croucher at Macquarie University for providing me with some fantastic sex statistics.

I especially would like to thank my informal "field researchers" who supplied me with their sexual secrets, naughty deeds, and deepest desires. You know who you are … and while you kissed and told, I swear to keep my promise to not reveal you, or those you kissed and told about.

Contents

Peckers, Boobs and Blast Off!

[*the body erotique*]

PENIS: dick, doodle, peenie, weenie, willy, winkle, winky, wowza, pecker, master member, limb, blue-veined custard chucker, donger, lance, purple-headed yoghurt slinger, sword, yang, tickle tail, lance of love, love dart, prick, cock, love torpedo, portable pocket rocket, spud gun, stick, glory pole, ramrod, wand, sweetmeat, banana, bacon, hairy sausage, love steak, buddy, Dr. Johnson, Jack, John, Johnson, little man, Moby Dick, old horny, Robin, General, hanging Johnny, blowstick, shaft of delight, joystick, jiggling bone, nob, one-eyed monster, Percy, schlong, fuck muscle, Cupid's torch, family organ, living flute, love pump, pink bus, trouser snake

ERECT PENIS: blue-veined root-on, boner, wood, hard-on, head, Irish inch, morning pride,

There is no evidence to suggest that men with huge noses, big hands or long feet have dongers rather than doodles.

stalk, stiffy, bugle, flag, guided missile, pink steel, prick pride, roaring horn

Peckers

The penis. Let's dive in head first and start with the obvious: size. We've all been told size doesn't matter, but when it comes right down to it, everyone wants to know what's normal and what's a "super-penis." Penises come in different shapes and sizes. Some hang left or right, others rise at an angle. This is normal. Men are naturally curious about how their package compares to others. A lot of surreptitious comparisons are made in locker rooms and urinals. Men, more often than not, compare their penis sizes when their penises are flaccid. This can lead to misleading concerns, because flaccid penis size can vary from man to man by many, many centimeters or inches. Penis size on full erection varies much less as most men have similar size penises on erection.

"Grow-ers" and "Show-ers"

Men are either "grow-ers" or "show-ers." Grow-ers are those men with short flaccid penises. As their penises become erect, the shaft grows much longer. The difference between their penis size soft and hard can be several inches. Show-ers are the donkey-boy types whose penises tend to hang long, even when flaccid. When their penises go from soft to hard, their length may hardly change. The penis simply fills with blood and becomes stiff, rather than longer. Never judge a softie; the stiffy is the key.

Size, Size, Size

Average Penis:

* As determined in scientific studies conducted by sex researcher Alfred Kinsey: 5.9 to 6.3 inches (14.75 to 15.75 centimeters long when erect.

* As reported in a composite of informal research and self-report questionnaires: 2.8 to 6 inches (7 to 15 centimeters) long when flaccid and 4.8 to 7 inches (12 to 17.5 centimeters) long when erect.

* Circumference: 3 to 5 inches (7.5 to 12.5 centimeters) when erect.

Largest Penis:

* As reported by Kinsey and Pomeroy studies: 10 inches (25 centimeters) long when erect.

* As reported by a composite of magazine surveys (unverified): 18 inches (45 centimeters) long when erect.

* Circumference (unverified due to self-reports): 6 inches (15 centimeters) when erect.

Smallest Penis:

* As reported by Kinsey studies: 1 inch (2.5 centimeters) long when flaccid.

* Very small penises (definitely those smaller than 1 inch [2.5 centimeters]) are usually regarded as a "micropenis" — a legitimate but rare condition.

Shrinkage

Penises are sensitive to temperature. In the cold, the penis will shrink up towards the body to stay warm. Some shrink so much they seem as if they almost disappear. The amount a penis shrinks up is completely individual, and the range is normal. Have no fear, he'll pop back out when the chill is gone.

Penises are like fish: the little ones you throw back, the big ones you mount!

GLANS: Bobby's helmet, helmet, Bobby's hat

FRENULUM: banjo string, bridle string, dick string

Parts of the package

The penis has some important bits on the outside, and on the inside. It's good to know the parts of the penis because if something goes wrong with it, you may have some idea of why it's "not well."

On the outside, the penis is made up of the shaft, the hood and the glans. The shaft is the body of the penis and makes up the length and width. The hood, or foreskin, is the piece of skin that is removed during a circumcision. The glans is the acorn- or mushroom-shaped head of the penis and is concentrated with nerve endings that make it sensitive to stimulation. Two very sensitive areas of the glans are the frenulum and the corona. The frenulum is the small stretch of skin on the underside where the glans meets the shaft. The corona is the smooth ridge of the head that separates the glans from the shaft. All of the parts of the penis

---

Measuring Up

Length: With a full erection, take a ruler and place one end firmly against your body, at the base of your penis, where the pubic hair is. With your hand, stretch out your penis along the ruler, straightening out any curves or bends. Read the measurement on the ruler at the tip of the glans of your penis.

Width: Using a measuring tape, get a full erection and circle the tape around the shaft.

---

are sensitive to touch (lick, squeeze, blow, caress, rub, kiss ... whatever tickles your fancy).

The main structures inside the shaft of the penis are three tubes that fill with blood during erection. The corpus spongiosum is the tube that runs inside the shaft on the underside of the penis. The corpora cavernosa are the two tubes that lie inside the shaft, side by side on the upper part of the penis. It is these two tubes that largely account for penile erection. Some erectile problems have their root here (the tubes don't, or have trouble, filling with blood). These three tube structures are spongy tissues that are dense with the blood vessels that allow for the engorgement of blood. When the penis is flaccid, these spongy tubes are collapsed; during sexual arousal they expand and fill with blood. Muscles around the veins at the base of the penis then contract to limit the amount of blood that is able to leave the penis. *Voilà,* erection.

Moby Dick: the blue whale, the largest mammal, has the world's longest penis, averaging 10 feet (3 meters) long.

Pecker problems

The most common pecker problems relate to sexual function, such as erectile dysfunction, low desire, premature ejaculation and orgasm difficulty. These are not simple problems so they are dealt with in detail in later chapters (see Speedy Gonzales, Little Boy Blue Lost his Wood and Gear Off).

There are, though, two problems that are rare, but important to be aware of, because if they ever happen you need to seek immediate medical attention.

Broken boner Even though the penis is not a bone, believe it or not, it can actually fracture. It's not easy to do, so even though you may experience severe pain at times in your penis, it does not necessarily mean your tool is broken. A penile fracture really only occurs when the penis is erect and rammed into a hard, inflexible surface. It usually happens quite by accident during rough intercourse, either by bashing against something like a bedpost, bedside table, or even a partner's pubic bone. If the penis has actually fractured, at the moment of impact there is usually an audible cracking or snapping sound. Naturally, this is scary and extremely painful, and if it ever happens you should go straight to the hospital. As embarrassing as it is, if you don't get medical attention right away, you will experience severe swelling and ongoing unbearable pain. Once diagnosed with a fractured penis, the broken tubes within the penis can be repaired by a doctor, and you will go back to normal sexual function.

Constant hard cock To some men and women, a constant hard cock is the ultimate fantasy. But in real life, it's a dangerous condition called priapism. A raging, throbbing erection that will not go away is cause for immediate medical treatment because it can lead to future erectile difficulties and dysfunction. Priapism occurs because of a blood drainage problem in the penis. Blood becomes trapped in the penis, producing prolonged erection, and this persistent engorgement can lead to pain, swelling, inflammation, and permanent damage to the circulatory system in the penis. Put your embarrassment to one side and get treated as soon as it occurs.

Remember: whether your willy is a weenie or a wowza, it's all about how you work it, baby.

TESTICLES: balls, bangers, bulbs, chimes, gongs, gonads, ding-dongs, danglers, goolies, happy sack, jizzbags, love apples, nuts, pounders, swingers, twiddle-diddles, velvet orbs, yongles, family jewels, bollocks

SCROTUM: ball-bag, bollock-bag, nutsack, purse, raisin, tadpole carrier, winky-bag

Balls

You can't play stick without the balls.

The testicles hang in the scrotum, the wrinkled sac of skin that hangs behind and below the base of the penis. The scrotum is very sensitive and it's also flexible and distendable. When pulled, tugged and squeezed (gently) it can produce feelings of intense stimulation. The surface skin of the scrotum is also sensitive, both to touch and temperature. When the scrotum is cold, it will contract up towards the body; when hot, it dangles down in the breeze. The scrotum also moves around during sexual stimulation. It will draw up tight towards the body prior to ejaculation. In fact, during the entire sexual arousal response, the scrotum and testes can contract and relax in a slow, wave-like movement.

The two testicles (testes) are each about the size of an almond and are egg-shaped. They should feel smooth, so if you ever feel a lump, get it checked. They hang at different heights, which is normal, so that they don't bump into each other, or produce pressure against each other. Even the slightest pressure can cause sharp and lasting pain. Usually the left hangs lower than the right, although the reverse is not uncommon. The testes manufacture sperm, and hormones that are responsible for sexual development and function. The testicles do not produce semen, which is why men still ejaculate after having a vasectomy. Semen is produced inside the body (see Juice section in this chapter).

The balls are not only the sperm makers, but also a site of primary sexual stimulation. When heading down, don't forget to play with those under-bits, because (almost all) men love it.

Blueballs

If a man experiences long periods of sexual arousal without the release of orgasm, he can experience mild to severe pain in his balls. This is known as blueballs, or love-nut pain. The solution, depending on the severity of pain, is to orgasm, but in many cases the pain will dissipate with time. While it's not in any way a pleasant feeling, it is not permanent.

ANUS: back-door, back eye, bumhole, butt pussy, chuff, date, flipside, moon, rosebud, third eye, round eye, trap two, workman's entrance, arsehole, batcave, blowhole, butthole, hole, ring, ringpiece, round mouth, round pussy, dirt road, flue, fudge tunnel, pooh chute, tan track

Flip Side

The anus is a word for which many of us like to use slang. Not all of us are comfortable with out-and-out talking about it, but the fact is, the arse, arsehole and perineum (the area of skin between the base of the back of the scrotum and the anus) are all areas of thrilling sexual pleasure for many men, straight and gay alike. The perineum, anus and anal canal contain many nerve endings which can be stimulated sexually. Back-door play is expressed in many forms, and a full explanation of the options are found in the sexual play chapters (see Blowing Kisses and Nude Twister, Anyone?).

SEMEN: juice, love juice, jizm, dicksplash, cum, cocksnot, goo, giff, lather, load, pearly passion potion, scum, snowball, splooge, spoof, spunk, wad, batter, cum juice, pearl jam, cream, dick drink, joy juice, love custard, man's milk

Juice

Most people think of sperm when they think of semen, but sperm makes up less than 10 percent of a man's love juice — the rest is just packaging for the sperm. There are between 120 and 600 million sperm in each average ejaculation — nearly enough, in theory, to repopulate the world. The remaining 90-odd percent of semen contains over thirty different substances which provide protection and nutritional energy for those hundreds of millions of sperm to survive the vaginal environment and make it to the end zone: the egg.

The seminal fluid (sperm-packaging juice) comes primarily from two organs found inside the body: the prostate gland and the seminal vesicles. As the sperm travel up from the testicles to the penis, the prostate and seminal vesicles release fluids which then join the sperm, and this ejaculate mixture then travels through and out of the penis. Prior to ejaculation, the Cowper's gland (also inside the body) releases a few droplets of pre-cum. The pre-cum neutralizes the acidity of the urethra which can damage or kill the sperm. Because men urinate out of the same tube that the ejaculate passes through, Mother Nature designed this system to protect sperm and enable the propagation of the species. Without the addition of these neutralizing pre-cum and seminal fluids, there might never have been an Adam or Eve Jr.

So what are these protective and energizing juices? The main ingredients are:

* Water.
* Simple sugars, to provide energy for the sperm.
* Alkalies, to buffer the acidity of the urethra and vagina.
* Prostaglandins, which cause contractions of the uterus and fallopian tubes, to aid the sperm to get to the egg.
* Vitamin C.
* Cholesterol.
* Zinc.

Semen is generally a pearly, milky-white to cream color. It can be yellower if a man has not ejaculated in a while. A pink to brown tinge in color can indicate the presence of blood. This is not cause for immediate alarm, however, if blood is persistently present in your semen, get it checked by your doctor as it could be a sign of infection or perhaps prostate cancer.

The average ejaculate is between 3 and 5 milliliters in volume, which is approximately a teaspoon, but the amount can increase if a man has not ejaculated for a while, or decrease if a man has experienced several consecutive ejaculations. In either case the volume of ejaculate will usually return to the normal amount by the next day. Extended foreplay can also increase the amount of ejaculate as prolonged sexual arousal gives the body more time to become stimulated and organs like the prostate then produce more fluid.

Despite the presence of sugars in semen, ejaculate is not fattening. Each ejaculate has between 5 and 25 calories, so swallowing will not make you fat.

Semen taste

The metallic taste many people describe of semen is probably due to the presence of zinc. In addition to tasting metallic, though, semen can taste salty, sour, sweet, or just plain foul. Experts do not agree on whether a man can affect the flavor of his semen by what he eats, however, people who have sucked a lot of cocks have offered up some key do and don't ingredients for tasty juice.

Yummy cum Ingredients that seem to enhance and improve semen tastiness: most fruits, including pineapple, kiwi fruit, plums, nectarines, oranges, lemons, limes, grapefruit, apples and mangoes; plus mint, parsley, green tea, lollipops and celery.

Funky spunk Ingredients that seem to make semen taste foul: tobacco, alcohol, drugs, red meat, chicken, garlic, onions, dairy, broccoli, Brussels sprouts, coffee, chocolate and, most especially, asparagus.

If you find it impossible to cut out the "nay" list of foods, there is a product offered on the web which claims to negate the icky taste of semen and make a man's love juice taste delicious. To find out more, visit *www.semenex.com*.*

---

* The author has not tested or researched this product and cannot endorse its claims.

If a good taste in your mouth is what you're after when blowing, it seems the solution is to suck a vegan, non-smoking, tee-totalling man's cock for spunk that doesn't taste foul.

Otherwise, deep-throat it, hold your breath and swallow thoroughly.

The Boy G-spot

Guys don't have a G-spot exactly, but since there is no sexual nickname for the prostate, some guys have hijacked the term G-spot to refer to the inner love button in men.

When it comes to arses, there are different strokes for different folks. Some guys like intercourse, some rimming, and some like their boy G-spot to be massaged. The prostate is a gland that has varying degrees of sensitivity in men, and some men love this area to be stimulated either before or during intercourse. Some men report intense orgasm when having their penis and G-spot stimulated at the same time. Others say their orgasm sensations last slightly longer and they ejaculate in a stream, rather than spurts.

Digitating your G-spot

Lie on your back either with your knees drawn up against your chest, or knees bent and your feet flat on the floor. The best digital appendix for access and leverage is your thumb. Insert your thumb and press it against the front wall of the anal canal (towards your belly). You will know when you have found your G-spot because it will feel like a firm mass, unlike the other wall tissue which will feel softer. Experiment with the type of motion that feels best — circular massage, pulses, hard presses, strokes — hey, whatever floats your boat.

Nipples

While nipples are generally thought to be a female erogenous domain, many men consider their nipples to be a prime sexual zone. Men have nerve endings in their nipples, just like women, however, the extent to which men find stimulation of their nipples arousing is as individual as it is for women. From light tickling to clamping, piercing, twisting and biting, every man is different in his degree of nipple excitement. Before heading down and under, try revving up the top rack.

Piercing

Described as a sex enhancer in the Kamasutra, piercing has a long history. In ancient cultures tongue-piercing was a way of humbling oneself before the gods; and nipples and genitals were pierced for aesthetics and eroticism. During the twentieth century piercing trends moved from the fringe dwellers to the punk culture, and are now embraced by the general public. People have become fascinated with piercing, and there are many theories as to why: some have to do with the expression of individuality in a culture of increasing anonymity, and others have to do with the desire to draw attention to one's perfection while at the same time mutilating or scarring it. Whatever the theories, a lot of men are having their penises pierced, and the why of it is all about sex.

Pecker-piercing

Piercing the penis is purported to enhance sensitivity. From rings to studs, there are many ways to pierce a pecker.

* Oetang: piercing through the foreskin or frenulum.
* Hafada: piercing a ring or stud through the skin of the scrotum.

* Guiche: piercing through the perineum (the skin between the scrotum and anus).

There is also a multitude of piercings that are placed along the shaft, base and glans of the penis.

* Prince Albert: one of the most common piercings, this is a ring placed through the urethra.
* Piercing rods can be placed vertically or horizontally through the urethra.
* Piercing rods can also be placed around the corona. Some men have more than one piercing on the ridge of their penis.
* Rings and rods can be pierced through the underside of the shaft towards the head or base of the penis.

FORESKIN: curtains, goat skin, opera cape, draw drapes

Foreskin

The foreskin, or hood, is the stretch of skin that covers the glans of the penis and is removed during circumcision. Circumcision is an ancient custom, still practiced today, but not without controversy. While in Australia 80 percent of boys were circumcized in the 1960s, that figure fell to about 10 percent in the 1980s, but is now increasing. Some circumcisions are done for initiation ceremonies and as a male rite of passage, while others are done shortly after birth for health or religious reasons. The idea that an uncircumcized penis reduces the risk of contracting sexually transmitted infections (STIs) and urinary tract infections is hotly debated. Additionally, there is no evidence that circumcision enhances sexual function or performance. The decision "to cut or not to cut" is largely an issue of cultural, religious and personal values.

Snip

How is a circumcision performed?

Modern circumcisions are often still performed without anaesthetic. Basically, a bell-shaped device is fitted over the foreskin-covered glans, and the foreskin is cut away around the ridge using a scalpel. The short-term effects are minimal, although there is no doubt that for such a quick snip, it is painful.

Stretch

There is a growing movement among circumcized men to reclaim or restore their foreskins. They believe their circumcisions are akin to genital mutilation and are angry that routine circumcisions are still performed today. There are several support groups and networks working to ban routine circumcision and provide therapies for circumcized men to restore their foreskins. It is not always possible to stretch the skin of the penis back over the entire glans, but there are men out there trying. A few of the Internet support groups are:

* NORM
* BUFF (Brothers United for Future Foreskins)
* NOHARM (National Organization to Halt the Abuse and Routine Mutilation of Males)
* RECAP (Reconstruct a Penis)

You can find these organizations, and others, online using a search engine. Also available online are various videos and products, such as "Tug Ahoy," that are designed to stretch the penile skin and restore a foreskin.

Mr. Big

No matter how many times you say it's not the willy but the working order, men are still curious about how to make a long schlong by surgery. There are actually two ways to make a penis larger: increase length and/or width. And while it's not necessary to go under the knife to achieve penile enlargement, many men wanting a permanent and lasting alteration opt for surgery.

Surgical penile enlargement

Technically known as phalloplasty, a penis can be made longer and wider through two procedures.

Lengthening the penis involves cutting the ligaments that connect it to the body. These ligaments are found inside the body, at the base of the abdomen, and are partially cut so that the penis can drop further down from the body, creating more length. To prevent the ligaments from contracting (and shrinking the length again after surgery), soft tissue is put between the cut ends of the ligaments. The whole procedure takes less than two hours. If the procedure is performed properly, there should be no nerve damage and the penis should return to normal function, although intercourse is forbidden for up to twelve weeks after surgery.

Widening the penis requires surgery on the shaft itself and is achieved by dermal fat grafting. The penis is removed from its sheath of outer skin through an incision made at the base of the penis. Fat, removed from the buttocks, is sewn in strips around the shaft of the penis under the skin. To wrap up, the new, fatter dick is slipped back into its skin sheath and then sewn up. A man must be circumcized to have this operation. It takes three hours and medicine is prescribed to prevent erection because hardening of the penis can break the stitches.

After surgery, the penis can look like it was smashed with a mallet, but within six months it should look normal again. Most men and their partners report being happy with their new Mr. Bigs, although, as with any cosmetic surgery, there are cases of disappointment or deformation.

Non-surgical penile enlargement

Not every man wants to go under the knife to enhance his pecker. There are surgery-free penis enlargement therapies and devices. Many of these use suction, stretching and even weights. These devices will not generally lead to permanent changes, but can give a man an ego boost or improve his body image if he has an issue with his cock size. A quick search on the web will lead you to many sites. To get you started, check out *www.penisimprovement.com*.

VAGINA: vag, cunt, poontang, Cupid's cave,
Venus's honeypot, box, cock pit, joy box,
love glove, home sweet home, love nest,
pole hole, glue pot, seminary, bullseye,
carnal trap, snatch, fuck hole, fun hatch,
fanny, glory hole, love hole, passion pit,
heaven, love canal, red lane, velvet tunnel,
front entrance, gate of life, way-in, garden
of pleasure, beaver, clam, pussy, gash, slice
of life, twat, cunny-warren, bunny, toolbox,
Cock Inn, groove

The longest vagina is 6 to 8 feet (1.8 to 2.4 meters) long, and can become even larger. It belongs to the whale, which makes sense, because it must receive a Moby Dick.

<u>Vag</u>

The vagina is shaped like a tube and is an elastic, expandable space. When not aroused, the walls gently touch each other; however during arousal these walls expand. The length of the average vag is 4 inches (10 centimeters). The inner two-thirds of the vagina have few nerve endings, and some women can barely feel stimulation there. The outer 1 inch (2.5 centimeters) or so has many more nerve endings that produce sexual sensations when aroused. The walls of the vagina are bumpy, rather than smooth. This is normal. These bumps on the lining of the vagina are called rugae. Just inside the opening of the vagina is a ridge of muscles which can tighten around the penis during intercourse. They contract during orgasm, as does the whole pelvic floor muscular system. Exercising these muscles can lead to a stronger, more intense orgasm.

<u>Pelvic floor exercises</u>

Also known as Kegel exercises, these can be done anywhere because no one can tell you're doing them. Squeeze the muscles, as if you are trying to stop a flow of urine, and pulse them both slowly and quickly. Many women find it simple to spend a few minutes doing this exercise daily while showering.

VULVA: down there, down under, fleshy part, naughty, the place, the bit, it, upright grin,

vertical smile, mouth, target, love flesh, muff, hairy doughnut, patch, lady flower, bearded oyster, fur pie, kitty, pussy, pink, mutt, mossy cottage, palace of pleasure, vertical cheeseburger, bearded oyster, cherry pie

Vulva

A lot of women refer to their vagina, when they actually mean their vulva. The vagina is the inside space, and the vulva is the entire visible outer area, including the mons veneris (also called mons venus or mons pubis), the pubic mound area that is usually covered by pubic hair; clitoris; labia (the inner and outer lips); urethra; perineum and anus. All those fleshy and hairy bits outside are part of the vulva.

You can remember the difference by knowing that *vulva* is Latin for wrapper or covering. Or just think the vag is the fucking-into part, and the vulva is the fucking-around part.

C-U-N-T: In Sanskrit, one of the ancient languages from which English derives, the female genital part we call the vag, or cunt, was called cushi. The Ancient Greeks called it cunnus, and then in Old English, it became queynt. Now we know it as cunt.

Source: *The Sex Chronicles: Strange-But-True Tales from Around the World*

CLITORIS: clit, bean, bud, bead, button, dot, joy button, love button, man in the boat, taste bud

Clit

The word *clitoris* is thought to come from the Greek for hill or slope or key, not button, as one might think.

The clitoris is the only organ in the human species designed specifically and purely for sexual pleasure.

News flash: the female love button is much more than that. It's not the size of a bean, bead or dot. It's much, much bigger. Just when men and women were becoming confident about finding and arousing it, it turns out there's much more to know about "the ol' man in the boat."

Anatomy of the almighty clit

Containing 8,000 nerve fibres, the clitoris is the most sensitive part of a woman's genitals and is composed of the same tissue as the glans of the penis. Most people think of the clitoris as being only the pea-sized knob of flesh just below the mons, where the inner lips meet. The clitoris, in actuality, is much more than just that one bit. It is made up of the glans, hood, shaft, legs, bulbs and muscles.

The glans is that button we all (mistakenly) consider to be the entire clitoris. In some women it only becomes exposed from the hood during arousal, whereas in others it is always partially exposed.

The hood is the fold of flesh that either partially or entirely covers the glans.

The shaft is located above the glans, under the skin. Press down on that area and you will feel a firm, moveable cord right under the skin that is highly sensitive to touch. In 1998, Australian urologist

Holy Clit!

Three-quarters of the actual clitoral size is hidden from view because it is under the skin. The size of the body of the average clitoris (including shaft and glans) is 1 to $1^1/_2$ inches (2 to 4 centimeters) in length. In a few women it has been known to be as large as $2^1/_2$ inches (6 centimeters) in length and almost 1 inch (2 centimeters) in diameter. When a clit is this size it can be as big as an average-sized penis, and can grow even bigger on erection, demonstrating the remarkable similarity in tissue between the penile glans and clitoris.

Helen O'Connell discovered that the glans of the clitoris is attached to a pyramid-shaped area of erectile tissue, about the size of the top half of a thumb. This area swells with blood during arousal and is very sensitive. This discovery helps to explain why some women can come by stimulation of the area around the glans alone, without the glans ever being touched.

Attached to the shaft are the legs of the clitoris. These spread backward into the body and attach inside to the pubic bone. They are between $3^1/_2$ and $4^1/_2$ inches (9 and 11 centimeters) long. Because they go deep inside the body, you can't feel them, but they do become aroused and fill with blood during the sexual response.

The bulbs of the clitoris are bundles of erectile tissue that extend down the sides of the outside of the vagina and encircle the urethra.

The legs and bulbs are surrounded by muscles, so when you contract your pelvic floor, all the muscles create tension and increase sexual arousal and orgasm.

So the love button is not actually a button at all, but more of a network of sensitive erectile tissues. All the parts of the clitoris swell with blood and become firm and aroused during sexual excitement.

Girly hard-ons

Because all the parts of the clitoris are composed of erectile tissue, they become engorged with blood during arousal, just as the penis does. In many women, the clitoral glans can become noticeably erect. It can increase in size, or just become harder. This is normal and the erection subsides after orgasm, as it does with men.

There is one dangerous condition of prolonged clitoral erection, called clitorism. Like priapism of the penis, extended erection of the clitoris can hamper normal blood circulation and lead to tissue damage. If you ever suffer from a painful or prolonged erect clitoris, see your doctor immediately.

LABIA: dew flaps, chicken wings, fish lips, fuck flaps, garden gate, passion flaps, saddle bags

Lips

The inner lips (labia minora) and outer lips (labia majora) of the vulva are the fleshy flaps of sensitive skin that fold over the opening of the vagina. The inner lips are much thinner than the outer lips, and are hairless. The outer lips are covered in pubic hair on the outside, but not on the inside portion, and are very fleshy. The lips are very sensitive to touch, and during arousal will become engorged with blood, darken in skin tone and move apart slightly to reveal the vaginal opening. The lips are the anatomical counterpart to the scrotum in men, and the degree to which women like their lips stimulated is as varied as it is for the all the ways men like their scrotums touched, tugged, licked and tickled.

G-spot

The G-spot has become a famous little organ in the female vagina, named after Dr. Ernst Gräfenberg, who discovered it in the 1950s. The jury is still out on whether all women have a G-spot, but it seems a lot of women do, and most of these women get great sexual satisfaction from its stimulation. It is a small mass of spongy tissue, about 2 inches (5 centimeters) inside your vagina, on the front wall, near the base of the urethra.

Finding the spot

It is best to sit or squat. Insert a finger inside your vagina and begin pressing firmly against the front vaginal wall (pressing up towards your belly). You will feel a firm spot about the size of a small bean, and when you press it, initially you may feel the urge to pee. If you keep stimulating the spot, that sensation will pass and the area will begin to become erect and feel pleasurable. Some women say that stimulation of their G-spot results in an orgasm that is felt deeper in the body than a clitoral one. It is more difficult to come from stimulation of the G-spot than the clitoris, but manual stimulation seems to be the most successful route. Intercourse positions such as rear-entry and woman on top can also enable the penis to rub against the G-spot, but it depends on the woman and the exact location of her G-spot.

A-spot

Sex researchers have recently discovered another supersensitive little area in the vagina known as the A-spot. If you're thinking, "A-spot? Come again?," well, you've hit the nail on the head. Technically called the Anterior Formex Erogenous Zone, the A-spot is located on the front wall of the vagina, like the G-spot, only higher up — about a third of the way down from the cervix. The theory around the A-spot is that stimulation of this little area increases vaginal lubrication and sexual pleasure. Researchers have found that among some women the stimulation of this A-spot increases moisture and helps women feel sexier and more turned on, which in turn helps them relax — and then they find it easier to orgasm.

If the jury is still out on the G-spot, then the jury is still in very early deliberations about the existence or pleasure potential of the A-spot. But, if you're curious, try finding and testing it out for yourself.

Finding the spot

Insert several fingers inside your vagina (it's better if your fingers are lubed up) and reach up until you can feel your cervix, which should feel like a firm, flexible lump at the top end of your vagina. Then slide your fingers down a few centimeters (an inch or so) along the front wall (belly side) and you'll feel a smooth area that's very sensitive. That's your A-spot and you can stimulate it best by stroking it vertically. If you want to try to stimulate it during intercourse, try a deep-penetrating rear-entry position.

VAGINAL LUBRICATION: vag lube, bitch butter, cream, cum, drippings, crotch oil, French dip, love juice, honeypot butter, girly goo

Vag Lube

During sexual arousal the walls of the vagina engorge with blood and release tiny droplets of lubricant which combine to form a slippery fluid. The amount of lubricant a woman produces during arousal varies from woman to woman, and throughout the life span — it can decrease during and after menopause. Vaginal lubrication helps the penis enter the vagina, but it also keeps the vagina moist, the walls healthy, and maintains the chemical balance in the vagina.

Some of the ingredients in vag lube are cervical mucus, exfoliated cells, vaginal wall secretions, lactic acid, complex alcohols, cholesterol and various other acidic compounds. The smell and taste of vag lube differs from woman to woman and depends on the chemical balance. Men and women who go down on women can like or dislike the smell and taste of a woman's love juice. As with semen, some argue the taste can be altered by diet. There is little research on the success and validity of this, so if cutting out nicotine, alcohol, meat and asparagus isn't your cup of tea, there are plenty of flavored lubes around that you can buy, or you can dribble something like mango juice around the vulva and have yourself a tasty snack.

PUBIC HAIR: bush, cunt curtain, fleece, fluff, forest, front-door map, fuzz, lawn, mossy bank, muff, pubes, pussy hair, short and curlies, snatch thatch, stubble, sweet briar, tail feathers, lady's low toupee, map of Tassie, tuft

Pubic Hair

The pubic hair covers the mons and outer
lips, and can spread out to the upper thighs.
Most women shave or wax some portion of
their pubes, at least in summer, and some
women wax or shave it all off (beware the
itchy regrowth). Waxing — the end result,
not the process — can be an artistic and
erotic expression of your sexiness. Women can
get a simple bikini wax, or a pussy wax in
which the hair is shaped into various designs,
such as a heart, racing car stripe, lightning
bolt, or whatever catches your imagination
and makes you feel sexy.

Anus

As with men, a woman's anus contains many
nerve endings, and can arouse sexual pleasure
when touched. Women can enjoy light or hard
stimulation, such as fingering, rimming,
sucking or tickling. Experiment with what feels
good. If you or your partner have never tried
stimulating this area before, give it a try —
you might delight in new, previously undiscovered pleasures.

Female Genital Alteration

Altering the genitals of women is often controversial. Female
genital alteration procedures, as described below, are undergone
voluntarily, for the purposes of decoration and *increased* sexual
pleasure. Most women wouldn't dream of letting a scalpel or

needle near their vulva, however there is a growing number of women who want to modify their clitoris and lips.

This should not be confused with female genital mutilation (FGM), which involves circumcision of the clitoris to reduce sexual pleasure. FGM is widely regarded as a criminal offense, but it is a practice still performed across many cultures and religions. It is a subject not in keeping with the focus of this book: details are readily found in news reports and other relevant books.

Piercing

Piercing the parts of the vulva is done for two main reasons: sexual pleasure enhancement and decoration. For women who have never appreciated the beauty of their genitals, piercing can be a means of celebrating their femininity and making them feel sexy. Clitoral glans piercings are rare, but provide a completely new level of sexual sensation during masturbation and intercourse. More commonly, piercings are placed through the clitoral hood, or along the inner or outer lips. Genital piercings can create intense sexual stimulation during sexual activities, or even just through the rubbing of the piercing against clothes as one sits or walks. This constant stimulation can create irritation in some women, who then remove the jewelry and put it on only when about to engage in sexual play. The majority of women with genital piercings report that they experience orgasm easier and faster than they did before they were pierced because the rings or rods make for easy manipulation of these sensitive tissues.

As with any surgical procedure, there are risks of infection with genital piercing, so if you are considering piercing an area of your vulva, be sure to visit a qualified clinic or piercing parlor.

Plastic surgery

Female circumcision While female genital plastic surgery is not as well known or discussed as genital piercing, it is gaining new vogue. The most common surgical procedure is a "female circumcision," which is the removal of the clitoral hood. Generally, women who have this procedure request it because their clitoral hood completely covers the glans of their clitoris, which prevents access for direct stimulation. Most women have a clitoral hood that retracts from the glans during sexual arousal, however some women feel their hood does not retract far enough, and like to have the hood removed wholly or partially to allow for greater glans stimulation. Most sex therapists agree that in any shape, a woman's clitoris is fine the way it is. In fact, the presence of the hood is seen as essential in most women because it protects the glans from too much stimulation. If a glans receives constant stimulation it often results in a great degree of pain. Regardless, some women opt for surgical alteration. Women thinking of undergoing this procedure should seek counseling first to determine whether their reasons for this surgery are healthy. Afterwards, a woman and her partner will need to learn new masturbation and sensory techniques as the exposed glans is extremely sensitive. No one should ever take the decision to have this operation lightly as it cannot be reversed.

Labioplasty In addition to the removal or alteration of the clitoral hood, the inner lips can be surgically altered in a procedure called a labioplasty. While it is completely normal for the inner lips to be uneven in size and protrude outside the outer lips, some women are bothered by the shape and size of their inner lips and request surgical alteration. Others complain of having long inner lips that get drawn into the vagina during intercourse, or pinched by the penis as it slides in and out of the vagina. These women want to reduce the size of their labia to prevent this kind of pain during sex. Most surgeons who perform labioplasties require counseling for the patient prior to surgery.

Mons liposuction Some women choose to have fat removed from their mons, the pubic mound area, to make their outer labia and clitoris more prominent. This is sometimes done for aesthetics, but also to make the clitoris protrude further and enhance sexual stimulation during intercourse. This is a relatively new procedure and not all plastic surgeons will agree to perform it without a medical reason.

Steroids

While rare, some women desire a larger clitoris and are prepared to use steroid creams to achieve it. The clitoris is made up of the same erectile tissue as the penis, so it does respond to steroids. Women who regularly use a steroid cream directly on their clitoris will eventually see that their clitoris has enlarged, and may even take on a penile glans shape. Another effect of using steroids on the clitoris is that the clitoral erection will be more pronounced. There is no evidence, however, that a larger clitoris or bigger girly hard-on results in a more intense orgasm.

Female body-builders who use steroids may notice that their clitoris becomes larger and more sensitive to stimulation. This is a side effect for any woman taking steroids. Other side effects such as heavy body hair, aggression and a deep voice are not so desirable. If a woman stops taking steroids, or stops applying steroid cream to her clitoris, the clitoris will shrink in size, but depending on the length of time spent on steroids, it may never return to its pre-steroid-affected state.

Vacuum

Some women desire an enlarged clitoris temporarily, so they use a vacuum pump device placed over the clitoral glans to suction it out of the hood and draw blood into the glans. After suctioning, the glans becomes very sensitive, but it is not a permanent alteration. Some suction devices are very strong and can lead to tissue damage. When shopping for a clitoral vacuum device (and there are many options available online), make sure that the product has been endorsed by a qualified medical practitioner.

NIPPLES: berries, buttons, eyes, raspberries, nips

BREASTS: boobs, chest flesh, globes of joy, handles, headlights, hangers, hooters, knockers, puppies, top set, tatas, tits, milk jugs, udders, grapefruit, lollies, bazookas, coconuts, fun bags, honkers, melons, party tits, shoulder boulders, rack, bongos, bouncers, pair, flight deck, dollies

Boobs

There has probably never been a culture in history that has not appreciated the female breast. Aside from nourishing infants, the breasts can be highly erogenous for many women. During arousal, the breasts, nipples and areola (the dark area around the nipple) become darker in skin tone. Some breasts swell in size, although this is more common in women who have not had children. Most women experience nipple erection, although a lack of erection does not mean a woman is not turned on. Because the nipples are separate from each other, it is quite common for only one to be erect. In fact, many women report that one nipple is more sensitive than the other.

🗣 *"It was so embarrassing. I always thought I was abnormal. My left nipple will stand to attention at the drop of a hat, but the right takes much more work. I felt so lopsided, but my partner and I have now turned it into a joke. We call one Miss Ever-Ready and the other Miss Take-Her-Time. My partner finds it a challenge to get Miss Take-Her-Time erect, and I don't mind the attention one bit."* — woman, 28

Boob play: although 90 per-cent of women report that their partners like to fondle their breasts during foreplay and intercourse, only 50 percent of women actually like it.

Source: *Cosmopolitan: Over 100 Truly Astonishing Sex Tips*

Breast augmentation

Breast augmentation, either breast implants or a breast reduction, is one of the more common plastic surgeries performed today. Breast augmentation surgery became available in the 1960s and has since developed into a relatively simple procedure. There are risks and benefits associated with it, which should be discussed with a surgeon before proceeding.

🗣 *"My wife opted to have her breasts reduced and, while I sometimes miss those big mounds of flesh, I understand that they hampered her exercise and active lifestyle. And to be truthful, it hasn't affected our sex life at all. I think she's just as sexy as she always was. Probably sexier, even, because she feels happier and it shows."* — man, 34

"After my divorce I wanted to make a change. I took my life savings and did two things: I moved interstate and got breast implants. I've never felt more in control, more feminine, or sexier. It was the best way to spend my settlement, and afterwards I felt confident and proud. I found a new man, and he knows my breasts have been surgically altered. But he says he still loves me for me. My new breasts were done purely for me, not for a man. I love them and wouldn't trade them for anything." — woman, 41

"I wanted to have larger breasts. I never really disliked my breasts, but I felt out of proportion. I'm a size 12 and have A-cup breasts. I thought having at least B- or C-cup breasts would even out my proportion. I went to have a consultation with a surgeon, and while I do believe the procedure is safe, going through the consultation made me see the superficial nature of the whole thing and I decided that I didn't need to change myself. I'm learning to like my shape, including my breast size, just as it is." — woman, 20

ORGASM: come, cum, thrill, the big O, final gallop, pop the cork, get home, paradise strokes, melt, pleasure pulses, let go, get off,

blow the load, blast off, release the build-up, shoot the wad, ring the bell, make the chimney smoke, gland finale

Blast Off

The Oh … Yes … Yes! Is it in the mind, or the body? Well, as it turns out, both.

In women, sexual arousal is characterized by increased blood flow to the genitals, dilation of the vaginal walls, lubrication, skin flush, muscle tension, heart rate increase and engorgement of the clitoris and outer one-third of the vagina. In men, the penis swells and hardens with blood flow, the skin around the genitals deepens in color, the muscles tense, the scrotum pulls up and the erection grows rigid. Before ejaculation, there is a sensation of not being able to hold back anymore, known as "ejaculatory inevitability." In both women and men, this erotic and tense build-up is released at orgasm, peaking in waves of pulsing pleasure. Technically, these pleasure pulses occur at intervals of 0.8 seconds in both women and men.

If orgasm were only about muscular contractions, though, it would not be the sexual highlight we all crave and enjoy. The magic of orgasm is that it scopes beyond the body and goes into our minds. Neurologists have found that during orgasm there is a release of electrical energy in the part of the brain called the

Jug jiggling: famed sex researchers Masters and Johnson discovered in their research that 1 percent of women are able to masturbate to orgasm simply by stimulating their breasts.

Source: *Practical Encyclopedia of Sex and Health*

limbic cortex. This is the brain's pleasure center, and also the area of the brain that controls awareness, which may explain why people sometimes describe orgasm as entering an altered state of consciousness, time and space.

But even beyond body and mind, orgasm enters our emotional state, often making us feel flushed with connection, whether for a moment, or a lifetime. This kind of connection is not felt by all, every time, but the capacity is there for orgasm to be a uniting, ecstatically shared experience.

Pleasure's purpose

Clearly, when it results in ejaculation, as it commonly does, male orgasm has the evolutionary purpose of propagating the species by releasing sperm to reach the egg. But what about the female orgasm? What is its purpose? Certainly women do not have to experience orgasm to get pregnant, so why does orgasm exist in women at all?

The answer to this question produces many debates, but there are three primary theories. One is that the clitoris was designed biologically to make sex pleasurable, thus encouraging women to have intercourse with males to ensure the ongoing propagation of the species. A flaw in this argument is that the clitoris is ill-placed for stimulation during intercourse. A counterargument is that before humans became civilized, it was important for only one partner to lose themselves in pleasure at a time, so that the other could be on the lookout for potential dangers.

The second theory argues that the position of the clitoris encouraged humans, over evolutionary time, to engage in intercourse in a face-to-face position, leading to a connection between male and female which would help fuse a bond between the man and woman having sex, and result in an inclination to raise the resulting children together.

The third theory is more physical and poses that muscular contractions experienced during orgasm in the female cause the cervix to dip down into the seminal fluid, helping to suction up sperm into the uterus and fallopian tubes. During orgasm, the vaginal walls also expand, creating a space in which the cervix is the "bullseye" for the sperm to reach.

Whether female orgasm is about pleasure, bonding, sperm motility and encouragement, or all three, the bottom line is it feels grrreat.

Orgasm for men and women may have evolved to ensure human reproduction, but it has the best side effect of all — undeniable, intense, melting ... oh yes, oh, oh, unh, unhh, aawheeuuuuwaheeeeaawngh ... pleasure!

Apparently Carnivale isn't the only show in which Brazilian women perform well: a 1996 Brazilian study revealed that 44 percent of women there have faked orgasm.

Source: *The Penguin Atlas of Human Sexual Behavior*

Deconstructing "Sally"

In the unforgettable scene in the film *When Harry Met Sally*, "Sally," played by actor Meg Ryan, demonstrated how convincing faking an orgasm can be. Both men and women can fake orgasms without their partner ever realizing the truth. The statistics on how many women and men fake orgasms are mysterious and unreliable precisely because those who fake it are not likely to admit to doing it, or to the frequency of doing it.

Faking orgasm occasionally is not always a bad thing. If they are tired or not enjoying sex, many women and men express a

The Big O

★ Only 26 percent of women report
reaching orgasm "all the time"
during sex; 43 percent fake it and
13 percent have never felt the
O with their current partner.

★ 78 percent of men versus
64 percent of women consider
the big O important to their
sexual pleasure.

★ Given these relatively low
numbers, there is evidently a
need for increased practical
information on sex and orgasms
— even for the sexually savvy
seduction masters.

Source: *Sex Life Survey,*
Courier-Mail, 2001

quick fake orgasm to finish intercourse. Once in a while, this is
natural and forgivable in a relationship, especially if you're honest
about it. If, however, you begin a relationship by faking orgasm, your
sex life with this partner will probably never improve, because they
will not know that what they are doing isn't stimulating. Similarly, if
you begin faking with a regular partner, your deceit will make you
the loser in the long run. Faking to make your partner feel good may
increase their ego, but it's your sexual pleasure that suffers, and when
you do get honest it will be an extra blow to your partner's ego and
can destroy the trust you have in the relationship. Many men and
women feel faking orgasm is a lie, so it is wise to be careful and think
of the consequences before you do it. Sex therapists agree that
preferable to faking is talking to your partner about why you didn't
come. Sometimes your inability to come has nothing to do with your
partner, but a lot to do with your personal stress levels or emotional
connection. Being honest with your partner will lead to a more
satisfying experience than doing a "Sally" every time.

"I've only faked an orgasm once and my girlfriend never knew. I was definitely turned on, but I was tired and I knew it wasn't going to happen. As soon as she came, I faked. My erection went down quickly and she never suspected. I didn't feel bad because it was only the one time. I'd never make a habit of it — it's not worth the trouble." — man, 29

"I am an expert faker. I find it really difficult to come through intercourse, so I just fake it. I guess I do it so the guy feels reassured that I'm enjoying myself. I love penetrative sex, even without coming, but I've found guys want to have me experience that release like they do. But I just don't. I only really come from a guy fingering my clitoris. When they do that, I never have to fake. So I really only fake during sex, and if I've already come from him playing with my clit, then I don't feel bad about faking an orgasm during sex." — woman, 31

Gland Finale Note

While the sexual response is designed to culminate in an orgasm, it is possible for men and women to train their response to result in multiple orgasms. For further information on this, see The Energizer Bunny chapter.

Rubber Dicky

[*safe sexy bits*]

Since at least the beginning of recorded history, humans have been concerned with preventing pregnancy and disease. Using methods ranging from the superstitious to the scientific, women and men have been trying to work out the best way to enjoy sex while controlling fertility. The methods outlined in this chapter are the most common contraceptives used today. Each has its benefits and drawbacks, and couples may choose to use different methods over time, depending on their life circumstances, and the strength of their desire to either avoid pregnancy or become pregnant in the future. If you are not in a monogamous relationship, or you and your partner have not been tested for STIs, including HIV, condoms are always recommended — either alone, or in conjunction with another method.

Dick Sheaths

Male condoms are tubular, stretchy devices generally made of thin latex, designed to cover the erect penis and prevent semen from entering the vagina. Some of them are rounded

Pregnancy Prevention Fallacies

* Prostitutes in first-century-BC Greece believed that grinding their pelvises during sex not only increased pleasure for men, but also encouraged sperm away from the womb.
* Second-century gynecologists believed that if a woman held her breath and arched her body back when a man ejaculated, the sperm could not reach the womb. Afterwards, she was encouraged to sit with her knees bent and sneeze several times to ensure the prevention of pregnancy.

at the top, and others have a reservoir tip added especially for catching ejaculate.

For condoms to be effective, you must remember to keep them handy, watch their expiration dates and put them on and take them off properly. A very small percentage of men and women report some allergic reaction to the spermicidal lubricant on condoms. Only ever use water-based lubricants with latex condoms. Oil-based lubricants break down the composition of latex and allow for the transference of STIs and HIV. There are plenty of water-based lubricants available, even flavored ones, from pharmacies and sex shops.

Condoms are effective against STIs and HIV for both vaginal and anal penetration. If you use a condom during anal sex, and want to switch to vaginal penetration, it is wise to take it off and use a new one. Using the same condom can lead to the transfer of bacteria from the anal canal to the vagina, which isn't always healthy for the vagina.

Advantages:

* Readily available in grocery shops, pharmacies and vending machines in men's and women's toilets in bars and clubs.

* Relatively cheap.
* Protect against most STIs and HIV.
* Proven to be an effective method when used properly.

Disadvantages:
* Partners need to be motivated to put one on.
* Can interrupt the spontaneity of sex.
* Reduce sensitivity of skin-to-skin contact.

Animal protection

Not all condoms are made of latex. Although latex condoms are the only male condoms that protect against HIV and some STIs, if you and your partner have been tested and cleared of HIV and all STIs, you may prefer using animal-skin condoms. Lambskin condoms are the most common. They are usually thinner than latex condoms and allow for greater sensitivity. Do not use these condoms if you are unsure of the HIV status of your partner.

Decorative sheaths

Condoms are not always used for contraception. Some of the gimmicky condoms often seen in the humorous sections of sex shops are simply for decoration or fun. They enhance an erotic experience by making sex a bit of a giggle. Some condoms come with decorative jewels, stickers, feathers, animal faces, and other "add-ons." These are for pure entertainment value. Do not use decorative condoms for true contraceptive or STI protection. And if the instructions on the box of a gimmick condom indicate it is not for vaginal or anal use, *follow these directions*. Allergic reactions could result, or some of those fun "add-ons" could not-so-funnily get lodged in the vaginal or anal canals.

Prophylactic Phacts

* The first dick sheaths were used by men in ancient Egypt, not for contraception, but for decoration, and as protection from insects and disease.
* The invention of the condom is attributed to Gabrielo Fallopia of Italy in 1564. It was a moistened linen sheath, tied at the base with a red ribbon, and was recommended for protection against STIs.
* Charles Goodyear invented the vulcanization of rubber in 1843, enabling condoms to be made from rubber. Prior to that condoms were made from animal intestines.
* Some attribute the word *condom* to Dr. Condom, court physician to King Charles II (1160–85), who was knighted for fashioning a sheath to protect the king from siring illegitimate children; however, most agree the "real thing" wasn't invented until 1564.
* Some say the name *condom* comes from the French town of Condom in Gascony.
* Others believe the word *condom* comes from the Latin condere, meaning to cover up, protect or preserve.

<u>Putting a condom on correctly</u>
Basic rules

* Place it over the head of the penis and roll it down towards the base.
* Hold the tip so no air gets in it (this can cause it to break).
* Never unroll it before putting it on the penis, or roll it on inside out.
* Hold the base of the condom afterwards, when pulling out of the vag.
* Save the environment and do not flush condoms down the toilet.

* If you're inexperienced with condoms and need to know more than this, most condom packages come with an instruction guide.

Before you start mouthing off about how you don't want to use a condom, make it an erotic experience, by mouthing-on the condom. With a little practice, anyone can use the "Look Ma, no hands!" method of putting a condom on. Partners: put the unrolled condom between your lips, tip facing in towards your mouth and open end facing out. Move your mouth over the head of the penis, and using firm but soft lips, slowly roll the condom down the shaft. If you don't want to deep-throat it, some final unrolling at the base with your fingers might be needed.

Ribbed condoms are great for the lady, but turn one inside out and they're stimulating for the guy. (Be sure to add some lube to the inside of the inside-out condom.) This is only recommended if using a secondary contraception method.

> *"I want to tell you a terrific story about oral contraception. I asked this girl to sleep with me and she said 'no'."*
> — Woody Allen

Bumper Stickers for the Bump'n'Grind

* If it's not on, it's not on.
* If you're entering venus, dress up your penis.
* Cover your stump before you hump.
* Don't be silly, protect your willy.
* Don't be a fool, vulcanize your tool.
* Before getting drastic, wrap it in plastic.
* If you slip between her thighs, be sure to condomize.
* If you think she's spunky, cover your monkey.

* When in doubt, shroud your sprout.
* If you go into heat, package your meat.
* Before getting laid, wrap your spade.
* If you can't shield your rocket, leave it in your pocket.
* Never deck her with an unwrapped pecker.
* You can't go wrong if you shield your dong.
* If you're not going to sack it, go home and whack it.

Legend has it that women in ancient Rome used goat bladders as an internal vaginal sheath to prevent pregnancy.

Vag Sheaths

The female condom is a loose polyurethane sheath with a flexible ring at each end, which is inserted into the vagina. Since it is relatively new, the jury is still out on whether women and men consider this method a pleasurable and reliable contraceptive. For those women who do not like relying on natural methods, experience side effects to hormonal methods, and don't enjoy inserting diaphragms, the female condom is a good way to control fertility and protect against STIs. For couples who want to share in male and female contraception, taking turns using condoms is one possibility.

Advantages:
* Can be inserted several hours before intercourse.
* Made of polyurethane rather than latex, so less likely to tear.
* Can be used during menstruation.
* Hypoallergenic and odorless.
* Provides protection against HIV and other STIs.
* Is reported to have an increased sensitivity for men and women compared with male condoms.

Disadvantages:

* Uninterrupted sex requires some pre-planning.
* Insertion takes practice to master.
* Expensive compared with male condoms.
* Can be noisy (think of a scrunching plastic sound).
* Some women and men do not like the sensation.
* Can move and shift against the vaginal walls.
* The penis can enter the vagina and "miss" the condom, pushing it up the vag, towards the cervix.

Barring It

Barrier methods for women such as the diaphragm and cervical cap are designed to prevent the sperm from entering the uterus.

The diaphragm

The diaphragm was introduced as a birth control method in the 1880s. A doctor must properly fit a diaphragm for a woman to make sure it's the right size. The diaphragm is a soft, shallow rubber cap with a flexible rim which is inserted into the vagina and covers the cervix. Before inserting the diaphragm, make sure it has no holes, and smear spermicidal cream or jelly inside the cap and around the rim. The diaphragm must be left in the vagina for about six hours to prevent sperm from continuing into the uterus, and to

To prevent pregnancy after intercourse, women in ancient Rome were advised to spit three times into the mouth of a frog. Greek philosopher Aristotle thought the ideal contraceptive was to mix olive oil with cedar oil, lead ointment or frankincense and apply it to the cervix.

allow the spermicide and normal vaginal secretions to kill the remaining sperm.

Advantages:

* Can be inserted several hours before intercourse.
* Can be used during menstruation without interfering with a woman's menstrual cycle.
* Provides some protection against STIs.

Disadvantages:

* Uninterrupted sex requires some pre-planning.
* Some women don't like inserting it, or find inserting it difficult.
* Can be uncomfortable if the wrong size is fitted.
* Rarely, a woman can be allergic to the rubber it is made from.

If you and your partner value spontaneity in your sex life, the diaphragm may not be the best method for you as it requires some pre-planning before sex. If you are not comfortable touching yourself or inserting objects into your vagina, you should also consider another method. Some women and men can be allergic to the spermicidal creams and jellies used with the diaphragm; some women may also experience some allergic irritation to the rubber of the diaphragm. If either of you experience burning, itching or inflammation, discontinue use and consult your doctor about another method.

Cervical cap

The cervical cap is just like the diaphragm only smaller. Its effectiveness rate is not quite as good, but some women prefer the smaller size in terms of insertion and comfort.

Shooting Up

Known as "the shot," because it is given as an injection every three months, Depo-Provera is a long-acting hormone solution containing progesterone. It acts as a contraceptive by preventing ovulation, thickening the cervical mucus so that sperm cannot enter the uterus and changing the lining of the uterus, making it difficult for a fertilized egg to implant.

Advantages:

* Highly effective and convenient because there is no daily action or thought required.
* Can be used to treat women with menstrual problems.
* Does not affect breastfeeding.
* Periods can stop altogether (some women love this, but it makes others worry).

Disadvantages:

* Follow-up injections must be timed accurately.
* The injection cannot be reversed or withdrawn, so side effects may last twelve to fourteen weeks.
* Some women experience menstrual irregularities in frequency and flow.
* There can be a delay after a final injection in the return of normal cycles and fertility.
* Does not protect against HIV or STIs.
* Can sometimes be associated with reduced bone density.

This method requires you to be mindful and consistent. You must remember to return for follow-up shots on time. There is no immediate discontinuation with this method, so if you and your partner would like to plan a pregnancy, you will have to wait for the hormones to exit your body before fertility returns.

Another hormonal contraceptive injection, based on the hormones in the combination pill (see below), is currently being researched and trialed. It is not yet available for use.

Pill Popping

The release of the oral contraceptive pill in the 1960s heralded the sexual revolution for many people. Women, who were now able to control their fertility reliably, could enjoy sex without worrying about the consequences of unintended pregnancy. Today, the pill is one of the most popular forms of contraceptive. There are two types, in more than twenty-five different varieties.

The combination pill

The combination pill is made up of two synthetic hormones, estrogen and progesterone. It works by preventing ovulation, thickening the cervical mucus, making it very difficult for sperm to enter the uterus, and changing the lining of the uterus so a fertilized egg cannot implant. There are many different types of combination pills, with varying degrees of hormonal levels and release strategies, so consult your doctor or family planning practitioner to choose a pill specifically tailored to your needs and body.

Advantages:

* Regular periods, lighter periods and improvement in many negative menstrual symptoms.
* Allows for spontaneity in your sex life.
* Research indicates a possible reduction in the incidence of cancer of the ovaries and uterus.
* Some women report improvement in acne problems.
* High effectiveness.

Disadvantages:

* Requires regular contact with health providers for prescriptions.
* Need to take a daily pill.
* Some women may experience side effects, which can include weight gain, acne and low libido.
* Does not protect against STIs or HIV.

The mini-pill

The mini-pill contains only the hormone progestogen. It works primarily by making the cervical mucus thicker, which prevents the sperm from entering the uterus. It is essential to take this pill every day at the same time to maintain the thick cervical mucus. If the mini-pill is taken carefully, it can be very effective.

Advantages:

* Same as for combination pill.
* Suitable for women who have problems taking estrogen.

Disadvantages:

* Same as for combination pill.
* Must be taken at the same time every day.
* Can cause spotting and unpredictable periods.

While the combination pill and mini-pill allow for spontaneity in your sex life, these are not methods for those who dislike the necessity of daily pill-popping.

The pill must be taken every day so is not a method for the forgetful. It is not recommended for women over thirty-five who smoke, or for women with circulatory problems. The pill is sometimes associated with a decreased sex drive, so if you have sexual desire difficulties, talk to your doctor before choosing a specific brand.

Emergency contraception

If you forget to take a pill (or two or three) and have unprotected sex, or if a condom breaks, or worse, if you are sexually assaulted or raped, it may be necessary to use a means of preventing pregnancy *after* you've had sex, rather than before.

The morning-after pill generally contains high levels of the hormones estrogen and progesterone. It needs to be taken within seventy-two hours after you have had unprotected sex, so it really is best to seek it out "the morning after."

This type of emergency contraception works by either preventing or delaying ovulation in that current cycle, or by making the lining of the uterus unreceptive to a fertilized egg. Research has shown that the morning-after pill prevents up to 75 percent of pregnancies that would otherwise have happened, so it is a reliable method of emergency contraception.

A second option now available for emergency contraception is the IUD. An emergency IUD can be inserted to prevent conception, however speak to your doctor or family planning practitioner about whether this is an appropriate option for you.

If you do seek emergency contraception, your doctor or family planning clinic may request that you get an STI check. This is usually a good idea after any unprotected sex, but most especially if you were not familiar with your previous night's sexual partner.

Patch Work

The hormones in the oral contraceptive pill are now being tested for use in the form of a patch. One patch is placed on the body each week and the hormones are absorbed by the body over seven days. The patch is designed to be used three weeks on, one week off. While a woman must still remember to slap on the patch every seven days, some would argue it's easier than remembering a pill every day. And an added advantage for partners is that they can see a woman is "on" the patch, and don't have to ask, or "take her word for it" if she says she's on the pill, and has promised she has been reliable. The patch is similar to other hormone-replacement patches and the nicotine patch, and comes in the lovely and convenient color choices of peach or clear.

Skin Deep

For those women who have been searching for an easy, "don't have to think about it" contraception method, Implanon could be the answer. The hormonal (progesterone-only) contraceptive implant called Implanon is a small plastic rod that is inserted under the skin, usually in the upper arm. It provides a woman with up to three years of very reliable contraception. The procedure to insert the rod only takes a few minutes and it can be easily removed. Once it is taken out, a woman's fertility can return to normal within a few days to a few weeks.

Advantages:
* Long-term, reliable contraception.
* Suitable for women who experience negative side effects of estrogen.
* Allows for spontaneity in your sex life.
* Can be used when breastfeeding.

Disadvantages:
* Irregular and unpredictable menstrual cycles.
* Relatively new, so there is no long-term research available about possible adverse side effects.

* Does not protect against HIV or other STIs.

If you are planning to get pregnant in the near future, this is not the method for you. Implanon is one of the more expensive methods and is administered for long-term pregnancy prevention. If you are prone to ovarian cysts, consult your doctor before choosing this method.

Jane Camel

In ancient desert nomadic cultures, camels were essential for transport across long distances. Legends describe how tribes would travel for months across the desert, and how dependent they were on the use of their camels. They needed their camels to be hardy for long periods of time, so nomads used to prevent female camels from becoming pregnant by placing pebbles in their uteruses. This is one theory about the first application of a contraceptive method that has come to be known as the IUD.

The modern (human) IUD, short for "intrauterine device," is usually made of copper and plastic and is a small coil or T-shaped instrument that is inserted into the uterus. Most have a plastic string that comes through the cervix into the vagina, and indicates the presence of the IUD. While scientists are not absolutely sure of how it works, it appears to prevent the implantation of an embryo in the uterus, and perhaps also affects the movement of the sperm through the uterus.

Also available now is the IUS — "intrauterine system" — which is similar to the IUD but also contains beads of slow-releasing progestogen. This makes it more effective than the IUD, and it is becoming a popular option.

Advantages:

* Highly effective and long lasting.
* Reversible.
* Once in place, no other effort is required, other than occasionally checking the string.

Disadvantages:

* Can lead to infection.
* Does not protect against HIV or other STIs.
* Possible increased pain and bleeding during menstruation.
* Periods can be irregular or stop altogether.
* Increased risk of pelvic inflammatory disease (PID).
* Possible complications with any unintended pregnancy.
* IUDs with hormones can lead to hormonal side effects.

The IUD is sometimes not recommended for women who have not yet had children, and who plan to have them one day. IUDs have been linked with an increased risk for pelvic inflammatory disease (PID), which can lead to sterility. If your body periodically expels an IUD, it means your body is not adjusting to a foreign object in the uterus, and you should consider another method.

Zap 'Em Dead

Sperm-killing potions and lotions placed in the vagina just before intercourse are among the oldest of all birth control methods. Records dating back as far as 1850 BC in ancient Egypt describe recipes for spermicides to prevent pregnancy. Ingredients included honey, carbonate of soda, acacia tree tips and (wait for it) the dung of crocodiles and elephants. As much as women today wouldn't want to insert these items into their

In 1885, Walter Rendell developed the first vaginal suppositive spermicide, using cocoa butter and quinine sulphate. Since the 1950s more powerful spermicides have been developed, and continue to be researched.

vagina (and shouldn't), ancient Egyptian physicians were on to something. Modern researchers have learned that gluey substances, like honey, slow down the mobility of sperm. Lactic acid, produced by the acacia tree, is deadly to sperm and some acidic ingredients, like elephant dung, hinder fertilization. Fortunately, we've come a long way since then, so stick with the spermicides available at your local pharmacy.

Spermicides are available in creams, jellies and pessaries or suppositories. Modern spermicides have been designed to effectively destroy the mobility of sperm, or kill them entirely. They can be used alone, or with condoms, sponges, diaphragms, cervical caps and other methods.

Advantages:
* No long-term side effects.
* Affordable.
* Easy to administer.
* Most can be used just prior to intercourse.

Disadvantages:
* Can cause allergic reactions in some people.
* Can be messy.
* Decreases spontaneity for sex as some preparation or planning is involved.
* Effectiveness rate is relatively low when used alone, without a barrier method.

Mother Nature

Natural methods of birth control are based on an understanding of the female menstrual cycle. There are several techniques to determine when a woman is fertile within her cycle. The three primary techniques are the basal body temperature method, the cervical mucus method and the calendar method. Women chart their temperatures during their cycle, keeping track of the days when their temperature dips, prior to ovulation. A woman's cervical mucus also changes during her cycle, enabling her to know when she is fertile. When a woman is ovulating, her cervical mucus becomes clear, slippery and somewhat stringy or "blobby" — a bit like eggwhites. Each woman's cervical mucus is slightly different, so regular tracking is required to become familiar with her own cycle. The calendar method is more mathematical and the menstrual cycle should be charted for a year before relying on this method. It involves keeping track of the length of menstrual cycles and then averaging this out over a year to find out which days are unsafe for unprotected intercourse. For further, specific information on carrying out these methods, there are many books available. Women can use these methods both for achieving and avoiding pregnancy.

Advantages:

* No side effects.
* Once learned (through books and notebooks), there are
  no costs.
* Enables a woman to have greater awareness of her cycle.

Disadvantages:

* Learning the methods and your cycle takes time and
  consistent effort.
* Stress and illness can alter body temperature and cycle length,
  making the methods less reliable during these periods.

* Medications can interfere with and alter cervical mucus. If you are on regular medication, which includes naturopathics and homeopathics, consult your doctor about the possible effects on your cervical mucus.
* Some women feel uncomfortable checking their vagina and vaginal secretions.
* Other forms of contraception or abstinence are necessary on "unsafe" days.

The effectiveness of natural family planning depends on whether a woman uses one method alone, or a combination. The more aware a woman is of her cycle, the more likely she is to be accurate about her fertile days. When used consistently and correctly, natural family planning can be very effective for avoiding pregnancy. Natural family planning is boosted by good organization and communication between a woman and her partner. Women and their partners must arrange sexual activity around the female body temperature and ovulation cycle. If you lead hectic lives and want spontaneity in your sex life, this is not the method for you. Body temperature can also be influenced by common illnesses such as the flu.

These methods require commitment and diligence. If you are not able to pay attention to your cycle, be prepared for the possibility of an unplanned pregnancy. If this is out of the question, perhaps another method is a better option for you.

Pulling Out

Bottom line: not a good method, unless you are willing to get pregnant (or have her get pregnant). Most men don't withdraw before releasing a bit of pre-cum, which can contain both sperm and HIV. Others mistime the whole shebang, which is just like using nothing. Pulling out can be effective if the man is practiced at it, but if he's not, it's basically a non-method.

Millennium Methods

There are a few cool contraceptive advancements coming our way this century.

His pill

The male pill is still not perfected, but research indicates that we may soon see men taking a pill for contraceptive purposes. The theory behind the male pill is to suppress the production of sperm. Men would still ejaculate, but without the small percentage of sperm in the semen. For those women concerned about the reliability of men taking a pill every day, there is also research into the male "shot," where a man would have occasional injections to prevent sperm production.

Ovulation indicators

Developed, tested and undergoing research trials are two methods for indicating ovulation. These methods do not protect against STIs, but can help women determine when they are ovulating. This information can enable women to conceive, or know exactly when to avoid unprotected sex.

There are devices that detect a woman's hormonal levels during her cycle, and illuminate with a green light on safe days and a red light on unsafe days. Another is a panty liner that operates on the same theory.

Latex Sucks

Men and women alike bemoan and complain about using latex for safer sex. Okay, okay, it's not the same as playing in your total birthday suits, but if you want to play risky, and have a lot of partners, latex is your best method for protection against STIs. Aside from condoms, dental dams are your next line of defence. Dental dams are square pieces of latex, available at most family planning clinics and some pharmacists. Some of them are flavored (ooh, a bonus!).

When sucking or licking the genital area, whether it's the vulva, anus or penis, use a dental dam or a cut-up condom. Granted, hardly anyone, aside from the most conscientious sex worker, uses latex for oral sex. But if you want to do it safely, latex is the way. Place the dental dam or condom section over the vulva or anus before performing any sucking or licking. For those who aren't really into this sort of act, but are doing it because it turns your partner on, the flavoured varieties provide a little more enticement.

When giving head, the safest way is to do it with a condom over the penis. The advantage: swallowing is out of the equation, as is having splooge spurt over your face, neck or chest (unless you're into that, of course).

Giving it a Miss

There is a whole chapter devoted to Not Doing It (see Been There, *Not* Doing That). However, abstinence is one of the methods some women and men use for contraception, so it deserves a brief mention here.

Being abstinent does not necessarily mean being chaste. In terms of using abstinence as a method of birth control, it only refers to abstaining from penile–vaginal intercourse. Abstinence from penetration is an effective method of contraception because without penetration, it is very difficult (virtually impossible) for the sperm to meet the egg. Only if a man comes between a woman's thighs and very near her vaginal entrance (read: *on* her entrance basically) is it remotely possible for her to become pregnant.

Abstinence is probably the cheapest form of contraception, besides pulling out, because there are no products to purchase, or charts and notes to keep.

Couples can often use abstinence as a method of birth control in times of high risk. If a woman is using natural contraception methods, a couple will need to use periodic abstinence during days on which a woman could be ovulating. Also, if a couple has decided not to use condoms, and she is in the first month of being on the pill, they may decide to abstain from intercourse during the first three to four weeks.

For couples using abstinence, there are plenty of other activities and sexual releases available, and this period can often be a time of intense experimentation and sensual play.

Advantages:
* Low to no risk of pregnancy.
* Reduced risk of STI transmission.
* Free.

Disadvantages:
* It might be difficult to maintain commitment to this method under pressure or sexual arousal.
* Both partners may not agree on the frequency or duration of this method.

Abstinence should be a joint decision, shared by both you and your partner. If one of you changes your mind about being abstinent, you should talk about your choices and discuss possible alternative contraception methods together.

No Through Road

There are a few options for both men and women who want to prevent pregnancy permanently. Tying of tubes is reversible in some cases, and completely and utterly permanent in others, so be sure to speak with your doctor or specialist before deciding on snipping or tying your tubes. A word about tubes: in women, it is the fallopian tubes, preventing the egg from reaching the uterus, and in men it is the vas deferens that gets the ol' snip, preventing the sperm from being released from the testicles. Men still ejaculate the same amount of cum (sperm being only a small fraction of a man's love juice). The advantages are both procedures, once done, require no ongoing cost, maintenance and, best of all, no thought. It allows for spontaneity plus. However, if you want to reverse the procedure down the track, it can be expensive, and may not always work. The disadvantages include no protection against HIV or STIs, and every once in awhile, a teeny chance, but it has been known to happen: oops, pregnancy.

Abortion

Abortion is not a method of contraception: it does not prevent conception. However, many women and couples turn to abortion if their contraceptive method fails. Many personal and ethical issues surround abortion, so if you and/or your partner are opposed to pregnancy termination, take care with your contraceptive choices, or you will find yourself becoming parents. If you are in a serious relationship and wish to consider abortion as your "fall back" method, in case of an accident, you both should be in agreement about this before you begin having sex, to avoid a potentially serious relationship conflict. If you are a single woman, be clear on your feelings about abortion so that you know what choices you might be faced with if you get pregnant unintentionally.

Take Your Chances

No method is 100 percent effective. Men and women are only human, and will make mistakes using contraception — miss a pill, or not put a condom on correctly. The table below shows the statistics for the effectiveness of various contraceptive methods.

Method	Efficiency
Abstinence	100%
Implanon	99.9%
Vasectomy	99.85–99.9%
IUD/IUS	98.6–99.9%
Combination pill	95–99.9%
Tubal sterilization	99.5%
Mini-pill	95–99.5%
Depo Provera	99.7%
Emergency contraception (pill and IUD)	96.8–99%
Natural methods	75–99%
Condom	86–97%
Withdrawal (this is at best a "guestimate" as there has been little reliable research)	81–96%
Female condom	79–95%
Diaphragm	80–94%
Spermicide	74–94%
Cervical cap	60–91%

Sources: *Contraceptive Technology*, 1998, *British Journal of Family Planning*, 1999, Family Planning Association of Australia.

Whether you're in a serious relationship or having a one-night stand, if you don't intend to have sex for procreation, both of you should be assured of contraception before hitting the sack. So, shoot the breeze before shooting your wad.

"I was a little drunk, but he was so hot and I was so horny. We were making out and there was a moment when it occurred to me to say, 'Do you have one?' or something like that, but I don't know, it seemed to spoil the moment and I just didn't. I ended up having unprotected sex with a guy I barely knew and I spent the whole time worrying. I had to rush out and get the morning-after pill and get tested for diseases. It was not worth all that hassle and I should've said something. I'd like to think I'll always insist on condoms from now on, but I know how slack I can be when I've been drinking. It might happen again, but I hope not." — woman, 24

"I was in a relationship and my girlfriend got pregnant accidentally. I went with her for the abortion. It was awful. She was crying, we were both traumatized, we called off the relationship and I swore I would never be careless with contraception after that. I was having casual sex with a woman about a year later and even though she told me she was on the pill, I didn't want to take chances. I wanted to make sure I was in charge of not getting her pregnant. She used to think using condoms was pointless since she was already on the pill, but I developed a way of talking, teasing and playing and getting her all hot before penetration so she basically begged for me to put the condom on and put my dick in her. I loved the control and I've used condoms ever since." — man, 31

The Golden Rules of Contraception

* Be honest.
* Don't hesitate to insist on contraception.

* Talk about using contraception before all your clothes come off.
* Always have condoms handy.

What It Ain't
Top ten list of what is NOT effective contraception

1. Douching with coke (the drink not the drug).

2. Douching with urine (hoping the acidity will kill the sperm).

3. Jumping up and down to get the sperm to drip out (same effectiveness as praying, really).

4. Using cling wrap or any home-made condom substitute (and bubble wrap is not a good home-made ribbed version, though I did give points for creativity when I heard this).

5. Re-using a condom (just plain gross, let alone ineffective).

6. Taking one pill, or a smattering throughout the month, and thinking it'll do the trick (oh, if I had a dollar for every time a girl did this . . .).

7. Inserting a spermicidal suppository the next day (too little, too late, baby).

8. Putting peanut butter on the cervix to "block" the sperm. (You're thinking: Who does this? But trust me, people have done it!)

9. Telling her or him, "Don't worry, I'm sterile" (if it's not true, and it usually isn't).

10. Getting drunk and thinking: What the fuck, it's just this once. (I see you cringeing, trying to hide your guilty faces, you naughty possums!)

Master of Your Domain

[*please yourself*]

MASTURBATION: diddle, beat off, do-it-yourself, grind, jack off, jerking, night exercises, fly solo, rub up, tug, wank, finger blasting, hand fucking, manual labor, wrist aerobics

MASTURBATION FOR THE MAN: crank the shank, ball off, dance with Johnny One-Eye, drive the skin bus, fuck palmela, go on a date with Rosie Palm and her five daughters, grease the pole, let loose the juice, pack the palm, pop the Peter, pump off, roll your own, shake the weasel, polish the knob, play five-on-one, slide the shaft, strike the pink match, stroke, tickle the pickle, make the hooded cobra spit, wax the surfboard, yank the crank, beat off, spank the monkey, beat the bishop, flog the dog, snap the whip, pound off,

hold the gherkin, make your own mayonnaise,
download the floppy, choke the chicken, free
willy, milk the lizard, feed the chooks, sperm
the worm, knuckle the bone

MASTURBATION FOR THE WOMAN:
apply lip gloss, baste the tuna, beat the
beaver, digitate, two-fingered shuffle, flick
the bean, floss the cat, lube the tube, play
with the home entertainment center, part
the red sea, poke the pussy, scratch the
patch, play with the little man in the boat,
dip in the honeypot, clitorize

Yeah, Right!

"It is a known fact that habitual onanism [masturbation] is very
dangerous, and often ruins both mind and body. It causes weakness and
tremor of the muscles, nervousness and lack of energy, weakens the
memory and creates despondency, irritability, etc."

Source: *The Natural Laws of Sexual Life* (1908)

Early twentieth-century advice to those who masturbated: "Now what
you have been doing is to be compared with taking poison and drugs. I
want you to stop it completely later on, but not at once, because your
system is not strong enough to bear immediate cessation of this thing to
which you have accustomed yourself. Look on it as though you were
taking a dangerous poison as a medicine, and endeavour to help
yourself to a cure by limiting your dose."

Source: *Sex and the Young* (1926)

Masturbation Myths

★ You will grow hair on your hands.
★ You will go blind.
★ You will grow warts.
★ You will become addicted to self-pleasure.
★ You will become nervous and agitated, until eventually you become insane and need to be institutionalized.
★ You will become infertile.

Why Masturbation Was Thought to be Baaad to the Bone

The heavy stigma of masturbation that existed for nearly 1,000 years was the result of several theories of the origin of life. Thirteenth-century Catholic theologian Thomas Aquinas believed that masturbation was a sin greater than fornication. He believed masturbation, for men, was a waste of valuable life force, and even the soul. Thomas Aquinas believed semen came from the brain and carried the substance of the soul and the power of life that form the fetus in the womb of a woman. To masturbate and carelessly, wastefully ejaculate without implanting this valuable soul-seed for the creation of life, was a moral crime against nature, religion and life.

This belief that semen contains brain and soul matter has existed for thousands of years throughout many cultures. The ancient Greeks, Chinese and Hindus, all at one point or another in their histories, held similar beliefs about semen's link to the brain. It was believed that unused semen in the body

The word masturbation *comes from the ancient Roman definition,* manusturbo, *meaning to defile with the hands.*

Source: *The Sex Chronicles: Strange-But-True Tales from Around the World*

Nineteenth-century American cereal magnate and health fanatic John Harvey Kellogg recommended harsh treatment for masturbators. If a boy was discovered to be masturbating, JH Kellogg suggested circumcision without anesthetic for the prevention of future wanking. For girls who masturbated, he proposed applying carbolic acid to the clitoris.

nourished the brain, so wasteful ejaculations would then undernourish the brain. The Chinese believed depleting semen stock reserves depleted the body's life force, and the Hindus believed semen came from blood and that the body needed over a month to create one drop of semen, so ejaculations outside of coitus were frowned upon.

With the very essence of the soul, brain, and life force believed to have been contained in semen, it is no wonder masturbation came to be viewed as a problematic pastime. Any release of life energy without the potential for creation became morally criminal. While we now know biologically that semen does contain sperm essential for creating new life, we also know the testicles manufacture new sperm constantly. If a man ejaculates five times in one day, he will notice less and less ejaculate with each orgasm. By the next day, however, supplies will be replenished.

Women don't even rate a mention in history, it seems. Much of the history of masturbation focuses on the male, primarily because of the emphasis on the ejaculate-as-life-force debate. Women in ancient Greece were thought to be inferior because they had thinner semen (vaginal lubrication), which the Greek philosophers interpreted to mean that women have lower life energy and weaker brains.

Masturbation for women was not considered to have existed (in the man's world), so women were not condemned in the way men were for threatening life force and creation.

Yes, Masturbation is Good for You

It is only since the 1960s that masturbation has become widely understood and truly accepted as healthy. Since masturbation has been taken out of the sexual closet it has become recognized as a natural way to discover one's body, sexual response and pleasure zones and techniques. Masturbation is not only viewed as a natural and healthy sexual expression, it is now understood to be good for your mind, spirit and body.

Masturbating to orgasm ignites the sexual response system in the human body. This sexual response does several things, including releasing hormones in the body that produce feelings of relaxation, pleasure, increased energy, and even euphoria.

The benefits of masturbation

Better sex The more frequently you engage in sexual activity, the better your sex life. Masturbation and orgasm increase sex drive, desire, self-esteem, and relationship satisfaction, especially among women.

Pleasure Masturbating to orgasm, or even just playing with yourself without coming, feels great. It feels physically good, and it also feels good to appreciate yourself.

Relaxation Masturbation helps you relax and unwind. It has no side effects and can even help people with insomnia.

Q. How did Pinocchio find out he was made of wood? A. His hand caught fire.

Masturbating can release hormones which induce sleep as well as relaxation.

Energy If relaxation isn't what you're after, masturbation can also lead to feeling "revved up" and horny. This could be before a date, or just on a day when you want a little extra boost. There is no need to "clean the whistle" à la the film *There's Something About Mary*, and masturbating before intercourse is not a sure-fire way to perform longer, however, masturbation can be a great way to get "in touch" with yourself, feel sexy, or even improve concentration. If you need a study break, a quick diddle can re-energize your focus and you can go back to those books with renewed vigor.

Relief Masturbation is great stress relief. It not only takes your mind off the causes of your stresses, orgasm is a physical release of tension within your body. For women, the contractions felt during orgasm can also provide pain relief from menstrual cramps because the uterus contracts during orgasm, and the spasms tense and relax the cramping uterine muscular tissue.

Safe Masturbation is a safe sexual expression physically and emotionally. There is virtually no risk of STIs* and none of pregnancy. There are no fights, games or emotional wringers. No angst over "When should I call her again?" or "But he said he'd call me, bastard!"

---

* Herpes can potentially be spread through masturbation. If you have a herpes sore on your mouth, touch it, then masturbate, you could end up with herpes on your genitals. Be careful during outbreaks.

Free! Masturbation is free. And it's always there when you want it. If your hand or toy is up to it, there's no communication, negotiation or debate as there can sometimes be with a sexual partner. No need for scheduling it in, or setting a date in advance. It's all you, baby.

Knowledge Masturbating allows you to figure out what techniques give you pleasure. You can learn how to make yourself come slowly, or come quickly. You can then share this information with your partner(s). Masturbation is an effective therapeutic tool for women who have trouble reaching orgasm, and for men who have premature ejaculation difficulties.

Positively indulgent Masturbation is for you, by you, and all about you. If you're just in the mood for a quick, no-fuss orgasm, it can be yours without having to search for a partner, or seduce one. It can save time if all you want is a "fix." Through masturbation you can experiment and play with toys and techniques without inhibitions — no one is watching. It can also be your time for fantasy. You can pick your own pace, and spend as much or as little time as you want pleasing yourself. Uninhibited, women and men often find they have longer, more intense orgasms.

How Much is Too Much?

The urge to fly solo and give yourself pleasure varies depending on your stress levels, lifestyle, time, sex drive and many other factors. People masturbate several times a day, once a day, once a month, or on rare occasions. Whether

"If God had intended us not to masturbate, He would have made our arms shorter."
— George Carlin

80 percent of women masturbate.

30 percent of women experience orgasm through intercourse.

80 percent of women experience orgasm through solitary masturbation and/or masturbation during intercourse.

94 percent of men masturbate.

(These statistics are from a composite of surveys, and, of course, reflect only those who admit to it!)

you masturbate twice a year or twice a day, it is a healthy, normal activity.

There can be a limit, though, to what's normal. Normal masturbation frequency is not determined by the number of times one masturbates, but by the space and attention it takes up in one's life. Masturbation is a natural component of a sex life, but should not be the focus of life in general. If you find you have become obsessed with self-pleasuring, you may want to ask yourself how far you will go to masturbate.

★ Will you make yourself late for work or school in order to masturbate?

★ Will you decline invitations to go out so you can stay home to masturbate?

★ Do you prefer masturbation to dating?

★ Do you regularly masturbate rather than find something else to do (hobbies, walks, movies, etc.)?

★ Do you find masturbation is the first or primary activity you do at home?

Masturbation has a place in your life, but it should not be an obsession in your life. If you find masturbation has taken center stage and has become an activity which impedes your socializing, you may have a problem. In fact, you probably do. If you feel you are obsessed with masturbating, make an appointment with a psychologist or sex therapist. They can help you place your wanking back into a healthy perspective. Obsession with masturbation is not like alcohol addiction. You will not have to go to group meetings, or commit to total withdrawal. But if masturbation has taken over your thoughts, desires and activities and you find you spend all your time doing it or thinking about it, talk to someone who can help you balance your sex life with the rest of your life.

If you are at the other end of the spectrum, and you never masturbate, you are not abnormal. While the vast majority of women and men engage in masturbation to some degree, this does not mean as a non-masturbator you're necessarily missing out. Masturbation is not a mandatory activity for a healthy sex life. Most people go through periods of abstinence from masturbation. Whether you masturbate several times a day or never, if you are happy with your sex life, your sexual response and function, consider yourself normal.

Masturbation Techniques for Men

The wank: isn't it just yank, yank?

There's much more to masturbation than the pump and tug. Men, in their infinite exploration of the penis, have devised more ways to masturbate than can be counted, or described. Here is an abbreviated run-down, from the basic to the not-so-basic.

Basic hands

There are four elemental hand positions: the fist, the backhand, the finger grip, and the "okay" sign. To masturbate with the fist, hold the penis with the knuckles facing away from the body. The backhand is the opposite, with the grip being so the thumb is down and the knuckles are pointing towards the body. The finger grip is a three- or four-fingered grip on the penis, with the thumb on the underside and two or three fingers on the top of the penis, as if holding the penis like a fat pen, or like how you might hold a joint (not a cigarette). The "okay" sign position is holding the penis in a ring shape between the thumb and forefinger, with the three other fingers extended out, or relaxed, so that the hand makes the "okay" sign.

Hand motions

Standard masturbatory motion is to pump or glide up and down the shaft and head of the penis. This can be done with all four basic hand positions. Speed and pressure can be experimented with to elicit intense or gradual stimulation. Occasional fingering and squeezing of the head is also very pleasurable.

A lot of men often like other hand motions in addition to the pump, tug or glide. Try cupping the head of the penis and jiggling it up and down at various angles. This can create an intense sensation in the glans of the penis.

Aside from changing your hand position from the base to the head of the penis, you can experiment with direction of motion.

Basketweaving Clasp both hands around the penis with the thumbs pointing towards the body and knuckles facing outward. Weave or wiggle your hands up and down the shaft and glans. This technique can be a pleasurable change of pace if you're used to simply pumping up and down the shaft.

Milking Think upward motion only. Clasp the penis with any basic hand motion and alternate hands, moving from the base to the glans. Start, for example, with your left hand, and as soon as it is at the tip of the penis, clasp the base of the penis with your right hand and follow the same upward movement. Keep the rotating motion at any varying speed and pressure. This is the ultimate "tug."

Dipping Using one hand, grasp the penis with your fist at the base. Glide up the shaft. When you reach the tip, flip your hand over so you have a backhand grip and slide your hand down the shaft. Keep repeating, so your wrist keeps making a flipping movement. This technique can result in an intense orgasm as it is constant and varying stimulation.

Palming Take one hand and hold the shaft of your penis. Then rub the head and shaft lengthways against the palm of your other hand. This creates amazing friction, especially for the glans.

Fingering For a slower masturbation and a longer orgasm, lie very still with one hand holding the shaft. Use the thumb and forefinger of your other hand to circle the glans. Keep circling slowly and rhythmically. Resist the urge to pump with the hand holding the shaft. If you ejaculate some pre-cum, glide that around with your thumb and forefinger. Occasionally you can use both hands to finger the glans. Keep resisting the urge to pump up or down the shaft. Eventually, you will experience a prolonged, almost orgasmic state, and your orgasm will be both powerful and long.

Webbing This can be done with one or two hands. The focus is on stretching the web of skin between the thumb and forefinger and rubbing it up and down the shaft. It can be done simply with one hand, or by loosely interlocking both thumbs and forefingers around the shaft and moving up and down. Movements can be varied in a circular motion.

What to do with your other hand

Most men find their scrotum and testicles almost as sensitive as their penis, if not more so. While masturbating the penis with one hand, use your other hand to massage, rub, tickle and pull your scrotum. If you're used to holding your scrotum from underneath, reach your hand across from the other direction so that it crosses over the hand that is on your penis so it reaches your scrotum from the top. It will give you the sensation and perspective that someone else is playing with your scrotum. The more you experiment, the more you'll work out just what motions and pressures enhance your response and orgasms.

If you want, you can always use your other hand as a "right-hand man" (or left-hand man, as the case may be) on your penis. You can place one hand on the head of your penis, and the other at the base, and move each hand in the same or opposite direction, at the same time, or in alternating rhythms.

Body positions

Most men like to masturbate either sitting or lying down. Kneeling and squatting, though, provide good access to the genitals and create muscle tension which can enhance orgasm. Squatting can provide dual hand access from the front and behind, and enables you to bounce your penis within your hand, in addition to moving your hand up and down.

On your side Lying on your side with your legs bent up towards your belly, you can grasp the glans of your penis and shift your top leg up and down to stimulate the shaft. Alternatively, you can stretch your legs out straight and move your top leg from side to side. That should move your penis slowly in and out of your hand.

Using your belly Lube up your penis and your belly from your navel to your pubic bone (where your pubic hair is). Place your thumb on the base of the head of your penis so your knuckles are facing away from your body and move it from side to side. Your penis will move from side to side and the friction sliding against your belly will feel great.

Full frontal Lie on your side and grasp your penis with the backhand grip. Roll over further onto your belly and push your hand into the mattress. Thrust into your hand. This will feel a little like intercourse because you're moving with your hips rather than your hand.

Temperature

To enhance erection and arousal, add some heat. This can be achieved by warming up an accessory, such as a condom, plastic sandwich bag or a glove, by briefly microwaving it (a few seconds only!) or by placing the item on a hot water bottle or heating pad. The extra heat will provide greater sensation.

You can alter this heat method by taking a blow dryer and blowing dry hot hair onto your penis or scrotum as you masturbate with your other hand. Beware that if you're using water-based lube, the hair dryer will dry out your lube very quickly, so you may need to replenish the lube often.

For a completely different sensation, try placing an ice cube or cold pack on your scrotum, or right below it on the perineum, just before ejaculation. It can make orgasm feel mind-blowingly intense.

Water sports

Shower heads aren't only for women. Men can make just as much pleasurable use out of them. Take a hand-held shower head, turn the water on and maneuver it around the base and glans of the penis and the scrotum. If you're uncircumcized, play with the water jet under your foreskin. You should be gentle with the scrotum and glans as these areas are more sensitive to pressure. Play around with temperature, and if you have a variable vibrating shower head, make the most of it!

Mock vaginas

There are lots of ways to simulate the sensation of thrusting into a vagina. You can create a mock vagina with your hand by creating a fist for the glans to enter as you pump the shaft with your other hand, but if you're looking for more creative alternatives, there are several you can try.

Latex Take a condom and fill the tip with a hearty amount of lube (you're not worried here that the condom might slip off and create a pregnancy/STI scare). Place it over your penis and when it's on snugly, squeeze the tip so that the lube moves down the shaft. Glide away. Or you can double the friction effect by placing a non-lubricated condom over your penis, then add lube and put a second condom on. Pump the shaft and glans with any hand position and the friction between the condoms will eventually lead to an intense build-up of arousal and prolonged orgasm.

You can also use latex gloves during masturbation to create a textured effect. Wearing latex gloves (available at pharmacies) with lube on one or both hands while masturbating your penis and scrotum can create a loose or tight friction sensation, depending on the size of the gloves. Tight-fitting gloves will give you a smooth sensation, while loose-fitting gloves will give more wrinkle in the latex, which will rub more roughly up and down your penis.

Plastic Take a plastic sandwich bag (not a grocery plastic bag) and put enough lube in it so that all the sides are lubed. You can either put your penis in this à la condom style, or place the bag between your mattress and bed base and, kneeling, pump away into it as you would into a vagina.

Pillows You can create a vagina of sorts with pillows. Push two pillows together and place your penis in the crack between them. Once you are in position, manipulate the pillows by pushing them together and angling and folding them so that you won't hit the mattress when you thrust. *Voilà* — pillow vagina.

Fruit With the comedy of apple pies aside, both oranges and bananas can be fantastic sources of self-indulgent pleasure. You can cut an opening in an orange that can be a terrific stimulus for the glans of the penis while you pump up and down the shaft. You will probably need to hold the orange with your other hand, and everything will smell like orange, so this is not for everyone.

The banana is the most popular fruit for masturbation, not for its phallic symbolism, but for its phallic shape. Peel a banana and after eating (or tossing) the banana, use the peel as a sheath around the penis. Move the peel up and down the shaft. The inside of the peel will provide lube and the sensation is unlike any other.

Vibrators Men don't often equate vibrator use with themselves — they usually think of them as a female domain. However, vibrators are as effective for men as they are for women. A shower vibrator or hand-held vibrator can be rubbed up and down the shaft and glans of the penis and result in amazingly intense orgasms. Specially made "penis sheath" vibrators are available in good sex shops, however, if you're totally strapped, even an electric toothbrush will do! (Though it's recommended to think twice about ever using it again in your mouth, and the sensation isn't for everyone.)

Accu-Jac An Accu-Jac is a masturbation device consisting of a penile sheath which makes a gentle "sucking" motion over the glans and shaft. Some come with a "buddy" sheath attachment so two men can masturbate together at once. Others come with a dildo attachment so a woman and man can masturbate simultaneously.

Anal

Not everyone wants to masturbate their arse. But a lot of men do. If you're a beginner (and even if you're not), here's a good start.

Kneel down and reach one hand back to your anus. Lightly clasp the head of your penis with the other hand. Start lightly rubbing your anus in a circular, vertical or horizontal movement (or whichever combination you prefer) and then start caressing your penis. You'll start to feel sexual arousal from all parts of your body. If this is your first time, you may feel overwhelmed by the sexual feelings, and want to stop. That's fine. If not, proceed by inserting your finger(s) into your anal opening and use a massaging motion. You can mirror this motion with your other hand on your penis and you will find your body will release an explosive orgasm.

Some men like to use a vibrator to give themselves more stimulation around their anus and perineum. If you're using a vibrator make sure that you hold onto it if you insert it in your anus. The anal canal can sometimes create suction once something is inserted, and you don't want to take an embarrassing trip to hospital if something gets stuck.

Masturbation Techniques for Women

You may think it's simple. Reach down, diddle, diddle, and unh, uhn, uhhnngggahhhhwoweee!

It can be that simple. It can also be more ...

There are nearly as many ways for a woman to masturbate as there are women in the world. Women masturbate by stimulating their genitals, but they are also turned on by touching all areas of their bodies. Most women have their tried and true technique, but to add some variety to spice up your self-pleasuring life, here are some variations. The techniques detailed below concentrate on genital stimulation. To enhance genital masturbation, many women also enjoy touching their hips, breasts, nipples, bellies, thighs, feet, face, ears, hair, throat and upper chest.

Hand jobs

Most women who masturbate have experimented with their hands. Not all women prefer using their hands, but a lot do. There are several hand-job techniques for female masturbation.

The fingers A common technique is to use one, two or three fingers to stimulate the clitoris, inner and outer lips, perineum and/or anus. This can be done in a vertical up-and-down rubbing motion, a circular or side-to-side motion or, most commonly, a combination of the above. Women who masturbate with their hands like to use varying motions, pressures and speeds to regulate and gauge their sexual response as they approach orgasm.

The fist Some women prefer the pressure they can establish on their clitoris and lips by using their fist. You can either place the fist at the top of the vulva where the glans of the clitoris is, or in the middle of the vulva, between the lips. Depending on preference, the fist can be placed with the knuckle of the thumb on the clitoris and the bent forefinger rubbing on the lip, or the knuckle of the pinkie finger on the clitoris and the end of the thumb resting and rubbing on the outer lips. Again, vertical, circular or side-to-side motions and combinations produce pleasure. Often, if a woman is in the habit of masturbating in one particular rhythm or direction, a change in routine will produce a powerful and intense orgasm.

The palm Many women who prefer a stronger pressure to induce orgasm will use the palm method. A woman may begin masturbation with her fingers and, as her sexual response grows, she may then turn to using her palm. Other women, though, use their palms from start to finish. Generally, those women who masturbate with the palm of their hand, do so with the base of the palm. The heel of the palm is used to stimulate the clitoris; the fingers are then free to play around with the lips, perineum or enter the vagina. By using the palm to stimulate the clitoris, the woman's fingers are able to arouse the lips and penetrate the vagina at the same time. Many women find this method of masturbation results in an intense orgasm.

The inverted V This is a variation on the finger method. The woman uses two fingers, generally the forefinger and index finger, placed in a downward V-shape, so the tips of the fingers are facing down, away from the body. She then massages the outer lips of the vulva, keeping the clitoris within the web between her two fingers. Occasionally she can "pinch" her fingers together, catching the glans of the clitoris and repeat this whole movement. Women like this technique because it builds up sexual tension in the muscles and allows for a great orgasmic release. The attention is not directly focused on the clitoris, but it involves the clitoris with nearly every movement.

Water works

Masturbating with water is a technique favoured by many women. The flow, texture and pressure of water over the clitoris and lips can often deliver a powerful orgasm, and even multiple orgasms.

The shower If you're lucky enough to have a detachable shower head, you have a built-in pleasure center in your home. Take the shower head and maneuver it all around your vulva, lips and clitoris. You can play with pressure and motion. If your shower head has varying settings, play with the vibrating streams. You can pull the shower head further away for a more gentle tickling sensation, or close in for harder stimulation. You can also move the shower head around in rhythmic circular, vertical and horizontal movements. Moving at different speeds can enable you to gauge how fast you will come, and you can learn a lot about your sexual response.

The bath Logistically, this is trickier than using a shower head, because you have to position yourself in front of the tap, but it can be far more relaxing and deliver those melting orgasms. (You do need a combined hot/cold water tap.) Lying in the bath, slide your bum towards the tap and essentially move your legs above the tap and spread 'em. You'll have to tilt your pelvis to get the water to flow directly onto your clitoris. And you may want to use one hand to spread your lips apart for greater stimulation from the water. If the tub is only half full with water, you may be able to lie back comfortably, otherwise you can lean on your elbows. The bath is a terrific fantasy zone if you've lit some candles. You can also take your favorite erotic book and get really steamed up.

The spa If you've got access to a private spa tub (good hotel rooms often have spa jets in their bathtubs), you can relax in the tub comfortably and position your clitoris in front of a jet. Be careful because the force of water from a spa jet can be rough, and you don't want to end up bruised. Often women say they've never experienced an orgasm like it. The pressure of a jet is similar to a vibrator, yet the feeling of water is very different. Some describe their water works orgasms as an all-over body shudder of pleasure.

Toys

The vast array of toys available to women for masturbation is mind-boggling. There are two basic ways to play with toys: inside and outside.

Vibrators Most vibrators come with different speeds and you can experiment with where you like a heavier or lighter pressure. A lot of women like a harder pressure on their inner and outer lips, but a lighter speed on their clitoris. You can pull away or press in to the skin to tease your arousal to the brink of orgasm, and then deliver yourself a come-like-never-before experience. When you first try masturbating with a vibrator you may be surprised at how intense, forceful and long your orgasms are. You have entered a whole new world of pleasure. Just remember that prolonged play, especially with the vibrator set to high, fast or hardest, can make you a bit sore afterwards. Those sensitive tissues aren't used to that much stimulation, so be a little gentle. Some women prefer not to touch their clitoris with a vibrator as it can be painful. Try placing the vibrator on the cord (just under the skin) right above the clitoris. This can bring you to orgasm in a flash.

Always use lube when you masturbate with a vibrator as the fast rubbing motion of the vibrator can dry your skin or cause friction, which can hurt without lube.

Some vibrators can be placed inside the vagina, and some cannot. Make sure you know what you've bought. Some vibrators are designed for outside play only. If the shaft and head of the toy isn't smooth, don't put it in your vagina. The last thing you want is a piece of plastic pinching or catching in there.

Vibrators made specifically for sex are more powerful now than they used to be, but if you're embarrassed about buying one, buy a general-use muscle massager. They are usually just as powerful as clitoral vibrators, if not more so. (See more on vibrators in the "Humdingers" section in the chapter Lick 'Ems and Stick 'Ems.)

Butterfly This is a flat, latex vibrator that is used against the vulva, lips and clitoris. Some have straps that wrap around the legs and waist to hold it in place so it can stimulate all the genital erogenous zones at once.

Dildos Vibration isn't for everyone. Some women want to play with a dildo while masturbating their clitoris and lips with their fingers (or a vibrator). Dildos come in all shapes, sizes and colors. While penetrating yourself with a dildo, try gliding it in and out at different angles. If you discover a motion you really like, you can try it out with a partner the next time you have intercourse.

Dildos are great for women who have a G-spot. They can be used to massage the vaginal walls and the G-spot, and this can give a tremendous internal orgasm.

Be safe. Always, always make sure anything you put in your vagina is clean, non-toxic and harmless. (See more on dildos in the chapter Lick 'Ems and Stick 'Ems.)

Temperature

Women are divided on this: many prefer warmer temperatures; others prefer the cool effect. When it comes to masturbating with water, most women say they prefer warmer water. (Never pour really hot water on your vulva as it can damage the tissues — and hurt!) But when using vibrators and toys some women like to keep them in the fridge so that when they start masturbating they get stimulated by the cool tingles of the toy, and then melt along with the toy as it heats up. Some women also like to play with ice cubes around their lips and clitoris. Others hate this, so try it and decide for yourself. Some apply ice just before orgasm, or alternate between a vibrator, which gets them hot, and an ice cube, which can feel very sensitive on the skin that has just been vibrated. Switching between temperatures can prolong the amount of time you're in that pleasure zone, just on the brink of orgasm, so that when you do come, it's a gush of warmth and pleasure pulses.

Pillows

A lot of women report that they discovered masturbation in bed while rolling around and rubbing against pillows, and this often becomes a favorite way to masturbate. Women straddle pillows, teddy bears, folded blankets — any kind of soft bedroom accessory. You can lie on your back, front or side, with the pillow between your legs. Move the pillow back and forth. Or, alternatively, you can do a humping, rubbing motion against the pillow for hands-free masturbation.

Fruit

Women who are turned on by soft, squishy things generally love playing with fruit. There are lots of ways to play with fruit, however mangoes, bananas and kiwi fruit are common favorites. This is because the inside of the peel is soft, and comes with its own lube. For a different sensation from your fingers or a plastic toy, try rubbing the inside of a banana or mango around your clitoris. The slipperiness will make you come surprisingly fast.

Tickling

If you're not in the mood for a hard, pumping session and want to be more delicate with yourself, grab a clean feather, some make-up brushes and some fresh flowers. Lightly stroke the brushes, feather and/or petals of the flowers around your vulva. You can tease yourself by tickling over the clitoris without applying any pressure. It will take longer to come this way, but will be worth the wait.

Riding

Women can masturbate by riding nearly anything. Of course, your basic ride is on a horse. Sit forward, wriggle around in the saddle and presto! But for the un-horseywoman, there are lots of other pieces of equipment that are just as ride-able. Women can ride the edge of the bed, the edge of the washing machine during the spin cycle, the edge of a bathtub — there are many options: just take a look around and think about all the handy household objects you haven't christened.

A favorite "riding" masturbation technique is often referred to as "riding the seam." If you've got jeans or other cargo-type pants that have a thick seam running down the crotch, sit up off your sitting bones and tilt your pelvis forward so the top of your vulva is facing down. Rotate your

A centuries-old practice among peasant women was to tie knots in their underclothing around their pubic area, so that they could masturbate by rubbing and riding against the knots.

hips so that the clitoris rubs back and forth along the seam. It's hands-free, and can even be done while sitting at your desk.

A variation of seam riding is thigh riding. Often women have more success at this if they start teaching themselves the "thigh ride" by sitting upright in a chair with one leg crossed over the other. Squeeze your thighs together in a pulsing rhythm so that the squeeze is centred on the clitoris. This will bring you to a slow orgasm. Some women find it too slow. Others find it's not enough stimulation. With practice, though, it can be a fun pastime during those boring Monday meetings.

Anal

As with men, lots of women love anal masturbation. Techniques for this are similar to those for men (see page 80).

There are too many ways for women to masturbate to describe them all here, but you should now have the general idea. Get creative. Enjoy your sexy self.

Female Ejaculation

Men come. Women come. Men ejaculate. Women ejaculate. *Women ejaculate?*

For centuries there have been reports of women discharging fluid from their vaginas during sex and masturbation. The source and nature of this fluid, which is very different from female vaginal lubrication, is not clear. Debate has raged about whether this fluid is a result of bladder incontinence during orgasm, or something else.

Most women's accounts of ejaculation incorporate having their G-spot stimulated. Some women report ejaculating through masturbation of their vaginal walls, and others experience ejaculation only when their partner massages their G-spot, regardless of what they do when they masturbate. However, there are also reports of women ejaculating from cunnilingus and clitoral stimulation, without experiencing any contact with the G-spot.

The area of female ejaculation is still a mystery in sex research, and it is not known why some women ejaculate and some do not. There are few universally accepted facts about female ejaculation, except that the fluid ejaculated is not urine. Research suggests that this fluid comes from the Skene's glands — glands composed of tissue surrounding the urethra. The Skene's glands are similar to the male prostate and the fluid is similar to that produced by the prostate. Studies of women who ejaculate show that the amount of fluid released is highly variable. Some women produce a few drops, while others ejaculate a few tablespoons.

Research currently says that not all women have the capability to ejaculate. There are gimmicky instructional products and services that promote teaching women how to ejaculate and these should be viewed with scepticism. The sex experts are still not clear on the biological and physiological processes that explain female ejaculation, so snake-oil peddlers who claim to have the potion or the motion to induce all women to be able to ejaculate are not worth your time or money.

Descriptions of intensity and length of orgasm from women who ejaculate and women who do not are very similar, and indicate that learning how to ejaculate will not make orgasm any more intense, pleasurable or longer.

Sex experts in the scientific world at this point accept that some women ejaculate, and for them it is completely normal. For those who do not, again, normal, normal. The ultimate goal in our sexual response, especially through masturbation, is pleasure — whether that is orgasm, ejaculation, or just a plain good time.

Sweet Sleep: Nocturnal Orgasms in Women and Men

A nocturnal orgasm is an orgasm that happens when you're asleep. It's as if your brain and your body are masturbating for you.

In men, it's commonly known as a wet dream. It usually occurs when a man has an erotic dream, but some men can't remember whether they'd been having sexy dreams on a night they experienced a wet dream. A nocturnal orgasm is a normal biological function of the body. It generally happens if a man hasn't been having regular ejaculations while awake. The body has an ongoing, active sexual response, awake and asleep, which keeps the "plumbing" functioning, regardless of voluntary masturbation habits. If a man is masturbating regularly (daily or so), he will find he has few or no nocturnal orgasms. This is normal too.

Some men who have never had a nocturnal orgasm, or who have enjoyed the pleasant surprise of a nocturnal orgasm so much, have chosen to abstain from masturbation for weeks, hoping to spark the body into producing a wet dream. The success of this varies from man to man. The body will generally produce a nocturnal orgasm if a man has not experienced an ejaculation for a month, however, this is only a general rule, and many a man has sacrificed masturbation without nocturnal reward.

Women have nocturnal orgasms too, although this fact is not as well documented. As with men, female nocturnal orgasms generally happen if a woman has experienced an erotic dream. Most women report waking up during the orgasm. Because female nocturnal orgasms are so under-researched, it is not really known whether women can induce them, or if they occur under certain sexual response, lifestyle or sex drive variables.

🗣 *"I've only ever had one orgasm in my sleep. I woke up and I was coming! I didn't know what was going on at first, and then after a few seconds, when I realized, I just lay there and enjoyed it. The whole thing only lasted a few seconds, but it was an intense throbbing in my clitoris and vaginal muscles. Afterwards I couldn't believe it. I've never had an orgasm without touching myself, or having a partner touch me. To think that my brain conjured up an orgasm for me without any physical stimulation — wow. I wish I knew what I had been dreaming about, because I've never had one since and I'd love to have it happen again — what a gift!"* — woman, 28

Masturbation as Meditation

Masturbation is not only about pleasuring the body and releasing stress. Some use masturbation as a form of meditation. They close their eyes, massage and caress their body, masturbate their genitals, use deep breathing and quiet their mind. Often after orgasm, they sit or lie in the post-orgasmic glow, releasing more energy and going into a deeper meditation. Experiencing orgasm during meditation can trigger a deep release of physical, mental and emotional energy, after which you emerge calm and balanced.

🗣 *"One of my most memorable masturbation experiences came as a gift — literally. I got a gift certificate to enjoy a relaxing hydrotherapy tub at a*

spa. I'd never experienced hydrotherapy before, and
was I in for a treat! The tub was body-form fitting
and was lined with big and small jets aimed all
along my body: feet, inner and outer legs, torso,
shoulders and neck. What I was most surprised at,
though, was one nozzle, on a bar arching over the
top of the tub, centred in the middle, which only
moved up to waist height. It was conveniently aimed
at the vulva and clitoris. The jets in the tub moved
automatically through hard and soft water sprays,
and this clit jet was the only adjustable one. I was
amazed that a beauty and health spa provided
women with this extra dimension of relaxation, but
I thoroughly enjoyed it. All bathtubs should have this
magical fitting!" — woman, 31

Masturbation as Therapy

Masturbation is a helpful tool in the treatment of some sexual problems. For women who have trouble reaching orgasm, masturbation exercises are often recommended by sex therapists. There are also masturbation exercises for men who experience premature ejaculation. For more information on these exercises, and how to do them at home, see The Energizer Bunny and Speedy Gonzales chapters.

Blowing Kisses

lip smooching and
deep-throating — top and
bottom oral techniques

Oral sex — face-to-cock, face-to-vag or face-to-bum action — is a deeply intimate experience, physically and often emotionally. Oral sex can be experienced as part of foreplay, prior to intercourse, or as an activity in itself, leading to orgasm, with no intercourse in the equation. In the purist view, this is true oral action. Many men go down on women prior to intercourse to rev her up or give her a pre-fuck orgasm. Other times, men may do it for the sheer pleasure of going down, without intercourse on the agenda at all; just pussy galore for his special Bond girl. And as for women, some love to go down on a guy as a special treat, or because they love it and are in the mood to do it.

While for some, oral sex can often be just hot, horny, fun, erotic lickage and suckage; for others, the close face–genital contact makes oral sex more intimate than intercourse. Oral sex can be an emotionally intimate experience, in which partners tune in to each other's subtle non-verbal cues and feel the shared bond of giving and receiving.

DIVING: muff diving, pearl diving, muff munching, eating out, going down, licking off, giving face, go fishing, heading south, lick a box, eat at the Y, yodel up the valley, eating pussy, eating pie, carpet munching, dive in the bushes, eating a furburger, eating a hair pie, lip service

THE DO-ER: carpet muncher, lap lover, lip servicer, pearl diver, fish king/queen, head jockey, gash eater, lipkisser

CUNTYLINGUIST: a talented, expert linguist fluent in the tongue of cunt.

Basic Diving Instructions (Earning Your Cuntylinguist Diving Certificate)

High on the list of top sexual experiences is receiving good head. Those women who do not enjoy it may have issues of self-consciousness about their body or vulva, or may never have experienced it done well. Women who love it say it makes them feel hot, sexy, desired, and the orgasms are like nothing else.

It's Orally Natural

* According to sex researcher Dr. Alfred Kinsey, most mammals, when sexually aroused, engage in lip-to-lip and tongue-to-tongue contact. They use their tongues to touch and manipulate every part of their companion's body, including the genitalia. Animal oral–genital foreplay can go on for hours before leading to intercourse.

* In one US survey of 18 to 44 year olds, 33 percent of women and 50 percent of men said they enjoyed receiving oral sex; 19 percent of women and 37 percent of men enjoyed giving it.

Source: *The Penguin Atlas of Human Sexual Behavior*

Men are hot and cold about muff diving. Some men can't wait to get down there. They love the experience of their tongue on her clit and vulva. It's like French kissing the most intimate part of her and they find her pussy to be erotic, sensual and delicious. They want to give their partner ultimate sexual satisfaction. And they also probably want a killer blowjob in return. Others, while they can't wait to stick their dick down there, avoid heading south with their face at all cost. These men can be brought around to loving it, though, with some practice. If his issue is about taste or smell, don't jump straight into it by sitting on his face; start slowly. The bath is a good place to begin, or right after a shower. Gradually, with positive reinforcement, he may start to see the benefit of watching you come from his mouth, and how much you hang out for a good fuck as a result.

> *Graze on my lips; and if those hills be dry, Stray lower, where the pleasant fountains lie.*
> — William Shakespeare

No matter what size your penis, if your lips and tongue can deliver, you'll have earned your cuntylinguist stripes and will get rave reviews as a star lover. Each woman's likes and dislikes are different, so the techniques and tips in this chapter hold no money back guarantees if she doesn't come. You earn your stripes yourself.

Teasing

First off, it's a dive, not a dunk. You're not dunking your head down there for a quick probe. Start slowly — a good dive takes a bit of time. Don't aim for the love button target straight off: make her wait, or even beg, for it. As you're heading south, try not to jump from face to vag in one fell swoop. Women like to be warmed up, so give her body attention. Kiss her body as you go down. The inner thighs are very erogenous, so spend a bit of time licking and swirling around there, before brushing across her lips. Be daring and unexpected. Surprise her. Use your fingers to slide around and play teasingly, with quick and slow movements. Now, if she's really throbbing and grinding for it, go ahead and tantalize the clit. But once there, keep focusing attention on

---

Muff Diving Accessory

Muff divers who want extended play, or to go down under water, say, in a spa, and still breathe, can use the Pussy Snorkel, found at *www.pussysnorkel.com*. The Pussy Snorkel comes with nostril inserts attached to a "breathing tube apparatus," but before you go thinking the whole thing is a bit silly, it also comes with a handy (or rather handless) clitoral stimulator.* Check out the site for more information.

* This is not an author endorsement of the product, but an illustration that diving accessories can be obtained and may be helpful.

---

other areas: it's not like once you hit the bullseye the rest of the dartboard disappears. You can use your lips to suck her clit, and use your tongue to reach in and lick inside her vag. Pearl diving is not only about tongue-on-clit action. Make your initial dive like a tray of hors d'oeuvres: a light smattering of varieties. Watch and listen to her cues so you can get an idea of which techniques really drive her crazy. And for God's sake, please eventually use them. If you know she's hanging to come, don't keep endlessly fiddling about somewhere out on her left outer lip. As hot as she is, it can cool down fast if it stops working for her.

Lippy loving: get your lover to kiss your upper lip when kissing you before diving. Eastern sexuality beliefs purport that the upper lip is the key to the clitoris.

Tools

Your main diving apparatus is clearly the tongue. It's warm, wet, soft and feels great because there is so much you can do with it. There is almost nothing you can do with your tongue that won't feel good, so rest assured that just putting your tongue down there is Correct Move Number One. You can vary between soft tongue and hard tongue. It's usually best to start off with a soft tongue as not all women like hard stimulation of their vulva, and neither do they like a hard poke straight off the bat. This is the seductive art of diving, after all, not fucking. Move your tongue around and vary it. If you're bored licking up and down, or from side to side in the same motion over and over, she probably is too. Always try different combinations and eat in an unpredictable order. If you know one particular movement really works for her, you can alter the pressure and rhythm for variety. Creativity should be near the very top of your bag of tricks.

In addition to tongue action, you've got your lips, teeth (careful!), the tip of your nose, and your fingers at your disposal. You can rub your nose against her clit in "Eskimo kiss" style, quickly shaking your head from side to side, and your lips are very good for both light brushes and hard sucking. Many women like a man to use his fingers when he's giving head because it allows him to draw back her lips for full clit exposure, and women often like the contrast of firm finger pressure and soft tongue, as well as fingers inside/mouth outside manoeuvering.

Techniques

Tongue tickling You can flatten and widen your tongue to lick larger areas, or just use the tip of your tongue for more specific attention to detail. For those of you who can fold or roll your tongue, you can try to cup the clitoris within the fold of your tongue (depending on the size of her button).

If you stiffen your tongue, you can probe it in and out of her vag. This feels good for a lot of women. It most likely isn't going to make her come, but it's nice for a change of pace. You can also use a stiff tongue over her clit, but a word of warning: not all women like hard stimulation of the clit, and some can find it painful. Make sure her grunts and shrieks are from ecstasy, not agony.

Vary your pressure, rhythm, motions and direction. In general, the rule of tongue is whether you're darting or lingering with it, mix it up and follow her signals.

Mouthing her off After a bit of lip brushing and nibbling, use your lips to create suction on different parts of her lips and clit. The contrast of your hot, soft lips and firm vacuum pressure is highly pleasurable for many women. While sucking, you can also flick with your tongue. Make sure you don't suck too hard: again, some women don't like it. And go easy with your teeth; grazing, yes, biting and chewing, no.

Blowing the trumpet Place the front of your lips so they completely surround the clitoris, then blow out gently, as if blowing a trumpet. When you need to breathe, breathe in and out through your mouth. Occasionally pull your lips back and allow the vibration between them to vibrate against her clit. It makes some noise, but then all vibrators do. And you thought you could never compete with the vibrator in her bedside table!

Caution: It is not safe to blow air into a woman's vagina, especially if she is pregnant — internal damage can result, so do not attempt to blow the trumpet on her vaginal opening.

98 percent of women are as sensitive to having their inner and outer lips licked and stroked as their clit. So go lip to lip.

Source: Kinsey Institute, as reported in *Cosmopolitan: Over 100 Truly Astonishing Sex Tips*

Finger-licking good In addition to tongue and mouth, most women like some finger action for firm pressure to help deliver the big O. Find out from her what gets her off, because you should be at least as good as she is in bringing her to a climax if you want the Great Lover Award for O-Achievement. Using your fingers inside, reach for her front and back vaginal walls, and play in the outer portion of the vag where there is greater sensitivity. You can also press or rub the heel of your hand on her mons, clit or shaft. Alternating between fingering and licking her clit in rapid succession is another pleasure potential.

In Tahiti, women used to refuse to blow a man, yet cunnilingus was routinely practiced and expected. Both men and women considered mouth kissing perverse.

Tackling the O

Here's the Number One Tip. When she starts to come, or is on the edge, do not let go of the clit. You've brought her this far, now keep hanging in there. If you're using your lips or tongue, many women may have prolonged orgasms because the pressure is not as hard, allowing for a longer orgasm before the clit gets too sensitive. So don't feel a few throbbing pulses, assume that's it, mission accomplished, then let go. Have her guide you as to when she is done, either by guiding your head with her hands, or simply ask her to tell you. Some women can achieve multiple orgasms through continual stimulation, but most women attain their second, fourth, sixth orgasms after a mini-break, so once she comes, keep licking and/or fingering, but gently. She will be sensitive. A lot of women feel that asking for more is greedy, so if you voluntarily keep diving for a second treasure, the bonus points will be huge. Remember, it's not over till the fat lady sings, and that red bulging clit can sing a few encores.

"Almost there" Sometimes it just ain't gonna happen. You've done everything right, she's hot, wet, wanting, but ... nope. This can happen for lots of reasons: her, you, the time of the month, how she's feeling, self-consciousness, stress, distractions — nearly anything, really. If you've given it your best shot and it isn't happening, what do you do then? First, ask her if there's anything you can do to get her there. Women can sometimes be shy about giving direct or explicit instructions on how to get her off, but more often than not, she'll know exactly where and how you slipped off the mark. The answer may be a simple, "more left, less pressure."

But even if it's not that simple, as long as she doesn't have a sexual problem with attaining orgasm in general (in which case she should consult a sex therapist), and this is a one-off, you shouldn't let it worry either of you too much. Kiss, cuddle, shift the focus to another area of the body; do whatever makes you both comfortable. If not coming via oral sex is a pattern — if a woman can come by fingers, masturbation, intercourse, but not by oral sex — then she may want to seek a professional sex therapist's advice. If this is the case, be supportive, and help her get over any issues she may have about her vulva, vagina and oral sex by telling her how sexy and beautiful she is, and how much you enjoy performing oral sex on her. First, she will need to practice letting go, receiving your face down there, and releasing the goal of orgasm so she can enjoy it. After that, tackling the big O gets easier and easier.

🎤 *"It wasn't that I hated it when my boyfriend went down on me, but I just never thought it was that great. I rarely came, and if I did, it was just barely, not for long, and a very gentle climax. Nothing like my friends have described. It just felt like he was licking me, but that didn't excite me. He really liked doing it though, and made it his project to get me to like it too. He started experimenting with pressures and I began to get into it. It took a few months, but one time it was so hot, he actually came without me* touching him — just from him sucking me. That was a huge turn-on, that my pleasure was so explosively hot for him. I'm happy to say that oral sex is now something we both love." — woman, 26

BLOWING: blowjob, blow, give head, head job, suck off, suck dick, suck cock, tongue job, gob job, go down, deep throat, dick lick, gum job, hummer, knob job, meat whistle, mouth fuck, sac suckling, white swallow, goop gobbling, drink from the fountain of youth, clean his pipe, blow the skin flute, kneel at the altar, tongue lash, gnaw the bone, kiss the worm, smoke the blue-veined havana

"I love blowjobs. What man doesn't? My wife gives great head, and she likes doing it. She often surprises me by going down — I rarely have to ask for one. Sometimes she jumps in the shower with me and gives me one, or before we go out, or even in the morning before getting out of bed. She's got some great moves, and can make me crazy before letting me come. What I really like is when she lets me watch her do it in the light, and when she's got my dick in her mouth and looks up at me with those beautiful eyes. That's nearly enough to send me over the edge, right there." — man, 32

"When I was fifteen, I accidentally walked into a room where a porn movie was playing on TV, and saw a scene where a woman was giving a man a blowjob. She looked gross, disheveled and submissive, and him coming all over her face, neck and hair was disgusting to me at fifteen. That image stayed with me and I was always afraid of going down on a guy because I thought a good blowjob meant I had to look like that porn star, and I was scared that the guy would come all over me like in the movie. Years of that fear built up a complete aversion to oral sex, and it's only now, fifteen years later, and only after a few drinks that I will ever attempt it." — woman, 30

The Legend of Cleopatra

It is said that Cleopatra of ancient Egypt loved giving head. She was a famous fellatrice in the ancient world, and is purported to have blown over 1,000 men, including a few hundred Romans in one night. Move over, Casanova.

FELLATRICE: a woman who is an expert in blowing. She specializes (and trains) in the art of stimulating a man's genitals with her lips, mouth and tongue.

Blowing Basics

As Samantha from "Sex and the City" said, they don't call it a job for nothing. Blowers must negotiate the jaw stress, teeth placement, nose breathing, bobbing, licking, hand/mouth rhythms, gag reflex, and the spit or swallow dilemma. There's a lot to think about, and that's why it takes practice and know-how to suck good cock.

There are two main problems that face women when giving head. No, not the dick and scrotum. The first is how much dick to take in. The second is what to do with his cum. To be considered a "top job" blower, a quick poll of sex workers and amateur oral sex aficionados reveals the popular answers are: (1) all of it; and (2) swallow.

These answers are maybe not what every girl wants to hear. After all, giving good head can make some women anxious. This is because it is so plainly obvious when it's not good: his dick doesn't get hard or he doesn't come; she doesn't enjoy sucking away with no reply and no result; and he is probably lying there wishing she'd do something else or give up. Everything seems to scream "failure": his soft cock, her ego, desire to please, and his sense of satisfaction. So, when faced with this degree of potential rejection (because if his dick doesn't get hard, many women automatically assume it's because of her), women en masse will do anything to stay away from the blowing zone. Or, if facing pressure to do it, will round their mouths and bob up and down until he comes. But really this is mouth-fucking, not blowing.

Giving head is not something every single girl is going to love doing, or even do, full stop, for that matter. Some girls who are shy or nervous, or grossed out about oral sex, can get over their fears with some practice; for others, giving head may never be something they become entirely comfortable with. To those who want to have oral sex in their repertoire, I say this: Every girl should have a blowjob bag of tricks. To learn how to give great head, first learn a few techniques that appeal to you, then practice them, and put the best ones in your lucky dip. There is no foolproof formula for giving good head, because each penis is different, as is the man it belongs to. Once you become comfortable with your head-job style and have a variety of techniques in your bag of tricks, though, you will be expert enough to satisfy just about any man, have no fear.

Two to three men in 1,000 can suck their own cock to orgasm and ejaculation.

Source: Kinsey Survey of 5,000 men, as reported in *The Illustrated Book of Sexual Records*

Teasing

The most common tactile error many women make is to head straight for the member and go for broke. If men wanted a straight tug, mouth or not, they could basically wet their hands and do it themselves. One of the keys to good blowing is in the tease. When men realize you're going to go down on him, they get excited just thinking about their cock in your mouth. So don't give them the prize right away, tease them and make them wait. Lick your lips, make them really wet, look at him, hold his balls in one hand and the base of his dick in the other. Kiss his inner thighs, drag your tongue across his sac. Toy with the head of his penis along your wet lips, but again, don't take him in your mouth right away. Breathe on the tip of his dick, and tantalize him by reaching your tongue out and circling his penis. Lick his shaft up and down. Let him watch you do this. Don't fuss about too long, though. A little teasing heightens his excitement, but too much gets tedious. When he really starts squirming, it's time to get serious. When they finally take his penis in their mouth, some women like to give a short groan or hum. This creates a slight vibration, and it can also turn him on more, by making him feel that resisting the urge to suck his cock has been as torturous for you as it has for him.

Techniques

There are no hard or fast rules about blowing techniques. Keeping your teeth out of the way is about the only firm guideline.

Do not simply mouth-fuck a cock. Good blowing is far more than up-and-down motions, in and out of your mouth. Try taking him in and sliding your lips up to the head of his dick, flicking his glans with your tongue, still inside your mouth, as you reach the tip. Twist your head around, rotating your lips around the coronal ridge of his head. Vary how deep you take him in your mouth. If you go deep consistently every time, he's likely to come right away, but if you vary between deep and shallow, you draw out the job a little longer. If you don't want to take all of him in your mouth, grip his shaft with one hand. You can pump your hand in the same direction as your mouth (both up, both down) or alternate your hand and mouth, meeting halfway (hand moving base to tip, mouth moving tip to base). Your rhythm can also vary — watch and listen to his body responses to detect whether to slow down or speed up. Remember, blowing isn't about one technique: don't just use a fast motormouth, or a slow, long drawl, but use a bit of both. Most women like varying speeds, and so do men. As you're doing all this, bear in mind that the tongue is an aid. Don't just make your mouth an open cavity. Let your tongue rest and slip along the bottom of his cock as you twist, slide and pump.

Sucking When a man says he loves having his cock sucked, he isn't only referring to licking and lips. You just have to stick your thumb in your mouth and suck it to feel the difference on your tongue. Think how good that must feel for him. You can vary suction pressures from soft to really quite strong. Just be careful you don't go overboard, suck or pull back too hard, or allow your teeth to get in the way. There are two main sucking techniques: the deep suck and the shallow suck. Taking only his head in your mouth, you can create suction on both the up and down movements on his glans, or alternate one or the other. With the deep suction, take as much of his shaft in your mouth as is comfortable and suck him off. You may even want to suck him all the way off, pulling your head off his penis entirely, like pulling a lollipop out of your mouth — this can make a smacking-type noise, but if he's into that, he'll love it. With the deep suck, you can pull back slowly, or in one sweeping move.

Licking Using a flat, wide tongue, you can lick him from shaft to tip, blowing your hot breath on him at the same time. You can also flick your tongue from side to side, tickling his dick as you move up and down his shaft. Circle the head and ridge with your tongue, dipping your tongue in the opening. If he has released pre-cum, pull your head away and let this droplet stretch out. Let him watch you do this, and dip back onto his head, taking him in. You can also alternate pressure strokes using your hand with licking strokes.

Minty fresh Some women and men swear by hot peppermint tea. Drinking a cup of peppermint tea heats up your mouth, which can increase sensation and blood flow in his penis. Some also swear the leftover mint taste in the mouth gives him a tingling feeling, especially in his sensitive head area. Women also report that using a bit of toothpaste on his balls to heat up his sac drives men crazy. It's better not to smear the paste directly on the skin, as it may be too intense or painful. Instead, put some paste on your tongue before licking and sucking the area.

Humming Some women can feel like right fools doing this, while others love the result so much they don't care. The louder and sometimes lower you hum, the stronger the vibration of your lips and tongue. Only hum around the head of his dick, because that is where it feels most intense. Some guys are not into this; they don't like the distraction of the noise. All you can do is try it and see if it works for you, or for him. Nothing ventured, nothing gained.

Throating

The first thing women think of when they think about taking a dick down their throat is "gag." Not gross gag, but the automatic gag reflex that occurs whenever any foreign object enters your throat. It's generally not too difficult to get his cock down your throat, but it is challenging to get your throat to accept its presence there. A penis is flexible and will bend in your mouth and down your throat. Your throat, though, will want to close off and eject it right out of there, at first. Tricks to calm the gag reflex are to think about relaxing the throat, breathing deeply and evenly, and occasionally swallowing the saliva that builds up in your mouth. Your throat will swallow with a cock in it, and it will soothe your response to gag. The best way to learn to deep-throat is to suck on a few lozenges, which slightly numbs the throat, then practice with a dildo (a shot of tequila beforehand wouldn't go astray either). Almost any woman, who wants to, can learn to deep-throat, but it takes patience, practice and perseverance.

Once you've mastered getting his dick down your throat, and it feels comfortable, you have two choices: deep-throating or throat-fucking. Deep-throating is the woman moving her head back and forth, taking the penis in and along her throat. Throat-fucking is the man thrusting his cock down her throat. Most women prefer deep-throating because she retains control over depth and tempo. Throat-fucking takes a lot of trust and communication. Whether you're doing either of these techniques, they should feel comfortable and pleasurable. If anything hurts, stop.

Spit versus Swallow

When asked what they prefer, the majority of men will choose swallow over spit. But in saying "swallow," what they really mean is that they want to come in your mouth. What you do afterwards is secondary in importance, although some men view swallowing as a symbol of acceptance and love. If you think about it, you can understand why he would want to come in your mouth. You've done a great job of bringing him to a climax, and if you take his cock out of your warm, soft mouth, just when he's about to feel amazingly intense pleasure pulses, you prematurely bring to a halt his luscious experience of you, and he comes instead either in the air or into a towel. Given the choice, most men will go for the mouth option every time.

But, for those of you who have the heebie-jeebies about actually swallowing cum, you may find that you don't have to. You can still spit it out, after he's come in your mouth. A discreet wipe onto a towel, shirt, tissue or bed linen is nicer than a hacking hurl. For some women, though, this is small consolation, as the issue for them is the taste of semen, the general repulsion of cum, or the demeaning feeling some

Law of sexual pleasure: for every action, there is an equal and opposite reaction.

women can experience when a man blows in their mouth. For the spitters of the world, bear in mind that you are the blower, you are the woman in control. He's generally happy enough that you want to take his cock in your mouth, so if you spit at the end, well, it's really not a major blow to him (pun intended). It may take some practice getting to know when your partner is about to come, so you know when to duck for cover. Many men's shafts will pulse just prior to ejaculation, but with some it's so slight that it's easy to miss. A little practice and attention and you'll be able to read your partner's telltale signs. And if you can't, well, ask him to tell you right before he's about to explode.

If you're intent on being a "top job" blower and swallowing, but truly, truly don't like semen (and let's face it, I know of no woman who would volunteer to drink a glass of the stuff), well, choices are limited: put up with the taste, learn to love it, or learn the trick to "down the hatch" (see below).

PEARL NECKLACE: drops of cum ejaculated on the partner's neck after a head job.

SNOWBALLING: holding the semen in your mouth, then French kissing your partner and sharing the semen in both your mouths.

Down the hatch

In any standard swallow, the goal is usually to get him to come towards the back of your throat to make swallowing quicker and easier, and to avoid the taste. Some swallowers like to taste their man's semen, to swirl it around their mouth, and even kiss their partner back, sharing his juice with him (snowballing). For the "down the hatch" maneuver, there is actually no swallowing involved. If you can deep-throat (see pages 108–9 for techniques), you can get him to come straight down the back of your throat, literally, "down the hatch", without having to take a single swallow. The downside of this technique is that just prior to climax you must deep-throat, which not every woman likes to do, and your throat cannot play with his head just prior to ejaculation like your tongue can, making variety and suckage out of the question.

Testicles

For women who are hesitant about sucking dick, well, the balls often perplex them even more. The skin of the scrotum is very sensitive, as is the area of skin between the base of the penis and the sac, and the perineum, behind the sac. Light stroking and licking of this whole area is almost always welcome. Pay attention to the skin of the sac as well as the balls themselves. Lightly scratch the skin with your fingernails. Use accessories at hand (food, feathers, toys). Lick his sac wet and take one ball into your mouth. You can try taking both in your mouth, but not every woman is successful at this. His testicles are sensitive to pressure, so be gentle, but not too light. Judge your pressure by his responses. Many men love to have their sac pulled. Circle your thumb and forefinger around the sac and pull. You can pull quite hard, but don't think "yank," "choke" or "squeeze"; think rhythmic pulling and massaging.

Who Goes First and Why

Most couples who both want to get off from oral sex think the man should go down on the woman first. There is a simple answer for this. If he has come first, his body switches off and goes into post-orgasm mode (technical term: refractory period). A man is much more likely to give good head if he is horny, hard and anticipating orgasm. His intensity and desire to please and feel turned on by her sexual noises and response is higher if he has not yet come. A woman can stay excited and multi-orgasmic for up to an hour after her first orgasm, so she can still feel hot, wet and into it when going down on him after she has come. Of course, a man who really, really wants to go down on a woman can do a good job after being sucked off; just because his body may not respond, doesn't mean he isn't loving it.

If you can't decide about taking turns, 69 is always an option.

Tongue Wagging

Whispering sweet nothings, dirty talk, groaning, shouting his/her name, yes yes yes, are all good forms of communication, but they aren't particularly helpful in terms of giving good head. If something isn't working for you, speak up! Or if you're wondering whether what you're doing is hitting the right spot, ask. Now, there is a line to draw with this, and crossing it often means you've gone from potential-rock-god lover to completely-insecure-unable-to-take-initiative lover. Random, brief and occasional checks with looks or words are acceptable. Or even a discussion before or afterwards to learn more about what your partner likes is often a good call. It is not good form to drop cock every half-minute to ask, "Like this?" or "How about this?" And neither should he stop every ten seconds to ask, "Here?" or "What about if I do this?" It's not a discussion time. You'll end up wanting to shout, "Just get on with it!" The compromise is somewhere between over the top and silence. A little talking, a few questioning moments, and the rest of the time it's down to the business of tongue. And remember, talking doesn't have to be only about asking directions. Men usually hate doing this anyway. Talking dirty is a great part of giving head. Men love to hear what you like about his cock, and why you love it in your mouth. And women love to hear how beautiful they are, how much you desire her and how turned on you are by looking at her pussy and seeing it get red and wet for you.

If you are the receiver, you may want to talk a little more — after all, your mouth is free (unless you're doing 69). In addition to your pleasure sounds, help your partner out by giving instructions. If they are on to a good thing and you don't want them to stop, say something, before they move on or away. If you want them to go that little bit to the left, well, how will they know unless you pipe up?

Body talk is another feature of communication in oral sex. Hip movement is a dead giveaway, as are facial expressions. Some men and women can lie back with a relaxed poker face while receiving, while others thrash and toss in ecstasy. Learn to follow what your partner's expressions mean. By and large, if she is grinding her hips up towards you, or up and down rhythmically, you are doing some good work. And if he is thrusting his dick forwards or tilting his pelvis towards you, he's getting worked up and wants more, deeper. Watch and listen for cues, so you know what your partner is silently asking for and responding to, as well as what they say out loud.

Positions

The two main considerations for oral sex positions are access and comfort. If you're in for a long session, comfort is the key. The receiver needs to be comfy to relax, let go and get into it with no niggling distractions ("What is that under my left shoulder?" or "This floor is getting cold"), and the performer needs comfort for focus, talent and duration. If they can't get comfortable, they will have trouble sticking to the job at hand (er, mouth).

Diving

Any position in which you can get access to the muff will work. For longer sessions, she may want to be sitting or lying down, rather than standing. She may want to watch you, in which case sitting in a reclined position against a few pillows enables her to see you, and it's easier for you to look up at her. If you are both lying down, you can lie on your sides; some men think access is slightly easier this way. Men who lie between a woman's legs sometimes experience neck pain after long sessions, but if you tuck one or two pillows under her pelvis, her muff is raised and access is more comfortable. Another solution is to slide her all the way to the end of the bed. In this position it is preferable to let her spread her legs over two chairs, or a bedside table and a chair, with you sitting on the floor, face aimed for the honeypot.

Blowing

Again, any position allowing access will work, though some are better than others. If you do not have to worry about your body weight, or your hair getting in the way, you are freer to concentrate. If you are lying down on your side with your body weight on one side, or propped up on one or both elbows, you might find you will tire more quickly than if you have your weight evenly distributed. You also might find holding your head up while you bend over him is tiring after a while. One solution is to have him lie on his side facing you, or rest your head on his thigh, but you compromise some access and technique in these positions. A popular position is for him to be standing or sitting, and for you to be kneeling in front. You have total control over his dick and balls, and are free to move your head, and his dick, in any direction. He can easily watch, and you can simply glance up to look at his face. Face and eye contact during oral sex is not only erotic, but adds intimacy and a sense of connection between partners.

69: soixante-neuf, flip-flop, flying sixty-nine, heads and tails, loop-the-loop

<u>Sixty-Nine</u>

"Doing the 69" — diving and blowing at the same time — is a famous way of having oral sex, and people tend to love it or hate it. Those who love it say it's the ultimate shared sexual experience, where you both get the two sensations of receiving and giving at the same time. Men love tasting a woman's pussy as he's being sucked off, and women say giving head is so much better when they're riding their own waves of pleasure as his tongue is feeling her. In the "Don't Care For It" camp, men complain about access and having their nose close to her bum because he's licking her upside-down. Women say they can't concentrate, and they have a harder time giving a good job because the position requires them to hold their body weight on their elbows (if they are on top), or limited head movement (if they are on the bottom or side by side).

Q. Do you know what 6.9 is?
A. A good thing fucked up by a period.

Q. What is 69 squared?
A. Dinner for 4.

Q. What is 68?
A. You do me and I owe you one.

The 69 tends to be high on entertainment and experiment value and low on technique benefit. For the shared, simultaneous mouth–genital feeling, though, 69 is your bet. Main 69 positions include side-by-side, man-on-top, though more commonly, woman-on-top. Side-by-side is the most common, as it is the most comfortable and least tiring; woman-on-top makes some men complain about how wet their face gets; and man-on-top can make some women feel like they are choking on a mouthful of cock, but for those women who like deep-throating, this is a prime position.

> *"I don't like 69. I think I'm too selfish. It's not as much fun if I can't moan and groan, and it's hard to say 'Oh, yes, baby!' with a mouth full of balls."* — woman, 33

Etiquette

It is poor form in 69 to abandon your end of the bargain because your partner is doing such a good job. Remember the Golden Rule of 69 is to please and be pleased. Some couples like to match or contrast rhythms together while others like to each do their own thing. Other couples like to play music and match their tempos and pressures to the beat. You and your partner will figure out what turns you on and gets you off together, in time. If you are new to 69, remember practice makes purrfect.

Bloody Hell

You're not a true Captain until you've sailed the red sea.

Not a lot of men jump to the head of the line to go down on a woman when she has her period, but there are some who honestly don't mind it. A lot of women are horny during their period and want to orgasm, but aren't happy to have intercourse, because their vaginas may ache, or they simply don't want to deal with the mess or fuss. If a woman is suffering from cramps, an orgasm may help relieve them. Head jobs, hand jobs or masturbation may be the preferred way for her to come during this time of the month. A woman can wear a tampon, and get off by her partner stimulating her clit, without any contact with her vag at all. Men may want, or agree, to go down on her, or not. It's really an individual preference, and if you are a man who gives good head on the other days of her cycle, she's more likely to understand if you want no part of diving during menstruation. So, women, respect his wishes, and if you know he's not into it, tell him if you're bleeding, or may have just started.

Safety

Oral sex is relatively safe sex in that there is no risk of pregnancy, however, there is the possibility of giving and catching sexually transmitted infections if you play orally with no protection. For truly safer sex, blowing should be done with condoms, and diving should be done with a dental dam or latex square placed over the vulva (see "Latex Sucks," in the Rubber Dicky chapter). The simple fact is the majority of us do not do this, even in casual and random encounters. If you decide to throw caution to the wind and give the latex a pass, be sure you at least avoid the following.

If he or she has a cold sore, herpes lesion, or anything even slightly suspicious on the mouth or lips, don't let them near your below-the-belt zone. Herpes can be transmitted from the mouth to the genitals.

If you have had recent dental work, or have open mouth-sores, or bleeding gums, be careful about holding cum in your mouth, or getting any menstrual blood in there, as HIV is potentially transmitted this way.

RIMMING: anilingus, bilingual, rim job, brown job

AROUND THE WORLD: a tongue bath, licking all over the body, including genitals and anus.

Bum Pashing

The bum pash, licking the bumhole, isn't for everyone, but hey, don't knock it till you've tried it, say many a rimming convert. It isn't much different in terms of basic technique than licking pussy. Some men and women like sucking sensations, but tongue action is a bit easier. Your tongue can be soft or hard, fast or slow, depending on what your partner likes. The anal opening has many sensitive nerve endings, so even quick, light and/or brief tickling with the tongue can drive your partner wild. For the uninitiated: this might be something to try in a bathtub or spa, if you're a bit queasy about any anal smells.

♟ *"It's my rosebud. I like it nuzzled, fingered, licked, sucked, blown on. Basically I like anything my partner does with it. It's so sensitive down there, that it intensifies my orgasms."* — male, 24

PASH RASH: stubble graze on a woman's chin, nose, lips or cheeks from prolonged or fervent pashing. Can range from mild redness to severe scabbing. Treat with aloe vera, vitamin E and a good skin care moisturizer. Men: Shave closer next time!

While kissing, 72 percent of people keep their eyes firmly shut, 8 percent open them and 20 percent sneak an occasional peek.

Source: informal magazine survey

Art of Pashing

Why do we love pashing? The face-to-face, lip-locking, tongue-hockey, spit-swapping mouth-swirling act is a ritual sacred to our feelings of sensuality and eroticism. The art of kissing is a central human expression, from our teenage to our twilight years. There are hundreds of different types of kisses; and there are kissing Kamasutras available in bookshops to help you add variety to your pashing repertoire. From the air kiss to the deep French kiss, there is no limit to variation, save the limit of your imagination! Kissing arouses, excites, humors, settles, teases, comforts, calms, tickles, plays, intoxicates and expresses. There are as many descriptions, emotions and motivations for kisses as there are kisses.

Ten things to hate about pashing

1. Beards.
2. Neck cramps.

"Whoever named it necking was a poor judge of anatomy."

— Groucho Marx

3. Knocking teeth.
4. Biting or bruising kisses.
5. Having my mouth searched dentist-style with their tongue, like they lost something.
6. Tongue too far down throat.
7. Sloppy, inattentive kissing.
8. Repetitious rotating tongue movements — boring!
9. Dribble and drool.
10. Smoker's breath/bad breath.

Ten things to love about pashing

1. Sharing and switching sides/head positions.
2. Tongue licking lips as well as mouth.
3. Sneaking a peek at the same time and looking at each other.
4. Hearing "Mmmmm" under their breath as they kiss me.
5. Light lip-sucking.
6. Alternating between deep and shallow kisses.
7. Being caressed and having my face held in their palms.
8. Bit of teasing biting of the bottom lips.
9. Exploring kisses on my neck, face, ears, eyelids.
10. Smiling or laughing while pashing.

Go Fish

Fish like to kiss, especially the Kissing Gurami, which pucker up, fish-lip to fish-lip, for up to twenty-five minutes in their fishy courtship ritual.

Gear Off

[*switching gears when sex drives differ*]

SEXUAL FRUSTRATION: feeling purple, blue balls, fuckstrated, night starvation

DESIRE AND EXCITEMENT: juiced up, gagging for it, freaking, horny, getting jiggy, feeling fuckish, hot, randy, hungry, rowdy, rooty, sexed up, wet, in heat, wide open, throbbing for it, have the hots, bedroom eyes, feeling on fire, red-eyed, looking with my fuck-me eyes, feeling come hither, feeling primed, warmed up, turned on

LACK OF DESIRE OR EXCITEMENT: dead down below, switched off, permanent headache, chilled, cold as ice, frozen, passion pass

Primal Urge

Humans have less than a handful of primal urges. Our very, very basic drives include the needs to eat, drink, sleep and screw. The part of our brain that is responsible for our desire to fuck is also responsible for our need to eat, our defense and protection and our emotions. These needs are commonly known as the Four Fs: food, fighting, fucking and feelings.

Our very basic urge to fuck, known as our libido (Latin for desire, lust), is for both making babies and making love. Whether we are in the procreation age bracket, before it, or well past it, our libido naturally waxes and wanes. Whether our sex drive is strong or weak depends on many circumstances and factors, including age, drugs and medication, stress levels, emotions, relationship status and health.

The stereotypes are that men, no matter what age, are always up for it: they are horny little boys until they are dirty old men; and women are supposed to be vampy hot-for-it vixens until "the change" and then they become cold crones, who wouldn't want sex even if bribed with a lifetime's supply of bargain shopping vouchers (or, well, maybe only then ...). Of course these are untrue: both men and women have libidos that dance around, that both jiggy and wallflower throughout their lives.

Generally the male sex drive peaks earlier in life, averaging in the early twenties, while a woman's sex drive peaks much later, in her thirties. However, because over a lifetime the sex drive fluctuates, a particular man may find himself hornier than ever at fifty and a woman may find herself feeling overwhelmingly, orgasmically nymphy at twenty-two. It is more common, though, for women to be hornier than men in their late thirties and forties, and men to be greater hound-dogs than women in their teens and twenties. Older women can be attracted to younger men because they have matching high libidos, while older men scope out younger women not only for "trophy" looks, but because they are more likely to have in-sync libidos and expectations, and accept less sex less often, with both tending to have lower libidos. Hugh Hefners of the world, take exception. But as an example, look at Tony, forty-seven, and Alice, twenty-three. They have lower sex drives than the insatiable Rod, twenty-one, and Kerry, thirty-four. One might think young Rod and Alice should be fucking like bunnies, and mid-life Kerry and Tony should be in domestic bedroom harmony, however, matching libidos alone pairs Kerry up with Rod because they both have far more voracious sexual appetites. This is not to say that every older woman and older man should be dumping their old mate for a newer model. Gears can be reconditioned in old engines. We don't always need the youngest, latest edition to score. And with maintenance and TLC, our libidos can flourish throughout our lives. In some cases, though,

> *Of American women, 46 percent have said that a good night's sleep is better than sex.*
> Source: *The Penguin Atlas of Human Sexual Behavior*

Sexual Urgh!

A man and a woman go into therapy and have separate sessions. The husband says, "Doc, everything's great except our sex life. We only do it three times a week." The wife sees the same therapist later and says, "I'm completely happy in my marriage except when it comes to our sex life — three times a week! He wants it all the time!"

whether old or young, our libidos don't only go up and down, they disappear entirely.

When we lose something we cherish, we look for it. When our sex drive slows or even stops, we do the same, and hunt for the cause so we can fix the problem. There are a number of causes of lost libido. When our sexual gear goes into neutral, we look for the triggers to rev it back up, because when we get our gear off to find our partner's sex gears are off or completely burned out, it's time to find the cause — and the solution.

Sick, mate

If you're ill, you generally do not feel like having sex. Whether suffering from a headache, flu, or battling a serious or life-threatening disease, your sex drive is often lower when the body isn't well. The body naturally wants to conserve energy to battle sickness, not expend it on sex, and the libido reflects this natural urge by becoming suppressed.

Also, many of the medications taken to fight illness, from depression to cancer, have side effects that tamper with libido. Whether you are taking a homeopathic, naturopathic or orthodox medication, be sure to read all about it in the literature given to you by your practitioner. More medications than not have some sort of effect on your libido or sexual function. This includes hormonal birth control methods for women, such as the pill, IUD and injections and implants. If you notice a sudden decrease in your sex drive, check your medications, or visit your doctor for a check-up.

Sorry Honey, I Have a Headache Headaches are one of our most common excuses to avoid sex. Contrary to widespread belief, sexual headaches are not entirely psychological or pretense. Known technically as coital cephalagias, sexual headaches are those throbbing headaches that occur just before or during sex. And *men* are four times *more likely* to suffer from these sexual headaches than women. Researchers have distinguished four different types of sexual headache, each with its own cause and cure.

1. **Muscle contraction headaches**: Usually focused around the head and neck, they are caused by the tensing of muscles during sex. They intensify during sexual excitement and peak in skull-splitting pain at orgasm. **Solution**: muscle relaxation techniques can help reduce the severity and frequency of these headaches.

2. **Vascular headaches**: Caused by increased blood pressure during sex, they are characterized by sudden explosive pain at the moment of orgasm. **Solution**: see your doctor if you suffer from this sexual headache. Prescription drugs for blood pressure may be required.

3. **Postural headaches**: These occur usually when having sex either in a sitting or standing position. They are thought to be caused by low cerebrospinal fluid pressure due to slight damage surrounding the spinal column. **Solution**: have sex lying down. If they continue to bother you, see your doctor.

4. **Drug-related headaches**: A more common form of sexual headache, these are brought on by the combination of alcohol or drug use and sex. Drugs such as marijuana and cocaine can cause headaches by lowering or raising blood pressure.

Alcohol, especially red wine, can trigger vascular or migraine headaches. **Solution**: make your bed a drug-free zone.

If you experience severe sexual headaches that include nausea, vomiting or dizziness, consult your doctor. Sex should not be a headache and a headache should not be an excuse.

Out of lust-juice

The male sex hormones, called androgens, are linked with libido, the most prominent of which is testosterone. What is less widely known however, is that although the primary sex hormones in women are estrogen and progesterone, females do produce a small amount of androgens, including testosterone. Testosterone is linked with libido in women, just as it is in men. The body produces varying amounts of each hormone, and in men and women, if this balance becomes out of kilter, sex drive can decrease. There are testosterone supplements and patches available for men and women suffering from low sex drive, but low libido can be the result of many factors, and hormone replacement may not be the right solution in all cases. Depending on the country, testosterone replacement therapy is generally not approved for use for women with low sexual desire, but can be available through restricted private prescriptions, and under careful medical supervision. Check with your sexual health practitioner. (See also "Testing Testosterone" section in The Energizer Bunny chapter.)

One US study revealed that lack of sleep the night before reduced the inclination for sex that night.

Source: *Cosmopolitan: Over 100 Truly Astonishing Sex Tips*

Bushed

Too shagged to shag is a common complaint of men and women. Fatigue wears down our body so that even our biological urge to bonk hits empty. Whether you have too much on your plate, leaving you no energy to muster up sexual desire, or if the problem is lack of sleep, your sex drive requires energy to hum. If your partner would prefer to sleep rather than make love, it doesn't mean they don't desire you, but that their desire needs a recharge. And that's exactly what sleep does: it recharges your libido. Sleep enables the body to reduce stress hormone levels in the body, and leads to greater desire.

Arr-grrr-ghh

Negative emotions and experiences and confusion prevent our sex drive from flourishing. Desire can go right out the window if we are feeling angry or frustrated. Men and women seek connection, whether to make love or make whoopee, and anger or frustration will literally stop the sexual response, right from the word go. Of course there are exceptions — when we have a physically releasing fuck, or make-up sex. However, built-up anger and resentment slowly erodes sexual desire in a relationship. They say one of the golden rules of a successful relationship is never to go to bed angry, and this is true in terms of maintaining sexual desire.

Similarly, distress, anxiety or issues arising from previous sexual abuse or negative sexual experiences can shut down libido. The memory of a past experience or lingering anxiety can resurface in varying sexual experiences, or with a new partner, if a person has suffered from rape, abuse, sexual violence or previous negative emotions from prior sexual encounters. This can lead to several sexual problems, including low desire.

Frustration or confusion, whether conscious or unconscious, over sexual orientation can also hinder sexual desire. This does not mean that if your partner doesn't feel like doing it they have "turned gay" all of a sudden. However, in some cases, if a person is in a relationship and realizes they are feeling "the other way," it can bring a sudden halt to their libido function.

All over, red rover

It seems logical that one of the quickest killers of libido is the end of a relationship. If a break-up is near, if you've decided you don't love someone anymore, this will impact on your sex drive, and your desire for them will wane. The death of love and affection in a relationship is usually the death of desire.

Stressed out, man

Stress not only affects aspects of our mood, coping mechanisms, relationship and lifestyle, but our physical libido as well. Our sexual function is highly sensitive to our stress levels, and if stress is high, sex drive is, more often than not, low. Keeping a balance on the levels of your stress will naturally maintain balance of your desire levels.

Switched off

Boredom in your relationship or with your life will equate to a plummeting libido. If you're not feeling turned on in your life, how can you expect to get turned on? To be switched on sexually, you need to feel switched on emotionally and intellectually in your life. And by your body. Poor body image is a leading cause of low desire. Low self-esteem or self-image, for both men and women, can quickly flip the libido switch to off. Your ability to feel sexy is dependent on your ability to perceive yourself as sexy.

Bringing up baby

Babies. We do it to make them, and once they arrive we never seem to have the energy. Raising babies is exhausting, but it also takes time. Our priorities become focused on being a good mother and father, and sometimes we lose sight of being a good lover as well. With sex occurring less and less, the sex drive goes into hibernation. Constant vigilance is needed to maintain a balance between good parenting and good loving.

Trying too hard

Sometimes the cause of low sexual desire is simply trying to do it too much or trying too hard. If your sex life is filled with pressure — to make a baby, make use of fertility treatments, or use whatever free time you have to jump quickly in the sack and make the most of it — it can stop desire dead in its tracks. Pressure is a deadset desire-stopper. Conception attempts can make sex a chore rather than a pleasure, and are a quick killjoy for desire. It's better to slow down, stay in touch with desire, and do it for pleasure, not for obligation.

The big chill

Women have earned the nasty stereotype over the centuries of being "frigid" when they have low sexual desire. Women have just as many reasons as men to experience low libido, and "frigid" is one of those words we no longer use because of the negative connotations it conjures up of women viciously withholding sex or being prudish or as cold as ice in bed.

"Seems to me the basic conflict between men and women, sexually, is that men are like firemen. To us, sex is an emergency, and no matter what we're doing, we can be ready in two minutes. Women, on the other hand, are like fire. They're very exciting, but the conditions have to be exactly right for it to occur."
— Jerry Seinfeld

Sexual desire is just as important to women as it is to men, and experiencing a loss of libido is equally distressing for both genders. Women and men can have a naturally low sex drive, and this does not mean a woman is frigid or something is wrong with a man. Individual sex drives vary greatly, and problems are only evident when a person feels their normal levels are lower, or low desire is interfering with their sex life or relationship.

Living Libido Loca

Libido naturally goes through peaks and valleys during different stages in life, depending on circumstances. If you're busy with work, on medication, a new parent, dealing with a loss, or experiencing any range of events or emotions, your sex drive will respond by fluctuating. When libidos fluctuate wildly, though, it can test your sanity and your relationship. And when one partner is in high gear and the other is in low, it can feel as though the two of you are never going to get into gear together. Crazy, up-and-down sex drives or consistently mismatched libidos can drive a wedge between you and keep your gears in neutral, rather than revving up. When this occurs, it is crucial that you and your partner prioritize your relationship and your sex life. Do not simply assume your libidos will click back into place automatically. While it's perfectly natural for your sex drive to wax and wane, if you are dissatisfied with how often you and your partner are connecting sexually, you must take action.

While it takes work to get your sex drives compatible over the span of a relationship, it's worth it, because of the benefit to your relationship. Many couples report that during times of consistent sexual expression, the level of intimacy and effective communication is raised and the overall health of their relationship is better. The sexual intimacy shared in the bedroom spills over into other areas in their life, from the most mundane to the deeply spiritual, and deepens their connection as a couple.

🗣 *"We've been married for over ten years, and I know our sex life has a lot to do with the overall health of our relationship. When we don't have regular sex, we tend to talk less about everything in general. We wake up, get showered, dressed, and each go out and do our work, then come home, have a brief chat, and fall asleep. Without sex, our whole life lacks intimacy. But when we are having regular sex, we feel connected, truly like a unit. We feel amorous, we talk to each other about our days while we're each showering, we agree on who's going to do what chores, we send messages during the day, and they're loving, appreciative ones, not nagging or barking orders. Then we decompress at the end of the day together and our overall affection and love is at a higher level. I know that regular sex keeps us a couple, rather than two people living together. We share everything when we're sharing sex together consistently."* — Barbara, 35

> *Women complain about sex more often than men. Their gripes fall into two major categories:*
> *1) not enough*
> *2) too much.*
> — Ann Landers

Switching Gears for a Good Ride

To revive sinking sex drives or a flagging relationship, more than one strategy may be required to help you and your partner get into gear and get revving.

Talk and listen

Acknowledging that there is a gear stuck in your sex life is the first step to unsticking it. Talk with your partner honestly about your libido, their libido and how often you are or aren't having sex. Couples most often complain of lack of time and desire for sex, so know that you are not alone, and that it is normal for these issues to arise in the course of your relationship. Using "I" language can help. This is making statements using "I" instead of "you," such as, "I appreciate it when you come home early and we can spend more time together," rather than "You hardly ever come home to spend time with me." Using "I" language shifts the responsibility to you, sounds less accusatory, and can lessen the defensiveness of your partner. "I" language promotes open discussion, rather than a domestic.

Open discussion means listening as much as talking, so hear your partner out by actively listening. Fair and balanced give-and-take communication with each partner talking openly and listening actively is an important step in reviving your sex life.

Compromise

Life is about compromise, and so is your sex life. You may be a night-sex person, but if mornings offer better private time, compromise is in order. Similarly, if you prefer a long lovemaking session, a short shag may have to suffice. The more often you have sex, the more your libido increases, and the greater your desire for sex. You will make more time for sex if you are in the mood more often. Compromise is the key to getting those gears humming.

Counseling

If your mismatched libidos have really devastated your relationship and communication, it may be necessary to call in a back-up troop or two, namely a sex therapist or relationship counselor. A counselor or therapist will mediate between you and your partner, source the conflict in the relationship and/or address the reason for low or mismatched libidos of one or both partners. It is always best to see a counselor together, however, if one partner is unwilling, the other can go for individual help. If you are feeling emotions such as anger, jealousy, fear or rejection, or you are simply not feeling close to your partner, your libido can easily be affected. It is a good idea to seek professional help to sort through issues before they grow larger. There is no shame in seeing a sex therapist. We are socialized to believe that sex is natural and we never need to be taught how to do it, or negotiate it. Not only is this untrue, but thinking this way underestimates and undervalues the complexity of our sexuality. Sometimes we need a third person to help us see the nature of our problems and how to fix them. And more than likely, your relationship will be stronger and you will feel closer as a result of having sought outside expertise.

Medication

A qualified sex therapist can work with your doctor in recommending examination and treatment for low sexual desire. They can work collaboratively to determine appropriate hormonal and physical tests to ascertain potential causes for low libido. While it varies in availability from country to country, the use of the steroid DHEA (dehydroepiandrosterone) has been shown in studies to raise libido in both men and women. It is never used as a first-response therapy to treat low sexual desire because it has not yet been thoroughly tested or approved. But in coming years it may be an option for some.

Testosterone replacement, in the form of patches, creams and implants, is fast gaining a reputation as a successful treatment for low sexual desire, especially in women. Testosterone is the hormone of desire, in both men and women, and low levels can be a direct cause of low sex drive. Studies have found that women with low libido and low levels of testosterone and DHEA have benefitted from testosterone replacement, and report a marked increase in their desire for sex after treatment. Testosterone replacement is not available for general prescription everywhere, but is approved in some cases for use in post-menopausal women. In the future, after further study, it is anticipated that testosterone replacement will become a standard therapeutic tool in the battle against low sexual desire.

Romance

Desire very often goes hand in hand with romance, and not just for women, for men too. If you want to get your rocks off then you must romance the stone. It's cornball and cliché to think about redating, but after you roll your eyes, realize that romance does wonders. Reinjecting your relationship with romance is an effective way to kick-start your lagging libido. If desire is low, don't schedule in a shag straightaway, try some wining and dining first. Whether you're juggling kids, jobs and chores, prioritize your partner and ask them out on a date — just the two of you. You can also heat things up by sending erotic emails, or even by showing your appreciation and affection by doing the washing up, bringing tea and toast to bed in the morning, and hey, flowers are always welcome. These gestures go a long way in the desire bartering system. The idea behind redating is to fall back in love, and remember the "early days" and the person you fell in love with. With that romantic reminder comes the passion you had when you first started dating. One of the most common statements heard by counselors is, "I want it to be like it was in the beginning." Well, turning back the clock is manual labor; you've got to seduce it back.

In sync

If your lack of sex life isn't the result of mismatched libidos but mismatched schedules, then the solution requires sacrifice and reprioritizing. We often get into a routine with commitments and habits that leave our sex lives lingering somewhere at the tail-end of our priorities. We're either tired and would rather sit in front of the TV, or we overcommit ourselves to too many nights out, too much work, too many kids' activities. If life gets in the way of your sex life to such a degree that you notice it, and it stops working for you, it's time to change priorities. Make some hard choices. Give up a night class, skip the gym, arrange for someone else to ferry your children to their classes and clubs, give your "Thursday night drink" social group a miss, and tune out your favorite television shows. Sometimes it takes dedication to reprioritize sex, especially if the relationship has hit passive mode, or you're shift workers, or simply hard workers, or social butterflies. If you find it overwhelmingly difficult and think that there simply is no room for sex in your busy life, then make a list of every activity and commitment you have in a week. Look at the pros and cons of doing each of those versus getting laid. At least one will score lower than sex, and it can be replaced. If not, look again. We're talking about screwing, folks, not solving world hunger. It doesn't take a massive amount of time. Make it fit.

Dirty weekend

Flip the gearbox on its head and take off to get off. Having trouble getting horny? Having a hard time making time for it? Stop being so responsible with your duties and commitments, and go be naughty. Throw caution to the wind and go gallivanting on a dirty weekend. It's often a bandaid solution and not a cure for whatever problems you have with your priorities, time, bodies or relationship, but for a pleasure-on-a-stick superficial fix, it's saucy, raunchy, lusty fun, and if you do it right, it will feel right.

Stop, in the name of love

Very often, just when you're going mad from not having sex, *not* having sex is just what you need to do. Huh? If sex, having it, not having it, wanting it, not wanting it, has become a pressure-cooker issue, then sometimes it's wise to back up and hold off. Acknowledge with your partner that you're going through a hard time, or a busy time and the issue is creating stress in the relationship, and give each other permission to leave sex off the "To Do" list (temporarily only). This gives the bedroom some breathing space and allows the relationship to relax from the pressure of scheduling sex. The sense of failure that can compound the problem when you've tried and failed to fit "doing it" in is then eliminated. You should agree on a timeframe (a few weeks to a month) for when you will get back in the saddle again to giddy up. Spend that sex-free time taking care of the commitments that are taking you away from being intimate with your partner, or learning time management. No bonking doesn't mean you can't be affectionate and teasing though. Take sex out of the equation to raise your desire levels. Then when you agree to reconnect, you do so with your full attention and burning desire. If this does not work, do not attempt to continue putting your sex life on hold. A damaging cycle of sexual neglect can quickly spin out of control, so visit a sex therapist or relationship counselor for advice.

Rub down

Touch is one of our most sexually stimulating senses. Massage is a deliciously erotic way of connecting with your partner and yet few couples do it. Many couples become too busy to spend time on their sex lives, and making love can become routine. As a result, the power of touch between partners can sometimes be perfunctory, or even sexless. Touches outside the bedroom may be reduced to a pat on the back or a peck on the cheek. In the bedroom, sexual initiation can end up being an inquisitive touch on the back or breast, a few kisses, and then it's all on fast forward to orgasm, if it's on at all.

Even during foreplay, the places that partners touch each other are often limited to a few square inches of skin. Whole pleasure zones of the body go unnoticed. Gordon Inkeles, author of *The Art of Sensual Massage*, says, "It's entirely possible that a woman who's been married for years has never been touched behind the knee, or between the toes, by another adult since childhood." In fact, our culture is so starved for touch that many of us will have sex simply to be touched, when all we really crave is the wonderful warmth of skin against skin.

Meditation and relaxation raise the levels of the hormones (such as DHEA) which increase your sex drive.

Vitamins and minerals such as zinc, B and E and others that work on the nervous and circulatory systems are good libido enhancers.

Before you go rushing out to sign up for the next available massage training course, be assured that a professional massage certificate and knowledge of human physiology are not required for a sensual massage. A sensual massage is simply using your sense of touch to give and receive pleasure.

Massage is a potent sex-enhancer, according to Inkeles, because it induces a state of deep relaxation by dissipating the negative physical and emotional effects of stress. People tend to use sex as a means of blowing off physical tension or mental stress. But a far better approach is to drop into a state of relaxation first, through sensual massage, then make love.

Not only is this more effective against stress, but according to both massage and sexual therapists, it can also heighten the sexual response. The ascent to orgasm (which momentarily involves extreme body tension) is much more dramatic if you first go into a state of deep relaxation. The rise of sexual pleasure from relaxation to orgasm is longer and felt more acutely than if you were to start from a state of semi-aroused agitation or stress.

Things to remember about sensual massage:

* Generally, people tend to touch other people they way they like to be touched. So to make sure you are massaging with the degree of pressure your partner likes, don't be shy about asking for feedback.

* A sensual massage is about exploring the whole body, not about explicit sexual touch. You can use indirect touching to simultaneously relax and stimulate your partner by stroking

around the genital area, or even simply cupping the genitals without moving your hands. Touch in different, less obviously sexual ways. Your touches can get increasingly deliberately erotic, but a sensual massage is not about delivering your partner straight to orgasm.

* People hold a lot of tension in their faces. In addition to touching all over the body, massage the face, especially the forehead, temples and jaw muscles.

* Focus on areas where the skin is thin as these areas are very sensitive. Some of these places are around the ankles, the neck and the insides of the arms.

* Try giving touch with things other than your fingers and hands: you can experiment with your breath, fluttering your eyelashes, and brushing your lips across your partner's body. There are also massage toys to use such as massage rollers, feathers and vibrators.

* Use massage oils because they tend to make the skin more sensitive to touch. In Mediterranean cultures 5,000 years ago, people used to anoint each other using vegetable oil scented with drops of lemon. Now we have a huge variety of oils to choose from, even ones that heat up once rubbed on the skin.

The sensual massage can be a sexual appetizer, or it can simply be an expression of affection. Whichever the case, it's a fantastic way to explore your partner's body and make them feel loved and appreciated. And if your partner came home shagged from work, it's the perfect way to unwind and convince him or her a shag's in order.

Get real

Be realistic. Humans are more complex than cars, and their sexual engines are temperamental and fiddly. Switching from low gear to high gear takes work and time; an overnight overhaul won't fix the problem long term. You may experience some really "on" weeks when you get off more often than you have in years. And then you may hit a rough patch again, when gearing up to get your gear off is unthinkable. Measure your libido in small victories, with one come at a time.

McSEX: ordinary, fast-food type, mass-production value, delivery of simple physical release through "going through the motions" intercourse.

YUPPIE SEX: perfunctory, routine sex, planned in mutual diaries, with structured use of sophisticated sex toys, lingerie and lube. Mess kept to a minimum, standard three times a week, utterly lacks creative raw, primal passion.

Making Time for Making Whoopee

* Hire a babysitter. Yes, the orgasms and intimacy are worth the fee.
* Eat a meal in bed instead of in the kitchen.
* Throw the TV guide away, hide the remote and unplug the tube. Stop watching tele-sex, and get to it yourself.

* Skip a Friday night out, and opt for a wild night in.
* Skip the gym and work out together at home.
* Fake sick at work for a sexual health day. (Justification: an orgasm a day keeps the sex therapist away.)
* Have a quickie in the shower before work.
* Screw the Saturday shopping and screw each other instead.
* Skip yoga, postpone that golf game, take the kids to the in-laws, simply agree to do what it takes to get laid.
* Look to the lunar calendar: studies show our libido increases during the full moon.
* As a last resort, buy handcuffs. Use in case of emergency.

Masturbation increases sex drive. Research has shown the more a woman experiences sex and orgasm, in any form, the higher her levels of desire for sex.

Fancy a Quick One, Luv? How Quickies Can Improve Your Sex Life

Forget everything you've heard about quickies being a pale imitation of "real" sex. Contrary to widespread belief, quickies are not bad for your sex life, and they are certainly far more than a basic bonk with practically all the foreplay cut out.

In fact, among those who liked to seize the moment for a quickie were Jackie and Aristotle Onassis. In one of the latest books on Jackie, *America's Queen: The Life of Jacqueline Kennedy Onassis*, author Sarah Bradford records that they would have sex in all sorts of unconventional places, regardless of who might be watching. She writes of a friend who was shocked by the way Onassis would drag Jackie suddenly into one of the cabins on their

quickie: noun.
Colloquial.
*1. something produced in a short space of time, often on a low budget and of inferior quality.
2. anything taken or done quickly, as a drink, snack, etc. 3.* Cricket *a fast bowler.
4.* Colloquial *an act of sexual intercourse performed in a short space of time, often without fully undressing.*
Source: *Macquarie Dictionary*

yacht, *Christina*, and make love to her without even bothering to shut the door. Apparently he was prone to sweeping Jackie off her feet; they did it almost anywhere, anytime, and loved it.

Research shows that sex in any quantity or duration is healthy for your sex life, and your sex drive. A quickie, by definition, is quick, but can still be wild fun and very exciting. Most people tend to think of quickies as a substitute for passionate, romantic lovemaking. Many sex therapists, however, disagree with this view and encourage couples to incorporate quickies into their sex lives.

Couples today list lack of desire, time, fatigue, pressure and stress as five of the biggest obstacles to a fulfilling sex life. Many feel their sex lives are disappointing compared to the mind-blowing super-sex lives portrayed in the media. They don't have romantic interludes in remote getaways every month, they don't come home to candle-lit bedrooms with rose petals littered over the bed, and they don't have screaming orgasms as they make love for the fourth time that night. Sometimes, "Do you want to?," "Well I suppose so" and a half-hearted effort, before rolling over for much-needed sleep, is just about all some couples can manage. This type of scenario calls for a quickie fix — and fast.

Why quickies work

Sexual activity in general helps couples feel connected. Couples who feel sexually connected are more likely to get along in areas of their relationship outside the bedroom. They communicate more effectively, feel more energized and show more affection towards each other. Couples who do not engage in a regular sex life argue more often. Many become irritable, angry or depressed.

Lack of desire is still the leading sexual problem among women. Studies in the US have shown a direct link between engaging in sex and sexual desire. Sexual intercourse raises hormonal levels in both men and women, which increase the brain chemicals associated with desire. The more often you have sex, the stronger your desire for sex becomes. So while bonking like bunnies is part of the solution, life can get in the way. Since it is simpler to have frequent quickies, they can make an important contribution to increasing desire, especially for women.

Quickies are also excellent for reintroducing passion into a sex life that has been long neglected. Many couples have a hard time prioritizing sex in their busy lives. By the time they get to sex, after everything else on their must-do lists, they can feel too tired or stressed to bother. Couples also feel pressure to make each time they have sex a long, passionate, intimate session, with incredible orgasms for both, preferably at the same time. Sex therapists who advocate quickies certainly promote longer lovemaking as a component of a healthy sex life, but they do encourage couples to be realistic. Often a few ten-minute frenzied quickies can do more for your sex drive than waiting for that fatigue-free, private, uninterrupted night to come along.

When a woman doesn't have regular sex her erotic response system begins to shut down. She may find she is not

Fantasizing keeps your body in a higher sexual gear, so if you fantasize about sex throughout the day, your desire for sex that night will be more intense.

easily aroused. Orgasm becomes increasingly difficult to attain. When a woman does have regular sex though, her arousal response is greater and achieving orgasm becomes less of an effort and more pleasurable. Quickies may not always give a woman an orgasm, but they will maintain her erotic drive and response. In the era of fast-lane living, quickies keep our sexual gears running smoothly.

What about romance?

Most people assume quickies are a romance-free zone. In fact, many might say quickies are the *opposite* of romance, that they are just about the act of sex. When women complain to relationship therapists and friends about not having enough romance in their lives, no one suggests a quickie as the solution. Instead, the "date strategy" is the common prescription: take your lover out on a date so you can rediscover each other.

However, a structured dinner date can put a lot of pressure on a couple if they have time problems, performance anxiety in bed, or plain haven't been doing it. If romance is what you crave, have a couple of quickies and you'll discover that sex leads to romance in a relationship, not necessarily vice versa. If you want breakfast in bed and flowers, make love the night before.

Can quickies be a bandaid solution for sexual problems?

As good as quickies can be for reviving a tired sex life, there are also drawbacks to the quick fix. If a man suffers from premature ejaculation, quickies will only reinforce this dysfunction. A sex therapist would recommend slow intercourse using specific stop-start techniques, not a quickie. If a woman rarely experiences orgasm, or never has, frequent quickies will not benefit her sexual response either. The odd quickie, though, might help her relax and provide relief from the constant goal of orgasm. Generally, quickies should not be the only form of sex in a couple's life.

Good quickies

Quickies are a terrific way to inject some spontaneity into your sex life. If you've always been a night-oriented-long-session sex person, try a quickie during a morning shower. If you or your partner have been stressed, a quick roll in the hay is a great stress-relief remedy. Orgasms release mood-elevating endorphins that can make you feel very relaxed. Or if your sex life has been a little on the routine side, but you're not sure about your Kamasutra abilities, try a quickie in a new position. Trying a new position as a quickie takes the pressure out of having to do it fantastically the first time — before you know it, you've done it.

Quickies also make terrific alfresco sex. Many couples get a thrill from having sex outdoors. Next time you have a picnic, choose a secluded area, perhaps beside a lovely stream, and make a quick one your starter. Maybe when you next find yourselves on a long drive in the bush, pull over for a feral quickie.

Quickies can improve your sex life. They add excitement and intensity to an already healthy sex life. They reconnect couples whose sex lives have gone stale. And they can be enormously helpful for couples who have let sex become the last thing on their list of priorities. Many couples, though deeply in love, stop touching each other because they fear rejection. Too much time has gone by since they last made love. Week after week there's been pressure and stress, disinterest and fatigue. Headaches and more headaches. Proposing a quickie is usually easier than initiating a long lovemaking session simply because you're not asking for a lot of time. And having sex, no matter how brief, will end the relationship rut. Want the old fire back? Looking for a thrill? Next time you've got a spare ten minutes, grab each other and go for broke.

As every cricket fan knows, fast bowling generates a lot of excitement. Or, if you're more familiar with baseball, think fast ball, or fast pitch softball.

"I lost interest in sex after the birth of my baby. I was tired all the time. I gained weight during my pregnancy and had a hard time taking it off. I hated the way I looked. Months went by and whenever my husband and I did have sex, I didn't enjoy it and I didn't feel attractive. Soon we hardly did it at all. We became parents and not lovers. While sometimes I missed sex, I just didn't have the energy to do anything about it. Then one evening, my parents agreed to babysit at their place. My husband and I settled in front of the TV to relax. We started cuddling and he mentioned how much he liked my new 'curves.' He said I looked sexy. I saw myself then as a sensual woman and kissed him. Before I knew what was happening, we were having sex in the lounge — sex like when we were first married — passionate, intense sex. It was a quickie and it was fantastic! It reignited the passion in our sex life and I've felt like a sexy wife and mother ever since."
— Sandra, 31

"My partner and I are both shift workers. I'm a nurse and my partner is a doctor. Our careers are important to both of us and we work long hours. Our sex life began to suffer from the burden of our jobs and lack of time together. There would be days when we hardly saw each other, let alone made time for sex. And both of us were always exhausted. When we did try to have sex, sometimes we would start and then agree to just give up and save it for another time. It became depressing. I thought I was too young to have given up good sex, or even a sex life at all. One night we had a rare couple of hours together before we needed to go to a work function. I made dinner and afterwards, when I started the washing up, my partner started flirting with me in the kitchen. We shared a glance, our look that means, 'Do you want to?' And we ran into the bedroom and had a quickie without even taking off our clothes. The whole time we were at the work function, we kept looking at each other, sharing the secret that we'd had sex right before. It felt racy and exciting, and made me want more sex. From then on, we promised to always make time for sex . . . and we have." — Miriam, 29

Does Your Sex Life Need a Quick Fix?

For each statement, give yourself one point for *No* and two points for *Yes*:

NO = 1   YES = 2

* I am too tired for sex.
* Sex is saved for night-time.
* Generally I am too stressed for sex.
* My sex life lacks spontaneity.
* Sex outside the bedroom is unusual.
* Romance takes too much energy.
* I feel disconnected from my partner when we haven't had sex in a week.
* I'd rather watch TV or read a good book than have sex.
* Sex requires too much scheduling to bother doing it more than twice a week.
* Often sex is done in a standard position.
* I have trouble relaxing.
* I don't have time for a sensational sex life.

TOTAL :

If you scored:

12–15 points

Your approach to sex is good and your sexual life is healthy. You place sex as a high priority and make time in your life for varied sexual expression. Quickies can be incorporated into your life, not as a remedy, but for the extra thrill you seem to enjoy.

16–19 points

There is room for improvement in your sex life. You may wish to work on your time management and relaxation techniques with the use of the occasional quickie. You could infuse more passion and creativity into your relationship by adding alfresco quickie sex to your menu of delights.

20–24 points

Your sex life could definitely use a quick fix. Quickies are a good way to reconnect with your partner. Don't feel pressure to make sex unbelievable each time. Quickies will liberate you so you can have fun with sex again. Learn to arrange your priorities so your sex life doesn't suffer. You can indulge in quickies to help with your time management and passion.

Speedy Gonzales

[*solutions for premature ejaculation*]

See Dick and Jane kiss. See Dick fondle. See Jane grind. See Dick come. Oops.

Whether you call it premature, early or rapid ejaculation, rapid fire, fast bowling, the quick draw'n'shoot, trigger happy or quick release, it's all the same ... it's simply coming too fast. But the question beckons: too fast for whom? The man? The woman? Both? How fast is too fast? Five minutes? Five thrusts? One? Even before penetration? Well, yes, if a man plans on intercourse and comes even before penetration, then it's safe to agree he has ejaculated prematurely. Mostly, premature ejaculation is defined between a couple, when a pattern is established of the man coming quickly and without control, or faster than he wants, so that the sex is dissatisfying for either or both partners. Some couples think a fast and furious three minutes is perfectly acceptable, while others would be concerned if their lovemaking lasted less than twenty minutes. The average couple makes love a lot, for different lengths of time, depending on their availability, mood and situation. If the man has control over his ejaculation but doesn't last long, he is not a Speedy Gonzales. If he regularly fires rapidly and is out of control, though, then Houston we have a problem: Speedy has hijacked Dick.

A one-off accident is not cause for concern. It does not mean a man has lost his ability to control his ejaculation. Most men at some point will experience a Speedy Gonzales episode or two. A pattern of coming too fast, of not ever having ejaculatory control, though, is a problem. Thankfully and luckily, for the men and women out there living with this problem, the Speedy Gonzales syndrome of coming too quickly is one of the most straightforward sexual problems to treat.

Ready, Aim, Fire

There are many reasons why men lose (or never gain) ejaculatory control, so they come too fast. The causes can be physical or psychological; they can be situational, or have been conditioned over many years. The way a boy masturbated in his childhood and teen years can sometimes impact on whether speed messes with his ejaculatory control. If a boy masturbated in his room, or in his bathroom, and was always nervous about getting caught, then he may have begun a pattern of having a quick wank. The goal became coming, as fast as possible. Little boys do not think this is a problem, particularly

No Speed Zone

The Oneida Community was a nineteenth-century Utopian community in the northwestern region of New York State, in the US. It was noted for its liberal sexual attitudes and practices during a period most known for Victorian conservatism. In the Oneida Community, men were trained to control their ejaculation to lengthen the duration of intercourse. Post-menopausal women in the community, who were free from the risk of pregnancy, volunteered to help young men practise this ejaculatory control technique. There was no limit to the frequency of these lessons, as the goal was to help every young man perfect their ability.

because when they are young adolescents they can get hard and come again very quickly. They don't realize that this response will slow as they age. So, whether they are looking at magazines, or in the shower, they can jack off quickly several times in a row, and get faster, more frequent orgasms. If a boy continues to masturbate like this, he learns nothing of ejaculatory control; only about how to come really, really fast. This can be reinforced in those boys who participated in "circle jerks" when they were young. Circle jerking is when boys get together and have a mass wank. Some even compete to see who can come first. This race to the finish means the winner will eventually become the loser: the faster he trains himself to be, the more likely he is to establish a problem of learning ejaculatory control down the road. These boys of the quick-wank brigade are the ones who never understand the phases in their sexual response, and coming cues, and how to slow these phases down voluntarily if they are getting too stimulated during sex. And when they start experimenting with making out and sex, their partner can also mistakenly reinforce the quick come. The quick teenage bonk in the back of a car or before the parents get home is the death knell of any learning about control over sexual response. As a result, their approach to sex becomes one of Ready, Aim, Fire, when what it should be is Ready, Aim, Fuck around for a while ... Fire.

It's not me, it's my dick

There are few physical conditions that cause premature ejaculation. The majority of causes are psychological. However, the physical response of orgasm and ejaculation can be brought about faster than expected if, for example, a man is suffering from inflammation of the genital area, or a urinary tract infection. The pain and sensitivity of the area may result in a man coming quickly. Similarly, abnormal prostate glands have been associated with rapid ejaculation. Even more rarely, some men have oversensitive penises, or overactive pelvic floor muscles (the muscles that contract during orgasm) which tense and stimulate orgasm, making it occur faster than a man would like. If you think you may have one of these physical conditions that may be causing your rapid fire, visit your doctor. But since most causes are not physical, your doctor is more than likely going to refer you to a sex therapist or your nearest bookstore.

My dick has a mind of its own

Rapid ejaculation is more often than not caused by psychological issues. Our sexual response is a barometer for how our lives are going, and one of the first areas where we notice problems is our sex lives. If something is going on in your life that is causing stress, anxiety, upset or distress, you can bet it's going to express itself in your sex life. And in the case of many men, stress, anxiety and upset can manifest itself in the penis by shooting off its head without control. Men who have emotional turmoil or stress bubbling beneath the surface may not acknowledge any problems until it hits their sexual function and becomes something they feel they have to face.

Psychological causes for premature ejaculation include (but are not limited to):

* Depression.
* Financial woes.
* Relationship or work stress.
* Prior abuse or negative sexual experiences.
* Performance anxiety.
* Fear of intimacy.
* Fear of pregnancy.
* Anger and negative emotions.
* Extremely high arousal.
* Sexual inexperience.

While there is a range of causes of rapid ejaculation, the most common are stress and performance anxiety. Stress can get the better of ejaculatory control at any point in a man's life or relationship. Performance anxiety usually occurs in the beginning of a relationship, precisely when a bloke wants to impress a girl, and may continue due to ongoing anxiety as the situation grows from embarrassing to his worst nightmare. If you suffer from a pattern of rapid rooting, the first step in solving Speedy is to get to the root of the problem. You can try to do this on your own, or by seeing a therapist. If you have had the problem for a long time, or it is severe, a few visits with a sex therapist may be required. If you think you can sort out what is causing your premature ejaculation on your own, know when it began and what its root may be, then you can work on eliminating the problem by erasing the cause (by reducing your stress, for example) and treating Speedy through employing the proper techniques detailed in this chapter to learn how to slow the pace and gain control.

Bandaids

Coming too fast can wreak havoc on a man's self-esteem. Men pride themselves on their stamina and vigor, so coming too fast makes many men feel less "manly" or less virile. As a result, men, desperate to fix the situation but too embarrassed to talk with anyone about it, resort to bandaid solutions. But homespun, urban myth, do-it-yourself fix-it techniques always fail, especially in the long run. And when they do, the male spirit (and/or ego) is then doubly shattered. To avoid all this horrible hoo-ha, a Speedy Gonzales man and his penis should head straight to a doctor, sex therapist, psychologist, sex manual, or keep reading below. Because to really slow Speedy Gonzales down, you must use tested, tried and true techniques.

The bandaid approach to solving premature ejaculation is the fastest way to keep coming quickly. The bandaid quick fixes do not get at the heart of the problem, but mainly mask it. To really get rid of rapid rooting, once and for all, the treatment must address the cause, not simply desensitize the dick. Proper solutions investigate potential psychological causes, not assume the answer lies with the penis. You must untangle your mind if it's fucking with your ability to fuck well, not just slap a bandaid on the problem.

Some of the classic bandaid do-it-yourself fix-it techniques that usually don't do dick include:

* Using two condoms at once.
* Applying a topical desensitizing cream to the penis to numb it.

(No fun for him, and no fun for her, either, because it usually numbs her too!)

* Mentally reciting sport statistics or concentrating on something else.
* Thinking aversive mantras, like "Don't come, don't come, don't come."
* Prayer.
* Squeezing your bum cheeks together.
* Biting your lip.
* Masturbating more often.
* Hormone injections.
* Viagra (this helps you get rock-hard, but does nothing about rapid shooting your rocks off).
* Alcohol (getting drunk may make you a sloppy slow-shooter once, but doesn't make you a slower shooter overall, and certainly won't make you a better lover).
* Cock rings, erection bands or other gimmicks. (These erection aids may work to contain the urge to ejaculate in the short term, but do not solve the problem. And they have to be used every time, and often become a crutch, not a cure.)
* Keep-hard potions and pills. (Many claim the cause of premature ejaculation is biological or physiological, not psychological. This endorses their claim that a few supplements, for many many dollars a bottle, will be the cure to give you the edge to stop coming quickly. Most of these are based in little scientific fact or study and do nothing whatsoever for rapid ejaculation. Be an informed consumer: be wary of buying something that seems too good to be true.)

Take Charge

Don't throw in the towel, just because you used it too quickly. There are fixes for those who come quickly, but they require time and dedication. You don't want a quick fix for a quick problem. The real fix takes time, but it fixes the problem for good.

Because most of the causes of premature ejaculation are psychological, counseling should be a part of every comprehensive treatment program. A sex therapist or counselor will investigate your sex history and determine what may be the quick-fire triggers, and will work with you to ease the anxieties you may be feeling about sex, your life, yourself, your partner or your relationship. Not everyone will need to see a counselor long term to treat and cure premature ejaculation. In fact, in a great number of cases, only one or two visits with a sex therapist are required. Understanding the underlying root to your quick rooting is crucial to making sure it doesn't resurface. The combination of thorough counseling and therapeutic techniques (see later sections, "Tease it baby, yeah"; and "Red light green light," in this chapter) hits the nail on the head, effectively teaching a man how to gain, and keep, ejaculatory control.

Master it

Solving premature ejaculation requires an understanding of both orgasm and ejaculation and learning how to control them. Male orgasm occurs in two separate phases: one is orgasm and the second is ejaculation. While the two usually happen together, this is not always the case. It is possible to orgasm without ejaculating: a man experiences "retrograde ejaculation" when he comes internally, usually back into the bladder; he may experience "dry orgasm" due to the side effects of some medications; or he has frequent orgasms without releasing ejaculate (this is how men have multiple orgasms, but not all men are successful at it). Men can also ejaculate without experiencing orgasm, a condition known as "dripping."

The orgasmic phase of the sexual response is marked by two sub-phases: the feeling of ejaculatory inevitability and ejaculation. Just prior to ejaculation, there is a feeling of inevitability, the "I'm just about to come" feeling that occurs when the seminal fluid has reached the base of the penis, between one and three seconds before ejaculation. It's that feeling where you just know, no matter what happens, you're going to come — wild horses couldn't stop you.

Mastering control over premature ejaculation requires familiarity with your sexual response; knowing the point at which your body will reach ejaculatory inevitability, and learning to hold off just before that point. Men who have ejaculatory control know how to surf the plateau phase of their sexual response, tease and ride it to the point of ejaculatory inevitability, but hold off on coming as long as possible.

To master this ejaculatory control, masturbation is a helpful tool. Masturbating to the point of ejaculatory inevitability, and focusing on the physical feelings he experiences enlightens the man on the sensations he should be looking out for, instead of just letting fly. There are also tips for learning to last longer, by simple conditioning through masturbation. This is known as "punching the clock": masturbating to an alarm clock, and disallowing yourself to come until the alarm goes off. Gradually, the alarm is set for longer and longer periods of time, training a man to last longer. This is really only effective for learning the physical feelings of the plateau phase and sensations just prior to ejaculation, rather than a cure-all for rapid rooting.

Masturbation as therapy for premature ejaculation is highly effective when using the stop-start method (see "Red light green light" section) or the squeeze-tease technique (see "Tease it baby, yeah" section). There are therapy instructions for alternative and mainstream treatment methods available for sale over the Internet, which I cannot endorse because I have not tried them. There are manuals dealing specifically with the treatment of premature ejaculation for sale in bookstores, and generally cheaper than the products on these sites, and there are also information sites on the Net that give therapeutic instructions for free (see Carnal Knowledge chapter). When looking for exercises or solutions, always be confident in the credibility of the source of your information.

A rapid rooter needs to learn not only how to last longer, but needs to prefer to last longer by understanding that slower, unhurried sex with longer foreplay and intercourse increases the engorgement of the genital area, sensitizing all the nerve endings, and eventually leads to a stronger, more intense orgasm. The longer the shag, the sweeter the payoff.

Drug it

Not always a recommended treatment, but there are drugs available, such as antidepressants, that have the effect of slowing blood to the penis and decreasing the urge to ejaculate. Some doctors are reluctant to prescribe a pill to treat premature ejaculation, but in cases where therapeutic techniques fail, drugs are sometimes successful. For men who legitimately suffer from depression, which also causes rapid ejaculation, drug therapy may be a suitable solution. And studies have found that if a man is not depressed and takes antidepressants, such as Zoloft, for premature ejaculation, he usually does not have any other side effects. See your counselor and doctor for advice if you think drug therapy might be more beneficial for you than the treatment techniques.

Exercise it

Kegel exercises (see Peckers, Boobs and Blast Off chapter) help a man strengthen his pelvic floor muscles, the network of muscles that engage during sexual response and pulse during orgasm. Working these muscles does two things: it helps strengthen the muscles so that when a man needs to control or pause, he has the knowledge and ability to do so, and also, the act of exercising the genital region puts a man "in touch" with his body, and its sexual response. The stronger the pelvic floor muscles, the more intense the orgasm, and the more control a man has over prolonging the onset of orgasm.

Control It

Learning to control rapid ejaculation can be achieved through a series of therapeutic techniques developed by sex researchers and therapists. If you are still experiencing difficulty after reading this section, visit a sex therapist to get the techniques tailored to your specific problem.

Tease it baby, yeah

Developed by the famous sex researchers and therapists Masters and Johnson, the "squeeze-tease" technique is enormously successful in treating premature ejaculation. This technique is better if employed by a couple, however single men can choose between using this method and the stop-start method (see "Red light green light" section) during masturbation.

During the squeeze-tease technique, the goal is to teach the man about the sensations he feels during excitement and prior to orgasm, and to learn how to delay coming. This is achieved by gradually getting the man excited, and then stemming that arousal by squeezing the penis. It is the woman who does the squeezing, but this is not an S&M maneuver so please be gentle. The squeeze should be applied around the ridge of the penis, at the base of the head, with the thumb placed on the frenulum (the little flap of skin attached to the ridge on the underside of the penis). The squeeze itself should be firm, for a few seconds, enough to partially decrease the erection, and the release should be quick but not rough.

🗣 *"When we first tried the squeeze-tease technique, I was worried that my wife wasn't going to be able to do the squeeze part correctly. I was very aroused and I thought I'd come and the whole thing would be a failure. But instead, she shocked me by squeezing the shit out of my dick. I thought she was trying to strangle it and pop the head off — she squeezed it until it practically bulged. It hurt so bad that it was another few days before I got aroused again. It was worse than getting kicked in the balls."*
— man, 24

🗣 *"I learned to squeeze firmly but lightly after my husband screamed his head off, and then nearly bit my head off, after I squeezed his other head too strongly."* — woman, 23

There are three phases to the squeeze-tease technique and it is important to resist the urge to race ahead: slow and steady wins this race.

The first phase involves no intercourse, and no contact with female genitalia. The partners explore and touch each other's bodies, and as they do this, the woman occasionally squeezes the penis. This is in preparation for using the squeeze-tease during intercourse. During this initial phase, it doesn't matter whether the penis is erect when the squeeze is applied. The man is generally getting in tune with the sensations in his body as he experiences increased and decreased excitement. As the couple progresses, the idea is to apply pressure to the penis once he is aroused, erect, and as he is getting increasingly excited.

The final training in this first phase involves the woman bringing the man to orgasm through masturbation. As she feels him getting more and more excited, she delays his orgasm by applying a pressured squeeze. As a couple practices this phase, she may apply several squeezes to delay orgasm for longer and longer. A woman may find it erotic and powerful to be in control of her partner's orgasm, and also to connect with him during a very intimate exercise.

Phase two is a repeat of phase one, only it raises the stakes. In phase two, the woman's genitals come into contact with the penis. As the man's arousal grows stronger with increased stimulation, the importance of the timing of the squeeze is greater. There may need to be open communication between the man and woman. If he feels close to the brink of ejaculation, or overwhelming pleasure, he should feel comfortable enough to speak up before blowing: the squeeze-tease technique is a team effort.

The final phase is motionless intercourse. No, it doesn't sound like much fun, but at least you've graduated to intercourse. The best position is woman on top, and after penetration, there is to be No Moving Around! No thrusting and no twitching. The first time, the woman should dismount her mate nearly right away and apply the squeeze. The technique is designed to build stamina and control through gradual increases in stimulation and bringing the male arousal back from each brink, so that eventually he is able to control and manage the sensations himself. As the man learns to gain control, the woman does not need to continue dismounting periodically. Instead, she can lift up and simply squeeze the base of the penis. This enables the couple to continue intercourse stimulation (still without thrusting, though), and while the squeeze at the base of the penis is less intense, it still serves as an effective reminder to the man to slow down his sexual excitement response. From this point, it is up to individual couples to decide how often to use the squeeze-tease technique in their lovemaking. If stopping to squeeze the penis feels too much like an interruption, couples may want to switch to using the stop-start technique.

Red light green light

The stop-start technique is often preferred by men as a technique to use during masturbation, rather than the squeeze-tease technique. When a man is trying to focus on learning his inner sexual sensations and ejaculatory control, it is easier for him to simply stop until the arousal subsides, than to stop and apply a squeeze to his own dick. Better to be safe than sorry and just not touch himself. A few men have had the proper intention of applying a squeeze, but then somehow the squeeze turns into a massage, and oops.

The stop-start method can be used by couples in the same phases as the squeeze-tease technique, from touching through to hand jobs and intercourse. As he learns to gain ejaculatory control, he can indicate to his partner to stop moving, so that stimulation ceases and he can slow his arousal. When his response is slightly dissipated, then intercourse can continue. This is a technique employed by a great number of couples, not only those trying to battle premature ejaculation. Some men without a history of rapid rooting can occasionally be super-horny or excessively turned on, and find themselves getting too quickly to orgasm, so stop thrusting, or ask their partners to stop grinding. Or in some cases, a woman will ask a man to slow down if she thinks she might be able to come, but can see he is getting there first. Pausing during sex is a natural way to ride the waves of pleasure and connect your sexual responses. You may find it to be a technique you employ to lengthen your lovemaking, even after you have successfully cured your quick-release problem.

"My boyfriend told me that when he was younger, he suffered from premature ejaculation. I never would've guessed it because he has such incredible stamina in bed. He's really good at knowing when he's going to come, and about slowing down. He also checks in with me and tries to help me orgasm during intercourse. He has to stimulate my clit to do this, so when he gets overstimulated, he stops pumping and focuses on playing with my clit. He's the best lover I've ever had because he knows his own body so well and uses it to get in tune with mine. He says he wouldn't have stopped to learn so much about his own sexual response if he hadn't had to tackle premature ejaculation. He's also really open in bed and our relationship is strong because we communicate so well." — Angela, 27

Rooting for Speedy

If a man is in a relationship and experiencing chronic premature ejaculation, it is always more successful to address the problem as a couple. To kick the hare out of the bed and bring in the tortoise, both bedmates need to work together. Before jumping each other, it's important to talk about the issue. This is easier said than done, but an introduction might be to each review the stop-start and squeeze-tease techniques and discuss which one you'd like to try first, or feel is more suited to you. Communication is the first step towards successfully slowing Speedy down.

As the partner of a man who prematurely ejaculates, your role is critical. His self-esteem may be damaged, and he may find he doesn't want to face or deal with the issue. He may be embarrassed, and may be disappointed that he cannot give you prolonged, satisfying intercourse. Your role as the Down Boy Rooter is not only pivotal in terms of being in charge of administering the techniques, but you need to be a cheerleader as well. Cheering him up (or rather, down) is a vital ingredient in the successful treatment of rapid ejaculation. He needs to learn control, but importantly, you both need to feel connected and work together to solve the problem. When the issue is fixed, not only will your sexual satisfaction be much higher, your relationship will be stronger than ever.

While providing support, remember that the pattern of premature ejaculation is not quickly undone. Along the way, there will be times when Speedy rears his head and fires, despite your best efforts together to stop it. Accept that there will be failure while learning control. Your reassurance to your partner during these times is crucial. Rapid rooting is much more difficult to cure if the man's partner is uncooperative or unsupportive. Women should not be "anti-come bullies" (à la an Aussie film *Praise,* in which the lead female character abuses her partner each time he comes too fast), nor should they be insincere by faking pleasure or orgasm. Don't shoot yourself in the foot: premature ejaculation is your problem as much as it is his, because your sexual satisfaction suffers just as much as his. The key is honest support and open communication.

One Man's Slow Burn

The following is a condensed version of an interview with a man, 26, who wishes to remain anonymous.

"I grew up masturbating in the loo. I was the only boy in a house full of women. I lived with my mum and three sisters, and not only did we have just the one toilet, but I had to share a room with my littlest sister. And I was always last in line for the bathroom. My sisters always, always came and went, fluffing and primping, in groups, and with friends. If I stayed too long in the toilet, they would tease me. They never directly taunted me about wanking, but they rolled their eyes, laughed and hinted at it.

"As the only boy in the house the scales were tipped in their favor and they made me feel like wanking was dirty. I had to hide my magazines and sneak them into the toilet. I grew up wanking really quickly in the toilet, praying no one would knock on the door and harass me. Or I did it late at night, after my sister fell asleep, under the sheets, but I was in constant fear that she would wake up, so I got good at jacking off as fast as possible.

"Looking back, I know that's where my problem started. I didn't think I had premature ejaculation with my first

girlfriend — sex never lasted a very long time, but she never complained. Then I had a few one-night stands, but it was at nineteen, with my second girlfriend, that I knew I had a problem. The first time we had sex, I came just as I penetrated her, and then I went soft almost straightaway, so I couldn't even pretend that it had happened a little after that. I was so embarrassed. She thought she had just gotten me overexcited and didn't get too worried about it. But when it happened again the second time, her reaction of shock and being disappointed really humiliated me. I broke up with her and then had a string of short relationships where I tried to avoid having sex, and then when we did and I came too fast, I'd dump them.

"My self-esteem sank, and I began to avoid dating. I masturbated, and began not coming quickly through masturbation, but I know now that I still didn't know control over ejaculation. Mainly because the next time I tried having sex I was so frozen with performance anxiety that I came even before penetration. It seemed the problem had gotten worse, not better. Thankfully my girlfriend was understanding. She'd even been with another guy who'd had premature ejaculation too (or so she said, maybe she was just trying to make me feel better). We kept dating, and my control got better as I got less anxious about performance. Her love was a big help, and also made me feel better about my whole sex life. But I was still coming too quickly and we wanted to have longer sex, and experiment with different positions. Every time we switched to a new position it would be too much for me and I'd come. Not from the excitement, well, partly, but also stress and anxiety, I guess.

"I eventually went to a sex therapist who talked to me about my anxieties and my girlfriend and I used the squeeze-tease technique. Through that, and my own masturbation, I fixed the problem and now I can last as long as I want without coming too fast. It's a miracle to me, really. I never thought I'd be able to gain control, it just seemed way too hard. I couldn't even imagine how other guys did it. But now I do, and even though I'm not with that girlfriend anymore, I'll always appreciate how she helped and didn't make me feel bad or lesser because I had this problem. She never made fun of me. And now I'm single, but not scared of dating or having sex. I'm just like the next guy. The only thing is, I don't admit that I ever had a problem, why should I? It's fixed and a thing of the past. In fact, when the guys and I talk about sex, sometimes I think they might have a problem, but that's for them to fix. I'm not going to admit I used to have a problem. No more embarrassing moments for me, they're over. Bring on the women, I say, I'm happy to oblige, and take my time doing it, too."

The Energizer Bunny

[*keeping that orgasm going and going and going*]

Charging those love batteries to go on and on and on, so you can get off and off and off takes energy, focus and skill. Some bunnies, though, just want to be able to blast off once, never mind mining for multiples. Whether your goal is to come once, hard and strong, or come over and over again, there are relatively simple exercises to teach you, and your partner, how to do it.

"O" Obstacles

With all the advertisements for fuck-me-better sex aids, toys, enhancements, potions and lotions, the pressure to come, frequently and brilliantly, is enormous. So much so, that it can freeze one's sexual response from getting off at all.

Not being able to come is called, in the technical world of sexology, *anorgasmia*. Strictly speaking, anorgasmia has several forms. There is global lifelong anorgasmia, in which a person cannot come ever, and has never been able to, either by themselves through masturbation, or with a partner. There is also situational anorgasmia, where a person can come in some situations, but not in others. The most common experience of this is the ability to come through masturbation, but not with a partner. And there is temporary anorgasmia, where a person used to be able to come, but the ability to orgasm has disappeared. All cases are stressful for the person; those who have never come are anxious to be able to, and those who could and now cannot are desperate to fix the situation. While anorgasmia in all forms is far, far more common in women, it can affect men too.

About half of all women and one in five men will suffer from the inability to orgasm at some point in their lives, and like most other sexual problems, the inability to orgasm has both physical and psychological roots.

Body barring

Medications, especially antidepressants, can have side effects which block or delay sexual response, making orgasm very difficult or even impossible to attain. Painful sex, for both men and women, can halt sexual response by putting the orgasm switch in the permanent "off" position. Women especially suffer from painful sex, and often just put up with it, rather than seeing a doctor. Unless S&M is your thing, sex should not hurt, so if it does, seek professional advice. Even a small injury, such as an old niggling back injury, that makes sex slightly painful may prevent you from relaxing enough to orgasm. If you cannot orgasm, anything that causes pain should be redressed, and all medications should be investigated for potential sexual side effects.

Alcohol is the fastest, most effective way to stop yourself from being able to come. You may still be able to get wet or get hard, but you might not be able to come. Inability to orgasm from excessive alcohol or drug use is not anorgasmia. It's a temporary body-induced sin bin (time-out) from partying too hard.

Mental block

The list of emotional and situational causes of anorgasmia is huge. The reason is that our body–mind connection is highly complex, and our sexual response system is really quite a fragile one. There is constant feedback happening between the brain and the gonads, and when our sexual response is asked to rev up to the max, if there is an overload of negativity, it shuts off instead. The sexual response system is the body's barometer and circuit breaker. Lust juices flow well as long as everything is in balance: as long as we have a relatively good internal balance of positive and negative emotions, stress and coping mechanisms, relationship and personal issues, etc. But if something gets too high, if stress levels skyrocket with a work issue, or a death, or there is a relationship break-up, financial drain, fear, anger, boredom, irritation, anxiety or worry, then "click" goes the circuit breaker in the sexual response system and bye-bye blast off. Very often libido goes MIA as well, but in many cases, the circuit breaker is small, and lust juices can still flow around some of the system, but the last loop to the almighty O is shut down — No Through Road.

Popping the Cork

Learning to release pent-up sexual energy in an explosive orgasm can take one hour to several months, depending on what's causing your block, how you feel about your body, and how you approach orgasmic training. Orgasmic training focuses on your mind and body, teaches you about your sexual response and how to relax, and guides you to finding and freeing your sweet spot. It may take time, and you may experience frustration along the way, but once you've popped your cork, you can celebrate.

Counseling

If your doctor has ruled out a physical cause for anorgasmia, counseling should be the next step on your path to learning how to come. Depending on your situation, a sex therapist may want to treat you alone first, before treating you as a couple. The inability to come is embarrassing and frustrating for both men and women. For men who are in a relationship or marriage and wanting to conceive, it's not only worrying, it interferes with making a baby and needs to be fixed as soon as possible. (In these cases, especially with the strain of IVF programs, the stress and expense of baby-making can be the reason for male anorgasmia.) Qualified sex therapists will meet with you to ascertain the cause of your problem, and prescribe appropriate treatment.

The inability to orgasm affects the partner, too, and often a counselor wants to speak with them to address the shared issues of concern, worry and intimacy. A sex therapist will often give a couple "homework" that entails "backing the relationship up" to remove the pressure of the goal of orgasm: couples are forbidden to have intercourse or even try to orgasm. The relief of this for the couple is often huge. In counseling, it's important to eliminate all variables that may be blocking the person from achieving orgasm, and work on getting back to blast off one step at a time. Each couple's situation is different, however, so don't try to be your own therapist: always see a professional for serious problems. And consistently not being able to come is serious.

Orgasmic training

Once you've seen a sex therapist about your inability to come, you'll be put into training. Learning to orgasm is an individual experience, so there's no telling how fast or long it might take you. Some people find that the act of talking through their problem with a counselor creates such a relief that when they give masturbation a try, they are relaxed, have little expectation and either come close, or bang-on get a wowza their first try. This is not the norm, however, and most men and women who have orgasmic difficulty take a few or many practice sessions before they get there. Practice makes perfect, like anything else. If someone asked you to do the splits right now, you probably couldn't. But if you stretched and limbered up and practiced every day, soon enough, you'd be getting close, and one day you'd be there. Orgasm is like that. No harder, no easier. You have to train yourself to allow your body to experience it.

Training moves through several phases: masturbation, sensate focus, mutual masturbation, and intercourse. It's often best to do the masturbation training by yourself. Your partner might want to be involved in the process with you, but it's better to be alone at first, to minimize pressure and expectation, and maximize comfort and relaxation. Anything that could potentially block or distract the sexual response from flowing should be avoided. And the point of some of the masturbation exercises, in addition to pleasure, of course, is to learn the sexual sensations of your sexual response. This learning requires attention, and a partner lying next to you getting turned on could distract you and lead you into another activity ... Your partner will get their chance to participate down the track.

Orgasmic training phase one: masturbation Make sure you are alone, comfortable and, most of all, have privacy: remove the possibility of someone walking in on you. If you can hear distracting noises, such as your partner watching TV, or your children playing, put some relaxing music on to drown them out. Create an erotic space for yourself: light candles, burn incense, run a bath — whatever floats your boat. If you simply aren't into that, then just find yourself a comfy spot. If you need tips on exactly how to masturbate because you've never done it before, read the Master of Your Domain chapter.

If fantasy isn't your thing, either look at a porn video, flick through some porn mags, or read an erotic book (there are some great ones available in bookstores, see the Carnal Knowledge chapter).

When first masturbating to train yourself to orgasm, half the goal is knowledge rather than pleasure. As you feel aroused, close your eyes and concentrate on the sensations you are feeling, not just in your genitals, but in your whole body. Notice what parts of your body are hot, or sweating, what parts are relaxed and what is tensed. Focus on your blood flow, notice your pulse. Experiment with your touch: play with what kinds of touches work and don't work. Women should occasionally stick their finger(s) inside themselves to notice how wet they're getting, if they are at all. Some women are surprised at how wet they actually get, while others feel turned on without getting very lubricated. If this is you, apply some saliva or lube to make things a bit slippery. This is essential if you are masturbating with a vibrator. It can seriously hurt your sensitive tissues if you use a dry vibrator on a dry vulva. Ouch.

If you could once orgasm and now cannot, make sure you break past patterns by masturbating in a new way, either by using a new toy or by using a different grip, hand motion or movement. You want to avoid negative self-thoughts that can crop up if you try to come the way you used to and can't. Eliminate all possibility for distraction and negative thoughts.

There are five key things to remember when practicing orgasmic training masturbation:

1. **Exercise**. Remember to do your Kegel pelvic floor exercises (see Peckers, Boobs and Blast Off chapter). Some men, and especially some women, cannot orgasm without pulsing and contracting their pelvic floor muscles. The tension created in these muscles lifts the sexual response and stimulates blood engorgement in the area (which is what you want to happen). Also remember to contract these muscles during intercourse, when you get to that stage. Many women contract these muscles to make the vag tighter for their partner's sensation, but it's a critical part of helping the woman come, too.

2. **Play**. Experiment, play, have fun, be creative, break your mould. Fantasies, books and sex aids and toys can help you become orgasmic. If you are embarrassed buying them, they can be bought discreetly over the Net, or even through some sex therapists.

3. **Head down, bum up**. Try hanging your head off the bed. This will let the blood flow to your brain and alters your breathing, both of which can increase excitement and lead to orgasm more easily.

4. **Remember to breathe**. Many women hold their breath during sex, decreasing arousal and making it harder to reach orgasm. While practicing masturbation exercises, remember to breathe, fully and deeply, even matching your breaths to the contractions and relaxation of your pelvic floor muscles.

5. **Tense up**. If you're almost there but having a bit of difficulty, tense your body, including your legs, feet, stomach, arms — anything you can think of. This tension can bring about orgasm if you're on the brink. As you learn how to manipulate your pelvic floor and other muscles, you can play longer on the brink and control the timing and intensity of your orgasms. You can learn to surf the wave of pleasure, of "almost there," longer and longer.

Orgasmic training phase two: sensate focus

Sensate focus is a series of exercises conducted over time, depending on the level of orgasmic difficulty you are experiencing. A sex therapist will tailor a sequence of exercises to fit your needs. Sensate focus can be done on a single person, a kind of body worship, but is most often carried out by couples.

Sensate focus exercises are designed to slow down the sexual response. They help refocus your sexual attention and energies on the body and the process of sex, rather than the goal (orgasm). They encourage each partner to give and receive pleasure from caressing non-erogenous areas before concentrating on genital stimulation. The exercises build awareness of the body's sexual sensations.

Sensate focus is exactly what it sounds like: focus on sensation. Even if you have successfully masturbated to orgasm, the first stages of sensate focus concentrate on the body's non-erogenous zones, and are not intended to bring about a blast off. Partners are encouraged to receive pleasure selfishly, without feeling pressure to reciprocate, and to feel pleasure through giving pleasure. Sensate focus moves through many stages, and not all of them may be required for you, depending on your situation. Your sex therapist will steer you through appropriate sensate focus stages as your relaxation and orgasmic capacities progress. Learning to receive pleasure selfishly in non-erogenous zones eventually works towards receiving oral sex selfishly, without feeling self-conscious (a common issue for women). And it aids in learning to completely let go to the sensations of pleasure, putting aside any other worries or thoughts. Couples are taught to create a pleasure zone, an orgasmically friendly environment, that once entered, is about them, their shared pleasure, and nothing else.

Exercise boosts testosterone levels, improves circulation and increases blood vessel diameter and blood volume, which makes blood flow to the penis, vagina and clitoris stronger, orgasms more intense and increases sex drive.

Orgasmic training phase three: mutual masturbation

After the sensate focus phase, couples should feel comfortable being intimate and giving and receiving pleasure together. The orgasmic stakes are raised as the couple is encouraged to move on to mutual masturbation. Couples are not always prescribed a specific set of exercises to perform, as individual preferences for who goes first and who does what are respected. Most important is to avoid all perfunctory sex: only play when you're in the mood. By this stage couples are often anxious to get to the intercourse training phase and become tempted to rush this phase. Running the yellow light here will only land you at a red light in the next phase. The goal of being able to experience orgasm through manual stimulation with a partner occurs in two stages. Watch first, then do. Have your partner watch you masturbate to orgasm. Do not worry if you can't come the first time. A return to self-consciousness in this phase is natural. As you become more practiced at it, let your partner know when you are experiencing the plateau phase, and getting close. These cues and clues will be helpful to them when it's their turn. Be sure to let them see what you are doing. Don't masturbate under a sheet or angled away from them. To make the transition to their turn, have your partner either lie by your side, or, if the face-to-face contact is making you anxious, sit between your partner's legs and lean back on them. Let their hand cover your hand as you masturbate so

Blended Cream

Some research indicates we experience two types of orgasmic sensations. One is a sharp, intense pleasure, felt primarily at the base of the penis or clitoris. The other is a slower, melting pleasure, brought about through vaginal, lip and clit stimulation in the woman, and shaft and head stimulation in the man. Combining stimulations can lead to a mixture of orgasmic sensations, known as a blended orgasm. Try taking turns: the man stimulating clit, vag, clit, lip, clit, lip, etc.; while the woman stimulates shaft, head, shaft, perineum, shaft, head, shaft, etc. This can make excitement last longer and lead to a long, blended mutual blast off.

they can feel the motions and tempo. Then let their hand touch you, cover your hand over their hand, and guide them through the pressures you like. The first time you orgasm with your partner's hand, you will feel ecstatic emotionally and physically — many couples do. It is a huge victory for a lot of women and men. From here, open communication between partners, and practice, will lead you both into "Kingdom Come."

Orgasmic training phase four: intercourse For women and men, this is the final frontier in the land of anorgasmia. If any preceding phase has failed, make sure you discuss what happened with your therapist — you should be in regular consultation with a sex therapist throughout your orgasmic training. Keep in mind that the longer the foreplay, the more likely it is that orgasm will occur during intercourse. Foreplay enables the genitals to fill completely with blood, and raises the level of physical excitement and emotional arousal. Do not make the mistake of hurrying, and do not worry if you can't come the first time you try. If at first you don't succeed, try, try again. At this stage, a man who still can't come should hop back on the therapist's couch for more mental unblocking. A woman at this point should remember that she's "come a long way, baby" and not being able to come during intercourse is normal for millions of women. But there are many ways to learn how (read on).

Love lotions

As an alternative or in addition to therapeutic treatment, there are several creams now available (and also being researched) that stimulate blood flow to the genitals to enhance the ability to orgasm. Creams purchased over the Internet should be bought with care, as some are nothing more than a mint-based cream to induce tingling. It feels like it's doing something, but it's actually doing a big lot of nothing. Legitimate creams that increase blood flow are subject to ongoing study and hold promise as effective orgasmic aids. For specific creams and their current availability, check with your doctor or an MD or sexual health practitioner.

Viagra for vixens

Viagra is currently being tested for use in women with low sexual desire and anorgasmia. It is believed to enhance the blood flow to the genital region, including the vag and clit areas. For women who cannot orgasm because the nether region doesn't get aroused or fill with blood, Viagra could be the answer. In the female sexual response, engorgement of the clitoris and vagina with blood is as essential to excitement and orgasm as erection in men. It's not as visible, but it's as vital. Studies investigating Viagra are hopeful that it may work for women as it does for men. The jury is a hung one at present: some study subjects have reported promising benefits, while others have said it's made no difference. Like most treatments, it's going to work for some, and not for others. Viagra is currently not yet available to women for sexual treatment.

Testing testosterone

Testosterone replacement therapy is currently under investigation for women suffering from low libido. It is possible that testosterone replacement could have a therapeutic effect on women who cannot orgasm, especially in those women who cannot orgasm because of painful sex, conditions such as vaginal atrophy and vulvadynia (chronic vulvar discomfort). Studies are being conducted, but availability of testosterone varies in different countries.

Before, During and After

Having sex and coming are two separate functions. You can quite clearly have sex and not come, and come and not have sex. Both men and women deserve to come each time they have sex, if they want to. Sometimes sex isn't about coming, it's about connecting, and orgasm is incidental. But let's face it, most people who fuck want to fucking come. Women have a harder time at this than men, especially when it comes to coming during intercourse. Flip back to the Peckers, Boobs and Blast Off chapter if you're confused, but it should be clear that based on male and female anatomy, straight, "regular" intercourse does not stimulate a woman in the places she needs in order to come. Orgasm during dick–vag penetrative sex is possible with practice and attention for both men and women; it's a skill learned, and once learned, loved.

Before

In the majority of cases, women come before intercourse. During foreplay, her mate either manually or orally brings her to climax. In some cases, toys such as dildos and vibrators are used to bring her to one or more climaxes.

The benefits of this are that she gets well and truly hot and wet before fucking, and after he comes, she's not left unsatisfied. The downside is that it can feel a little like taking turns rather than a shared orgasmic experience.

During

Freud started the mass confusion among men and nightmarish frustration for women by claiming that clitoral orgasms were "immature" orgasms, and women who did not come during sex through a vaginal orgasm had, essentially, stunted sexual development. Men and women around the globe began to assume women should naturally be coming through intercourse, and if she didn't, she was probably incapable of doing so.

Sexual development and function has since been corrected, and we now know and acknowledge that clitoral stimulation is required by 99.999999 percent of women to achieve orgasm, and the women who come during intercourse come because the clit is being stimulated, not because they have special vaginas made of magical orgasmic tissue that the rest of us don't have.

There are a number of sexual positions that can deliver both partners to orgasm during intercourse. Once discovered, they are immensely popular and, with a little practice, the bed can become cloud nine for you both.

Meow Known as the CAT, the coital alignment technique is a favorite among couples who like to make love face to face, bodies connected, and with both partners able to come. The CAT is a variation on the missionary position, but the variation is a critical one. The man does a few things differently. One is that he rests his whole upper body weight on the woman, not on his elbows. When he has to support himself, he tends to come faster, and one of the requirements for coming together, or at least both coming, is to last longer to give the woman enough time to reach orgasm. Next, the man "rides high"; that is, he shifts himself up so that when he is inside the woman, the base of his penis is in contact with the clitoris. Deep thrusting is not the name of this game. Instead, the couple engage in a rocking and rubbing motion so that his penis gets stimulated, and her clitoris never loses contact with his penis. This is the key part: do not break the cock-base to love button friction. The man keeps contact on his downward-into-her motion, and the woman keeps the pressure on her up-against-him rocking. In this manner, both partners receive enough stimulation to come, and sometimes can come together.

Tilt Another variation on the missionary position is where a woman may use pillows under her back and bum to help tilt her pelvis forwards. With the pelvis tilted upwards, the clit and lips are more exposed and the man can press his pubic bone against them to stimulate them. Again, thrusting is not enough stimulation: constant rubbing against the clitoris with his pubic bone can lead to a deep orgasm for both her and for him.

For centuries, both the Chinese and Hindus have used a sex aid known as the horned pillow. Shaped like a half moon, this pillow is tucked under the woman's buttocks to lift her forwards for both clitoral stimulation and deep penetration. Westerners have since caught on, and generally a pillow of any shape does the trick.

Woman on top There are a number of benefits to the woman-on-top position. First, the man is not supporting his body weight, so he can concentrate on controlling ejaculation and lasting longer. Also, the woman's clitoris is exposed, especially if she is sitting up or leaning at a slight angle, rather than lying on top of him. The man or the woman can manually stimulate the clit to orgasm while in this position. Also, if the woman is lying down against him, she can rub her clitoris against his pubic bone as she is grinding, twisting and pumping along his shaft inside her. This position is also good for a mutual rocking back and forth motion, rather than thrusting, because it maintains genital contact and stimulation for mutual orgasm. For detailed "how to" information see the "Ride him, cowgirl" section in the chapter, Nude Twister, Anyone?

Leg lock The idea of a woman not spreading her legs to come may sound a tad odd, but once in the man-on-top position, with his penis inside her, both partners should adjust leg positions so that the woman's legs are firmly together, and the man's legs are on either side of hers (the opposite to the standard missionary position). This can create friction between the penis sliding in and out and the clitoral glans. For an even tighter fit, he can squeeze his legs against hers, and she can press her thighs together and contract her pelvic floor muscles. This increased body muscle tension adds to the overall tension required to climax.

Spooning In the spooning position with the woman's back facing the man, so that she is in the front curve of the spoon, the clitoris is exposed. She can either reach down, or he can reach around to stimulate it. Partners may like to tuck into a fetal position together, with their legs spooned together as well, or she may bend her upper leg, angle it upwards, or wrap it over or behind him. With one hand placed over her vulva, or fingers on her clit, stimulation is there to bring her to a climax, or sometimes just the pelvic motion created between hand and clit is enough friction to get her off. (See chapter, Nude Twister, Anyone? for more information.)

After

It's less common for women to get off after the man blows his wad, unless she does it herself. Climax during sex seems to be the last song on the set list of sex. There is no encore. So if she didn't come before, and she didn't come during, by modern custom, it ain't gonna happen after, either.

If he rolls over and asks, "Was it good for you too?," you could be honest and say, "No." But most men are not going to go diving down on a woman when their dick was just there and you're dripping wet, and he's all done and no longer turned on. You might get him to give you a hand job, or if not, you can do it yourself. Women who get off afterwards generally trot off to the bathroom and hand-deliver themselves their own relief. Men who guess that's what she's doing tend not to like it one bit; it doesn't reflect well on his prowess factor, and he should learn fast that he should be getting her off before or during. It's not just good form, it's sex etiquette.

Pleasure Pulses

Multiple orgasm is the ability to come more than once in a very short space of time. It sounds simple, but it's far from it. Learning to experience multiple orgasms requires your ABCDs: Arousal and Beating off, and then some serious Concentration and Dedication. The way a man might experience a multiple orgasm is vastly different from the way women can. It's not easy for anyone to learn to multiple, but it's much easier for women than men. The garden-variety orgasm is a fucking fantastic consolation prize, though, so if you can't master the multiple, it's not like you don't go home a blue-ribbon winner. In the game of getting off, everybody wins once.

Multiple blast-offs for her

Women may not be able to pee standing up, but men can keep that talent, since in the trade off of "look at me aren't I cool" tricks, women got the multiple orgasm. Blessed with not having a refractory period, which is the mandatory "cooling off" period experienced by males after orgasm, women can keep going and going — there is no such pause button in the female sexual response.

Women are more likely to achieve multiple orgasms after their sexual peak, around thirty-five, or when they are in their second trimester of pregnancy, due to increased blood flow.

See? There are benefits to getting older, and bigger.

Streams and rolls Women experience two kinds of multiple orgasms: streaming and rolling. The streaming multiple orgasm is more common than the rolling variety, and some women experience only one or the other, while the lucky, lucky ones experience both. The streaming orgasm is a continual orgasm, starting from the first one, without really ending. It can spike and plummet in intensity, but it continues on and on, as long as stimulation is applied. It is more than one long orgasm, because the shudders of pleasure, the "peaks of orgasm" come and go, making it feel like an echo effect: peaks of sub-orgasms on top of one long one. While the baseline is "Yeah! Yeah! Yeah! Yeah! Yeah!" at first orgasm, continued stimulation keeps a woman there, at that orgasmic threshold, and then the multiples kick in, spiking after the first orgasm, every few seconds or every thirty seconds, along the lines of "Woo! Oh Baby! Oh God!," as the orgasmic threshold reaches new heights. The streaming orgasm is a continual building up and not letting go, or rather, repeatedly letting go.

The rolling orgasm is slightly different. This variety is the kind most people think of when they think "multiple orgasm." It is a series of orgasms, one rolling on right after the other, and each one is quite distinct and separate. They can occur a nanosecond apart, or a minute or so apart. If orgasms are experienced more than about a minute and a half apart, they are more widely regarded as sequential orgasms, rather than multiple orgasms.

These sequential orgasms are seen as a sub-breed of multiple orgasms. They are separate orgasms, a few minutes apart, and requiring separate stimulation. Women have these most commonly of all, and all women are capable of them, but how quickly they have them in succession depends on how sensitive their vulvas are: some women are so sensitive after one orgasm that touching anywhere down there is more painful than pleasurable. It may take ten minutes or more before another orgasm can be delivered. Other women find that when touched again, after a few seconds of no stimulation, they can peak up to another orgasm very quickly, sometimes in a second or two. This is unlike the rolling orgasm, which is a series of orgasms that are felt with constant, continued stimulation. Women who experience one orgasm often then stop stimulating themselves, or their partner stops stimulating them, but if they continued, they'd find that they could keep coming in rolling orgasms. The first blast-off is usually the strongest one, but nearly as soon as it subsides, another crest comes along, and another and another, literally like waves rolling into shore.

Maxing the climax Whether you are trying to experience rolling or streaming multiple orgasms, the training is the same: masturbation. When first learning, it's best to practice on your own so you can concentrate. Once you've taught yourself, then you can show your partner how to do it. Because multiple orgasms are experienced quite differently in women and men, the masturbation training techniques are slightly different. While men need to practice holding off from the first orgasm, women should masturbate to orgasm straight off the bat.

Once you have come, the focus begins. This is where experimentation with continued stimulation occurs. For women who are very sensitive, avoid the clitoris and try to continue stimulation in another area, with the aim of maintaining a high level of orgasmic sensation. For many women, the streaming orgasm is the first one to aim for. The tools you will need are one hand and a vibrator, or two hands. Think of it as playing the piano: each hand (or one hand and the vibrator) is playing different keys at different tempos. Once you have come, keep one hand, or the vibrator, slowly stimulating to maintain the orgasmic threshold, like a warm, low humming engine that's continually coming. Popular spots for this include just below, or just above the clit, on the shaft. While you're experiencing this pleasure, your other hand, or vibrator, rubs or buzzes a personal sweet spot, usually the clitoris, to deliver encore spikes of multiple orgasms. This orchestration takes practice, and women who first try often have high expectations or anxieties about the whole process that block it from happening. Practice relaxing and enjoying it, and eventually it will come, and come and come.

To learn the rolling orgasm, a vibrator is very helpful, and almost necessary with some women. The difference in the training exercise is slight. Some women train themselves to attain quick sequential orgasms and then work towards the rolling multiple orgasm. Masturbate to orgasm, then release all stimulation. Yes, take the vibrator away. Then after about twenty to thirty seconds, apply the vibrator either to the clitoris, or if that's too sensitive, your sweetest big O spot, and make yourself come again. Each time you masturbate to orgasm, pull away for shorter time periods, and then reapply stimulation to orgasm. Experiment with different speeds and motions of the vibrator to learn what can get you to come quickly, so that eventually your orgasms are coming on top of each other, in quick succession, without ever releasing stimulation. Once you have learned the motions required with a vibrator, start masturbating without one, so that you can come by your hand over and over. Women have said that varying their masturbation techniques often helps. For example, they may use a three-fingered circular motion to get to the first orgasm, and once there, switch to an up-and-down motion right on the clit for their second, then quickly switch to a side-to-side on the clit shaft for their third. Each woman is different, which is why personal experimentation is needed to find what works for you.

🗨 *"It took me months before I had my first multiple orgasm. I'd been trying off and on, but I really wanted to experience it, because I wanted to know what it felt like. It was great! I can't really describe it. I thought they'd get weaker and weaker in intensity, because I was told to expect that, but I had four orgasms and they were all really strong. It was like a few jolts going through me. Now I can have them almost whenever I'm in the mood for it. I usually only have two or three, but once I had five."*
— woman, 24

🗨 *"I can have orgasms one right after another, within a period of a few minutes. That's what I call multiple orgasms. I can have as many as four in a row. My boyfriend is really good at giving them to me. It makes him proud that he can pleasure me over and over, and he gets off on it. He says he's not jealous, but if the tables were turned, I would be. I guess it's because he doesn't know what he's missing."* — woman, 21

"My first multiple orgasm came with a partner. I came unexpectedly while I was on top of him, rubbing against him, but not having sex. I kept rubbing and came a second time straightaway. It was almost like one long orgasm, except it was definitely two separate peaks, where my heart raced and my body jerked." — waitress, 31

Multiple blast-offs for him

Yes, men can learn to reach their sexual climax and experience multiple orgasms without ejaculating. Okay, well, the truth is: it's a qualified yes. Men generally have a refractory period, a naturally occurring "down time" after orgasm, when they usually cannot be stimulated to orgasm again. This time period varies according to age and health, from a few minutes to many hours. So for men to be multi-orgasmic, they must work around this refractory period issue.

Men experience multiple orgasms in the opposite way to women. A man's last orgasm is his big, releasing one; the one that comes along with ejaculation. For a man to have multiple orgasms, he must train his response to feel orgasm prior to ejaculation. So, in essence, he experiences a series of little orgasms prior to his main event, which is the coming and spurting simultaneously. To learn to do this, a man must first be in tune with his sexual response. He must already be able to control when he ejaculates. If not, there is little hope until he learns this control. So, once he has control over knowing when he is about to come, and is able to back off from that point, he can learn what's called surfing the "plateau wave." The plateau wave is the bundle of sensations just prior to orgasm, before the feeling of "Oh, I'm gonna come!" The moments before this feeling of inevitability are called the orgasmic threshold in a man. It is this threshold that can be lengthened and surfed, brought up intensely, and lowered. The hills and valleys of stimulation while on this threshold can feel like small orgasms, prior to ejaculation. Once he's learned to control these sensations, a man can stay at this orgasmic level for several minutes, rather than the nanoseconds an average male does. The orgasmic sensations felt while surfing this threshold are often not the intensity of an orgasm a man might feel if he were to let fly after not having sex in a month, but they are genuine orgasmic pleasure pulses.

Manual labor Masturbation is the key to learning. And the best way to learn is slowly, and in small steps. What you have to do, literally, is work up to it. Masturbate to mid-excitement, then stop. Take stock of the feelings and sensations both in your balls and penis, and in your abdomen and groin, as your erection subsides. Over the next few weeks, masturbate to higher and higher peaks of excitement (spread out the time you take to learn, to build up a good knowledge of your sexual response at different times of the day, and under different circumstances, like stress, relaxation, etc.). When you hit the plateau stage of high excitement, when it's all starting to feel really good and you don't want to stop, stop. Stop and concentrate on where the sensations are. Experiment with short bursts of stimulation to find out how long and how much it would take to come. Concentrate on the pleasure right at that point and play around to find what levels of bliss you can achieve without actually coming. Give yourself short, quick stimulation, then stop quickly, over and over, and you will find yourself going up and down like a yo-yo, experiencing multiple waves of pleasure. It's been described as like riding a wave of pleasure: up to the peak, down a mini-valley, up again, peak, valley, until you choose to blow. The first few times, you may only experience two, but with practice, men who have mastered the multiple say they can go up to ten.

Men can also go to alternative sexual health practitioners, such as Tantric sex gurus and Tao sexual health experts, who can give advice on coming without ejaculating. The ancient practice of male orgasm without ejaculation lies in breathwork, relaxation and control. Men who have ejaculatory control over the timing of their ejaculation have attained step one, but there is the advanced level of sexual response control, which is learning to experience orgasm without letting go of ejaculate at all. Once a man has mastered the ability to come without juicing, which takes much practice and concentration and is certainly not achievable by everyone, he can learn to do that more than once at a time. *Voilà*, the multiple orgasm. It is ejaculation that brings on the refractory period and prevents men from multiple O-ing. Once the trick of experiencing orgasm without ejaculation is learned, multiple orgasms are an attainable goal. This does not sound easy, and it is not easy. For the majority of Western men, orgasm goes hand in hand with ejaculation. To lengthen orgasm, or learn to multiple, your choices are to learn not to spurt, or to learn to surf the plateau wave. Most men opt either to surf it or fuck it.

"I masturbated until I think I memorized my body's response to every kind of stimulation known to man. I got close, I think. I don't know if what I feel is IT, but I can last a lot longer now, and I stay in that pleasure zone for much longer. Sex used to be about getting to that place, then coming. Now I get there and spend most of the time during sex in that pleasure threshold. It makes sex a whole lot better because where I used to spend five out of twenty minutes at that plateau phase, now I spend fifteen

Culturally Orgasmic

Anthropologists studied islanders such as the people of Mangaia, as examples of extreme sexual libertarianism. The people of Mangaia were sexually permissive, believed orgasm was crucial to sex, and especially fertility. Older women often taught younger men how to be good lovers, and how to deliver a woman to orgasm. Older men trained up the young women in this department too.

The Marquesans, who lived in the mountains of the central Pacific Islands, were also an orgasmic people, and had a wild sexual culture. They had erotic festivals, participated in orgies, alfresco sex, group sex, hospitality sex, oral sex, and especially, frequent sex: up to five times a night.

*out of twenty minutes there. And the sensations are
fantastic. I don't know how to come without
ejaculating, but I can recommend stretching out that
pre-orgasm phase. Plus when I do come, it feels huge
because I've really been building it up."* — man, 29

*"I tried. I even went to one of those Tantric workshops.
Made no difference. I get to that point, and I come.
Only once. I think all this multiple orgasm stuff is a
load of bullshit, myself."* — man, 27

Little Boy Blue
Lost His Wood

understanding and solving
erectile problems

Willy, Won't He

If getting wood is work, or simply isn't working, it's time to consider the idea that erectile difficulty has reared its ugly head (or not reared, to be more specific about it). Erectile problems can strike at any point in a man's life; it is not just a grandfather syndrome. Men who experience erectile difficulty in their younger years often suffer acute embarrassment, fear and worry, because they don't expect it to happen to them when they are young. The hard, strong, fast and ever-ready erection is perceived as a reflection of his manliness; that he is a strong man, hard, sexy, always at the ready and, above all else, virile. His ability to fuck is a primary one; to insinuate or state that he cannot is the ultimate insult. With all this male identity and purpose riding on one's erection, it's no wonder men don't like to talk about it when it doesn't happen.

The "I" Word

* The word *impotence* is derived from the Latin word *impotentia*, meaning lack of power. It was first used in a sexual context, referring to male lack of sexual power, function or ability, back in 1655.

* The first clinical description of impotence occurred in medical literature around 1833.

* In 1918, it was described as "the complete or incomplete inability satisfactorily to carry out heterosexual coitus per vaginam. Satisfactorily means adequate erection, time and control of ejaculation."

Source: *The Illustrated Book of Sexual Records*

Hard woods and soft woods

Erectile difficulty is the inability to get wood. But as we all know, there are different types of wood. A man, even without suffering from impotence, can experience softer erections at times, depending on various circumstances, including medications, drugs or alcohol. "Erectile difficulty" is the term used nowadays rather than "impotence" for two reasons: one is the lack of penis power does not mean a lack of male power (which is what the word impotence means — lack of power). Inability to get a hard-on does not mean a man has lost his machismo, or his power, and the health industry has stopped using a term that connotes that.

> *"It's not the men in my life, it's the life in my men."*
> — Mae West

But also, impotence implies that a man is unable to achieve any kind of erection, not even a whiff of a stiffy, ever. The term erectile difficulty is more accurate because most men who suffer from a few problems in the woody department can get partial erections, or only have intermittent problems.

Some typical wood problems include:

* You still experience morning erection, but you can't get hard with any sexual stimulation, through either masturbation or with a partner.
* You can get hard for masturbation, but not with a partner.
* You used to get erections, but never get them anymore, not even in your sleep or in the morning.
* You can get hard with visual stimulation, but not with a partner.
* You can get hard prior to intercourse, but then it fails.
* You can only get marginally hard, but not as hard as you used to get.
* Sometimes, not all the time, without taking drugs or alcohol, it just doesn't get up, and you don't know why.
* You can get hard, but it takes a long time, or much, much longer than it used to.
* You can get hard, but it doesn't stick around very long.
* You've never had a hard-on in your life.

Why the Compass Points South not North

Blood, sweat and tears

Blood is the lifeline of the hard-on. If the arteries that carry blood to your penis are damaged and not working well, then blood cannot fully or adequately enter the penis, and without good blood flow, the dick has trouble getting hard. High blood pressure is a serious problem and can directly contribute to erectile problems. Unfortunately, so do some of the medications used to treat high blood pressure. The best bet is to prevent arterial damage and high blood pressure by exercising right, which means working up a sweat at least three times a week. Good fitness goes a long way to keeping dick handy and hard.

In addition to keeping physically fit, it is important to keep emotionally healthy. The penis is a part of the body, just like any other organ, and is susceptible to negative emotions. Depression is a leading cause of erectile failure. Men who feel depressed may have trouble getting and maintaining erections, and clinical depression very often affects sexual function and ability to get hard. This is often a temporary wood problem, and will ease when the depression subsides. But, of course, this doesn't help in the fight against being depressed. If you feel you suffer from depression and are having erectile problems, visit a counselor, MD or sex therapist.

Softie at heart

Heart disease very often goes hand in hand with erectile problems. Men with heart disease often also have arterial or circulatory problems which affect blood flow to the penis. But also, men who have had a heart attack are sometimes afraid that sex will bring on another attack. This worry brings on erectile difficulties. Talk to your specialist about your concerns, and usually, after any heart surgery, you need four to six weeks to recover before you can slowly resume sexual activity and get back to normal. If you feel you need medication, visit your MD, or if you feel you need counseling, see a therapist.

Smoke 'em down

Cigarette smoking not only kills you, it kills your ability to get wood. Forget the lone, sexy Marlboro man riding into the sunset; his horse was probably all he could ride, because he was most likely impotent (ever wonder why he was always alone?). Smoking has been linked not only with cancer of the penis, but with erectile inability. The nicotine in cigarettes constricts the arteries, and the tiny little capillaries in the penis are the first to feel it. Smoking is also linked with heart disease. It's a vicious cycle, but the good news is that once you quit smoking the blood flow improves within weeks. There may be a few causes of your impotence, but if you're a smoker, quitting is your first step to getting your sex life back.

Death by chocolate

Your sweet tooth may be killing your ability to feel the sweet shudders of orgasm. Men with diabetes often experience erectile difficulties after years of the disease. Diabetes can affect the arteries, as well as the spongy tissue in the penis, leading to problems getting hard. This generally occurs if you have had diabetes for over ten years, and the best solution is to control your sugar levels, eat sensibly, exercise and avoid smoking and excessive alcohol. If the problem has already occurred, see your MD for medication options.

Body jam

There are a great number of diseases that can affect erectile function, and an even greater number of medications that have a side effect of jamming the sexual response and disrupting a man's ability to achieve or maintain a hard-on. Some of the diseases and their medications that can tamper with getting wood include cancer, heart disease, depression, diabetes, spinal cord injury (mild or severe), Peyronie's disease (an abnormal condition of the penile connective tissues that makes erection painful), and hormonal problems. If you think you may have any of these diseases, or are taking medications for any of these diseases, and are experiencing erectile problems, speak to your doctor or an MD.

Getting on

As you get older, your body ages, and like wine, some parts get mellower. The raging hard-ons you experienced when you were twenty are, at sixty, a thing of the past. Older men have erections less frequently, and the time in between them is longer. A man in his late seventies or eighties can expect to need a twenty-four-hour rest period (known as the refractory period) between orgasm and his next erection; and that is normal. Erections in later years may not be as frequent, or as hard, but they should still happen, so if you're not getting them, see your doctor or an MD.

Groggy cock

Grog is famous for bringing out the party animal at the pub, but then when you get home, there's no need to bring out the lion tamer, because the beast never rises from the dead, or if he does, it's half-heartedly. Limp-dick syndrome in youth is very often because of excessive drinking. While it may only be embarrassing at first, if heavy drinking continues, the problem can set in for good. The same goes with heavy or regular use of cocaine and/or pot.

Split down the middle

Sometimes, a man's ability to make love, or not make love, has everything to do with whether he is in love. If a man is experiencing relationship problems, or has just experienced a relationship split, his ability to get hard can fly out the window. Not all men who split from their partner want to rush out and fuck everything that walks. Some take a split really hard, and a side effect is that they can't get hard. Talking through relationship problems, grief and confusion is important to get your sexual drive humming again.

Worrywart

Stress. Anxiety. Worry. Financial frets. These concerns not only plague a man's mind, but his penis as well. Dick does not want to come out to play when there's all this shit going on. If a man cannot seem to work out why he is having trouble getting hard, take a look at lifestyle, workload, deadlines, performance anxiety and any other pressures. Chances are, the clues are there.

Saddle up

Studies show that men who ride a bike regularly without a proper seat or padding can do damage to the nerves and arteries in the groin that lead to the penis. Over time, this damage can become permanent. The solution: avoid the narrow bicycle seat and choose a wider, padded saddle, or you may find that's the only saddle you'll be doing the giddy-up in.

Help, Doc

Whether in search of a Viagra prescription or in need of a talk about some sexual and relationship issues, visiting an MD or therapist is always important if erectile problems are getting the better of you, and making your sex life worse for wear.

If you visit an MD, you can expect them to ask you questions about the frequency and firmness of your erections, and your sex history. Your doctor will also want to examine you thoroughly, which, depending on your age, situation and personal health, may include tests on your penis, balls, prostate, heart, blood pressure, blood, skin, hair, hormones, liver, blood sugar and urine. Additionally, your doctor may want to test whether you are experiencing nocturnal erections, by giving you a device to strap on which detects and measures whether you get hard during the night.

Depending on the outcome of tests, your doctor will prescribe a medication, maybe Viagra, maybe not, and may also recommend a counselor.

Seeing a counselor about erectile problems, even after medication is prescribed, is valuable, especially if the man is in a relationship that has been suffering or dealing with this issue for some time. Changes are bound to occur in and out of the bedroom after not being able to do it and then suddenly being ready, willing and able. And maybe even chomping at the bit.

Some couples have found that therapy has been valuable to:

* Discuss relationship and sexual issues that have surfaced or resurfaced.
* Cope with the stress that not being able to make love raised.
* Talk through cheating or leaving fears about whether a partner has sought sexual satisfaction elsewhere as a result of the man not being able to have sex.
* Talk about a woman's fear that he will leave her for a younger model now that he has regained his ability to have sex.
* Negotiate libido issues between partners.
* Mediate or jumpstart open communication between partners.

Whether you choose to see a marriage or relationship counselor, doctor or sex therapist, it is important that the two-way lines of communication between partners are kept open, and an atmosphere of support, encouragement and affection is fostered.

Gathering Wood

The little blue pill

Considering the staggering success of Viagra, it's amazing to think the little blue pill almost never was. It was sheer accident that sildenafil, the drug contained in Viagra, was discovered to be beneficial for hard-ons. Sildenafil was first researched as a treatment for angina (chest pains caused by a lack of oxygen reaching the heart), and didn't work. But during research, study participants reported a side effect: woodies. Naturally, that changed the direction of the research and eventually Viagra was born and hundreds of millions of men, and their partners, have cheered.

Viagra sales worldwide hit one billion in the first year alone.

How Viagra works is relatively straightforward. When a sexually functioning man gets aroused, a flurry of chemical messages, hormones and enzymes are sent between nerves, blood vessels and the tissues of the penis, resulting in blood flow, and erection. Messages and substances are also released in the body when erection comes down (either on purpose, after orgasm, or whenever you get started but then lose it). Essentially, in men with erectile dysfunction, these messages get out of balance and erection either doesn't happen, happens partially, or appears and then vanishes. Sildenafil works by boosting the substances that promote erection while blocking the substances that arrive to bring down the erection. Think of it like a Pac-Man game: inside the body there are little green pacmen blipping around, who go into action and head south when sexual stimulation occurs. Their mission is to raise the dick up hard. Then there are yellow pacmen who spring into action and come along, usually after the show, and their mission is to bring the dick down, after orgasm, or after a systems failure. These yellow guys outnumber and attack the green pacmen, so when they're around, they usually win. The yellow pacmen are important because without them the dick might stay hard too long, but sometimes the yellow pacmen arrive and attack the greenies too early, messing up the whole choreography of the game, and bringing the dick down when it should be up. So Viagra, the Big Blue Daddy, comes along and sorts them out: making sure the green pacmen get the chance to send their messages and have their hard-core show, before the yellow pacmen arrive on the attack, and if they dare try to gatecrash the show, Viagra is the bad-ass bouncer who doesn't let them.

Viagra does not work by popping a pill, downing a drink, and sitting back to wait for the love wand to come along. You must be in the mood for l'amour for it to work. Viagra works to help promote erection by removing the blocks; it does not whip up a stiffy for you, without your participation. Sexual desire and stimulation must be present for a hard-on to happen. So, yes, it's safe to take if you have a hunch you're going to get lucky, but aren't sure. You won't look foolish, or feel foolish, because your ever-ready Down Under salute will be on standby during the dinner or the movie.

Viagra is best taken without alcohol. It's not a good idea to pop one if you've come home drunk and think a fuck sounds like a good idea. It's a drug, not a completely fantastical love potion, and it can interact badly with alcohol. It's also best to take it on an empty stomach (again, so it has fewer things to interact with, and so it is absorbed faster). The best bet is to set a date for lurve, and pop the pill about an hour before you think you might dance the horizontal hula.

Blue light danger zone As miraculous as most men think Viagra is for transforming their sex lives, it is not perfect, and has a few side effects.

More common, can-live-with side effects include:

★ Headaches.

★ Indigestion.

★ Red flushes on face.

★ Nasal congestion.

A little stranger, but can-still-live-with side effect is:

★ A bluish tinge in vision for several hours.

Serious, can't-live-with, need-to-rethink-taking-the-pill, (but less common) potential side effects are:

★ Hypertension.

★ Heart attack.

★ Sudden death.

A doctor should discuss all potential side effects with you, and determine if you are in a risk group that should not take Viagra, such as those men who have had a stroke or severe heart attack within the preceding six months, those who are on medication containing nitrates, and those who have really high or really low blood pressure.

Popping a pill is never the be-all and end-all answer to a sexual problem, so be sure you address relationship and personal concerns as well.

What the blue wonder can't do The little blue pill is not a cure-all. It works specifically on hard-on problems, not on premature ejaculation or low libido. Men who have low sexual desire or rapid rooting problems should not turn to Viagra for the answer because it just won't help.

While there are trials currently testing the effectiveness of Viagra on women, it is likely that the dosage and exact make-up will be different for women. Don't both go pill popping and sharing a

An ancient Taoist Chinese cure for impotence was to have the man kiss and suck the vulva of passionate young girls. It was thought the sexual energy would transfer to him, especially if he swallowed all her cream.

Source: *The Sex Chronicles: Strange-But-True Tales from Around the World*

prescription with your mate until the studies prove that it really works for women's sexual arousal and function. (It is believed that sildenafil can stimulate blood flow to the vagina, lips and clitoris — in the same way it can to the penis — and enhance sensation and lubrication.) Until it is approved and tested for women, do not trailblaze your own study with Viagra and risk potential unresearched side effects. It shouldn't be too long before we know how Viagra can be used for women, and how it should be administered. Patience, ladies.

Blue urban myth Viagra is a sexual-performance-enhancing drug for men with erectile problems, not for guys who are looking for a sexual edge. If you are a normal sexual male, do not pop the blue pill thinking it will give you a stronger stiffy; it won't. It won't make you last longer or come harder. That's a total urban myth. Some men take Viagra after they've had a few drinks, as a way of helping their performance, but it's the alcohol that's preventing them reaching their peak sexual performance ability in the first place. Viagra should not be used as a crutch or a sex aid, unless you are being treated for a legitimate sexual problem.

"My mates told me they tried Viagra and it was amazing. They said it worked like an aphrodisiac and would make me horny, as well as make me last

longer. One bloke said it helped him stay hard for
over two hours. So I thought I'd give it a try. I pictured
it something like Popeye with his can of spinach, that
right after taking it, I'd get hard, really hard, like
Popeye's biceps used to grow. Well, nothing happened.
I couldn't even tell I'd taken it, and it made no
difference at all to my hard-on. I should've known,
knowing those blokes, that they were having me on."
— man, 25

Nature's wake-up call

Yohimbine is a natural chemical derived from the African yohimbine tree. It has been found to restore erections in up to one-third of men who try it. It works for men who have erectile difficulties stemming from psychological troubles as well as those who have erectile problems from physical illnesses such as diabetes or vascular disease. Unlike Viagra, men can use yohimbine to enhance their sexual function, even if they have no history of erectile difficulty. Yohimbine is available at most health shops and chemists. Some research has indicated that yohimbine affects blood pressure, so be sure to check with an MD or your doctor or pharmacist about its interaction with other medications or naturopathic remedies.

Stiff shot

The option of an injection in the penis to remedy erectile problems is far less preferable to men now that Viagra is available, however, it is still used with success. And in some cases, where Viagra is not suitable, men are willing to give themselves a shot if it means getting a stiffy. The

The ancient Greeks and Romans prescribed a tonic of animal semen to cure impotence.

injectable substance (called prostaglandin) enables the arteries to the penis to expand, allowing blood flow into the penis so an erection is possible with sexual stimulation (which occurs almost automatically as the penis needs to be massaged up and down the shaft immediately after injection to spread the prostaglandin around). A doctor will teach you how to inject the drug into the shaft of the penis so that you are able to give yourself an injection before intercourse, and will prescribe the correct dosage for your body and problem. The stiffy-shot should be administered about twenty minutes before intercourse, so clearly it's vital that a man learns to do it himself. While it sounds like a horrific experience, one you would think would make getting turned on afterwards impossible and unthinkable, men actually report that it doesn't really hurt, and they do get a hard-on within five to twenty minutes. Because of the potential for bruising and scarring, never inject in the same place twice, and keep the number of injections each week to a small number (discuss this with your sexual health physician). There are potential side effects to injecting prostaglandin into your penis, and you should be well aware of these before choosing this solution to your erectile problem.

WARNING: Injecting can lead to prolonged erections. An erection lasting longer than six hours is not only painful as all hell, but also dangerous, as damage to the member can occur. Consult an MD or your doctor if you experience long erections to adjust your dose.

"I nearly passed out the first time the doctor injected my penis. I thought there was no way I would be able to do it myself. But it's incredible, the motivation an erection can be. I learned to do it, and while it has taken the spontaneity out of our sex life, at least we

have one now. And yeah, mate, the honest answer
is that it hurts a bit, but surprisingly little, actually."
— man, 57

Fixing the leak

For men whose erectile dysfunction is directly related to arterial problems and has no psychological root, surgery is sometimes an option. If your penis suffers from "leaking veins," surgery can be performed to sew them up, or block them with special chemicals. For more serious problems, such as penile arterial blockages, delicate bypass surgery can be done, or a procedure known as venous arterialisation. In this procedure, a healthy blood vessel from your thigh or chest is taken out and joined to the artery in the abdomen that leads to the arteries in the penis, and then attached to the veins that take the blood out of the penis. The blood then flows into the penis via these veins instead of through the blocked arteries. It's a rather topsy-turvy, backwards route, but it seems to work in about 75 percent of cases. If it works, it's a semi-permanent to permanent solution, and you no longer have to take any little blue pills. However, only an MD can determine if you are a candidate for these surgeries.

Implants

While penile implants are the subject of many jokes, it's serious business to the men who need them. As popular as Viagra is, it is not suitable for every man because of its side effects, and because it seems some men develop a tolerance to it and need an option when it stops working for them. There are two different kinds of implants, and both have their pros and cons. The implants available are the inflatable implant and the semi-rigid implant.

Old Arab medical texts prescribed impotent men to attempt to sleep with a virgin to regain sexual function and power, and cure impotence.

Source: *The Sex Chronicles: Strange-But-True Tales from Around the World*

Pumped up The inflatable implant is a lot like the pump athletic shoes of the early 1990s, where you pumped the tongue behind the laces to fill the shoe with air. Only in this case, you're pumping an implanted pump in your ball sac to fill the penis with saline. A release valve is also in the sac to let the saline out to a reservoir implanted behind your pubic bone. It's quite a handy randy device, really.

Dirk Diggler The semi-rigid implant has made a number of advances. Silicone implants are placed in the penis, keeping it hard, but not too hard, all the time. The silicone is flexible enough that it can be bent down and tucked away when you're not in a sexual mood. When you feel like getting down and dirty, you simply massage and bend it straight for a permanent erection. Dirk Diggler, move over, Boogie Nights have come again.

The implants are placed in the two spongy tissue columns (corpora cavernosa) that run down the length of the shaft. The implants provide erection, and the rest of your sexual response is natural. You can still feel connected to your partner during lovemaking, feel pleasure through stimulation, fuck like an athlete, and orgasm like a king. The bonus: you can keep screwing until your lady has had enough, because you stay hard as long as you like.

Suck him hard

Men with partial erection problems still sometimes use a vacuum device to get hard. These devices are easy to buy in shops, clinics, or on the Internet. The basic principle behind them — and there are a number to choose from, ranging in price from a few bucks to a few hundred dollars — is to draw blood into the penis to make it hard or harder. Most of them have a plastic sheath, which covers the penis, and then air is pumped out of the sheath, creating a suction which draws blood into the dick. A man can then use bands or cock rings around the base of the penis and/or scrotum to prevent the blood from escaping. Some men, even without any erectile problems, occasionally use a device like this to get extra hard. It's not a good idea to do this very often, because the more you put unnatural, undue pressure on those precious arteries, the more likely you are to damage them. And then you run the risk of needing a device like this all the time.

The first vacuum device to treat erectile difficulty was made public in 1844.

HRT

Women aren't the only ones taking hormone replacement therapy. If erectile difficulty is deemed to be due to lack of sex hormones, such as testosterone (which is only one among many male sex hormones), then testosterone therapy can be considered. Still controversial, research results and practitioners conflict on whether it actually works successfully. It is available through implant, injection, tablet, cream or patch.

Wood alternatives

If therapeutic solutions haven't worked for you, or there are times when you'd rather not go through the fuss of pills or pumping, remember that a hard-on is not everything. It's pretty fucking important to fucking, I won't lie, but think of it this way: you can get a huge amount of pleasure from giving your partner pleasure, and she will really appreciate it, too. Cultures around the world, and throughout time, have exalted the prowess of a lover. And prowess is not always defined by being hard, but by being creative, skillful and generous. In ancient cultures, men used to have sex with women with strap-ons and dildos made from nearly every kind of material. "Happy Boxes" for better lovemaking included dildos of different shapes and sizes. Give having sex with your partner with a dildo a go, and you might find you experiment in ways you probably never would if you had a hard-on and made love "straight." Step outside the square and have some fun. Release the stress and performance anxiety, and if your rooting problems were psychological, it could be that all you needed was a little break from the pressure of performing penetrative sex to get back on track. Maybe, or maybe not. Let's be honest, change doesn't happen overnight, and while fucking is usually better than playing around, playing around is better than not doing dick. It's important to have a Plan B when Plan A falls down.

One-Night Wonders

[*when variety is the spice of your sex life*]

ONE-NIGHT STANDS: pash'n'dash,
blow'n'go, root'n'scoot, roll'n'stroll,
fuck'n'chuck, ruffle'n'shuffle, do'n'shoo,
pick'n'flick, tussle'n'hustle, snog'n'jog,
"have a shag, then grab your swag"

FOUR "F"-ING: Find 'em, Feel 'em,
Fuck 'em, Forget 'em

What's Your Sign?

"Hey, baby, what's your sign?" may be the age-old sexual pick-up line offered up by males in our culture, but other cultures have historically engaged in a variety of far more explicit signals to indicate their desire for intercourse.

For the Pacific Tikopia people, a man would proposition a girl he was interested in having sex with by flipping up her skirt.

Pick-up lines

* I may have lost my virginity, but I still have the box it came in. Want to play with it tonight?
* I'm going to teach you a lesson in math by adding you to my bed, subtracting your clothes, dividing your legs, giving you a square-root and multiplying your climax.
* How do you like your eggs in the morning? Scrambled or fertilized?

Among some North American Indian tribes, a young man wanting to spend the night with a girl would enter her hut with a stick. He would light the stick in her camp fire and if she then blew it out, he stayed the night. If she put the bedcovers over her head, he would leave, having been rejected.

A Jaluit man of the Marshall Islands indicated his desire for intercourse with a girl by saying "penis" and "vagina" and suggestively rolling his eyes.

The Siriono people of South America showed their interest in sex by picking lice out of each other's hair; picking wood ticks from their partner's body and eating them; picking worms and thorns from each other's skin; and decorating each other with feathers and paint.

So maybe being approached with the line, "I've lost my phone number, can I have yours?" isn't so bad after all.

CASUAL SEX: fuck around, get around, sleep around, dick around, fool around, screw around, muck around, bedhop, to play, to notch, "I'm working on my reputation," "I'm conducting my own sexual survey," fuck-hunting, hot to trot, feeling fucky

Busy Bunnies

In a survey of over 34,000 Internet users (in which half of the respondents were under 25 years old):

* 4 percent said they had slept with over 100 people
* 3 percent have fucked 50–100 people
* 7 percent have had 21–30 sexual partners
* 14 percent have had 11–20 lovers
* 20 percent have screwed 5–10 partners.

Source: *The Penguin Atlas of Human Sexual Behavior*

Once Upon a Night

Sometimes we just want to fuck.

As pleasure seekers prowling to connect physically for a night, or even a few hours, we hit the town, searching for the hook-up.

Casual sex. It's an ingrained part of our sexual pop culture, moral-objection brigades aside. Both women and men, whether they love them, hate them, regret them or swear by them, have done the one-night wonder. Some rationalize them by saying, "We really connected; it was deep and meaningful, even for a night." Others acknowledge that it was what it was: a fuck, pure and simple.

We cater to the needs and urges of our bodies, and aren't always looking for the "Once Upon a Time, Happily Ever After" story. Sometimes, we're just in the mood for a shag: no strings, no complications.

Singles who would go out with a married person:

17 percent

Source: Dr. John Croucher, Macquarie University

ONE-NIGHT WONDER HUNTER: Casanova, fuckster, love machine, fuck-artist, poodler, skirtchaser, playboy, ram, bun duster, ho, sex machine, rider, hustler, loverboy, fuckaholic, stud, lounge lizard, male slut, alleycat, rootrat

The Hunters

Traditionally, men have been regarded as the one-night wonder lovers. A quick root'n'scoot is the quest, and once they're off, they're off. The one-night wonder hunter can be found any night of the week, at many a venue, especially those that serve alcohol. Drink, more often than not, is the foreplay of the one-night wonder. Among other things, grog gives him the hunting bravado to pull.

"Yeah, sure, most of my one-night stands have been when I've been drinking. It gives me confidence, once I've had a couple of schooners, to chat up a girl. If I'm out to score, it's much easier if I've had a few. And if she's been drinking, it lubes the whole process."
— Andy, 26

"Sex without love is an empty experience, but, as an empty experience, it's one of the best."
— Woody Allen

While some women may consider the hunter the one-night wonder, leg-spreading, seed-spreading bastard (particularly women of the bitter, twisted, man-hating ilk), the truth is that not all men are in search of endless random one-off shags. Men too have deep souls wanting connection, companionship and mating mateship. That said, no matter how soulful and wonderful they may be in other contexts, men in search of a one-night wonder have their antennae tuned to short-term pleasure only. Do not attempt to adjust this tuning as the chances of success lie along the lines of flying pigs. Men who are out to fill their biological urge, male sluts hoping to sow their wild oats, are on a fucking mission. One-night stands are about the business of pleasure. They are about casual sex and physical satisfaction. That's the limited contract of a one-night stand. There are exceptions to every rule, but for every spontaneous and deep connection from a one-night stand, there are (at least) nine random, casual, body-only encounters.

Hunters argue that they are biologically driven towards casual sex and multiple partners; that it's their beastly playboy nature. If you buy that argument, it's best to know the hunting nature of the beast before doing it like it's done on the Discovery Channel.

What he wants her to know about one-night stands:

* It's a night, not a relationship.
* He does not genuinely want to spend the night, unless he wants a morning shag.
* He wants to do things girls in relationships often won't do, like anal sex, 69, fantasy role-plays, threesomes.
* He doesn't want to do things girls in relationships do, like cuddling, spooning and sleeping intertwined.
* He wants to be blown.

Q. What's the difference between a good girl and a nice girl?
A. A nice girl goes out on a date, goes home and goes to bed; a good girl goes out on a date, goes to bed, and then goes home.

Doing a "wombat": refers to a guy when he has a one-night stand because a wombat "eats roots, shoots and leaves."

* He wants you to talk dirty, or at the very least, tell him how hot and great he is in the sack.
* He wants to actually sleep, which means personal space in the bed.
* He may want to talk, to connect, but sharing a moment does not mean sharing a future.

Score cards

Men are famous for their little black books, but what's less widely known and appreciated are their secret score cards. Some men keep secret diaries of their conquests in which they rate their one-night-wonder girls according to factors including body type, attractiveness, sexiness, desire, creativity, talent and fuckability. Women may baulk at this reality, that men can be so objective and analytical about a sexual encounter, but for some men, sex is a hobby — an ongoing skill and practice, worthy of honing and scoring.

"I keep a record of all the women I've slept with on my computer. I use a program to maintain all my variables, for how well I think the sex went, and how sexy she was. Of course, I never let them know I do this, but it's my private record, so who cares? I do it to keep track of my sex life, what I do, what I think of previous partners, and how I can improve on previous performances. I would never show my files to anyone, because I'm not out to humiliate a woman, or make her feel like I didn't respect her. It's not about objectification, it's about knowledge and skill." — Todd, 29

> *"I keep a general record of the women I've been with. It's not serious, and I'm not out to be a Casanova or anything. I just like to keep a record of who I've been with and who they were, what they were like. I guess it's a pride thing."* — Matt, 23

> *"I keep a specific record of every woman I've ever been with. I rate them according to body, sexiness, how well they fucked, and what they did. A few of my friends know I do this and they heap shit on me, but I still do it. I like keeping track. It's like my victory lap."* — Chris, 30

ONE-NIGHT WONDER GIRL: tramp, bunny, charity girl, bike, good-time girl, loose, floozy, hottie, whore, ho, tart, spunk-bucket, easy lay, rep girl, maid, wench, zipper, hot box, hot pot, slag, slapper, slut, thrill seeker, the right sort

"Adam": slang for caveman, Neanderthal, sexist macho who treats women like dirt. It is not a compliment when a woman says, "He's a total Adam." Also used in sexual terms. To say, "He's a nice guy, but an Adam in the sack," means he's a grunting missionary type and not very creative, sensitive or generous in bed.

The Gatherers

Before 1900, overt premarital sex for women was virtually unheard of in the Western world, but since then, the number of females engaging in casual sex seems to be increasing with every passing decade. And while it cost generations of women their "reputations," women like Mae West paved a new way. Many of the promiscuous labels like "slut" have been reclaimed by women, and today, in some subgroups these words are part of a changing, powerful pro-woman and pro-sex vocabulary. Call it feminism, liberation or wising up: women have taken possession of their sexual freedoms and have come out to play.

The misunderstanding that women are the one-night-stand victims rather than initiators needs some clearing up. Welcome to the world of the PowerPussy: women in control of their pussies, their desires and their choices. The sex kitten in charge of having random sex without guilt has made her entrance and is flashing her liberated power. Vixens embrace the one-night wonder because it makes them feel sexy, irresistible, desired, desirable and powerful. And the most glaringly overlooked, previously hush-hush fact: women are just as horny as men.

SEX-JOHNNY: when a woman wants a fuck with no strings, and when pretty much anyone will do (a penis attached to a body), she's said to be on the prowl for a Sex-Johnny — a random partner for casual sex.

Women, traditionally, are the gatherers — they don't hunt the jungle quite like men, but they collect and pull for physical satiation just the same. They are as able as their male counterparts to draw in a mate, whether for a night, or a few hours. Girls are made of sugar and spice and so are their sex lives; every sweet angel has a craving for some spice now and then. Women are just as physically oriented as men when it comes to one-night stands. A woman will ditch her girl posse without hesitation if it means scoring with a chiseled hunk o' burnin' lover. If a woman is in the mood, and gets even a whiff of potential for a good lay, she's off with him, to get off with him.

> *"One more drink and I'll be under the host."*
> — Dorothy Parker

What she wants him to know about one-night stands:

* She wants to come.
* She wants to come.
* She wants to come.
* She wants to experiment.
* She wants you to go down on her.
* She wants you to get her wet before heading in.
* She wants to feel powerful and sexy.
* She wants to connect, talk, make some meaning out of the physical.
* She wants to have fun.
* She wants you to stay the night only if she invites you to.
* She wants to come.

Pash odyssey

Not so famous as men's black books, but just as personal, are women's pash odyssey diaries. Keeping track of lovers, casual and meaningful, and rumbles in the jungle is a rite many women observe. Keeping abreast of things is natural to women: they keep track of their cycles, and many little girls kept "Dear

Alpha male: the leader of the pack, like the silverback gorilla. An alpha male is not determined by muscles and machismo, necessarily, but is rather the kind of guy who makes heads turn when he arrives in a room. A man among men. Major mojo. Alpha males are born, not made; they simple are, without trying.

Diaries," so it's a natural extension to keep track of their desire cycles and pash experiences. Some women even take this journalizing of jungle roots to complex heights, rating performances and penises. Others use this chronicling to record safe-sex encounters, and risk-taking ones, including HIV- and STI-risk behaviors.

MOJO: sex appeal, sense of siness, hubba-hubba factor

Cocktail

The cocktail is the usual and reliable prequel to cocks and tails getting it on.

Alcohol probably birthed casual sex. Without a few cocktails, the cock probably wouldn't have stood a chance getting a piece of tail. Saturday Night Fever hits, shots get slugged, and the sexing-up hours begin: the cock sure gets hunting and the eager beavers start to gather.

The prowl for a one-night stand is all about "mojo" — having it, and getting it. Men and women who are desperate to get laid have next to no mojo. Desperation is a mojo killer. And those who are constantly horny, or haven't been laid in months and are nearly purple with frustration, will go home with anything that walks and says "yes," but that's just about sexual release, not real mojo. Less drunk, the standards are (somewhat) higher. Eyes meeting across a crowded bar will detect mojo from the slightest glance because they will instantly feel sparks, chemistry, lust. When two people connect on a mojo level, they're in for a hot night.

FREEMUFFING/FREEFURRING: going without underwear (women)

FREEBALLING: going without underwear (men)

Heading out specifically for a shag means dressing to pull, or rather, in some cases, undressing to pull. Skipping on underwear makes some feel sexy, and for some it's simply more convenient not to have to fiddle with that under layer if it's only going to come off anyway. Others make sure they've got their best undies on — or for some guys, their "lucky" undies (yuk!). For women, Murphy's (twisted) Law is that if she's shaved her legs, and has her lacy, sexy, matching bra and panties on, she'll go home empty-handed, or rather, to her own hand. But if she's wearing her best set of granny-pants, or something worse, like a girdle (think Bridget Jones), and her bikini line and legs are a jungle, then her chances of pulling are greatly increased. The CK-jocks Law is similarly true for men: if he came out in his ten-year-old Captain Kangaroo boxers, he's more likely to get his pants down and get lucky than if he decked himself out in his tight, black Calvin Klein briefs. While those who dress to pull and those who freeball and freemuff do often successfully complete their missions, sometimes,

Slurp'n'Send: sending SMS messages or emails after excessive consumption of alcohol, most of which are overly flirty or downright dangerous. All outgoing messages should be saved for added humiliation in the morning, so you know how much sin-bin time is required as punishment for dastardly or plain stoopid sends.

we go out not planning for sex, having said fuck it to nice underwear and fuck off to the razor, and that is when we're nearly guaranteed to get shagged.

BEER GOGGLING: the phenomenon of finding a member of the opposite sex attractive after multiple drinks when, sober, you would not find this person remotely appealing.

No spiking

The use of alcohol and drugs with the practice of one-night stands may be widely acknowledged and even widely accepted, but what is not acceptable is the unethical (and illegal) use of alcohol and drugs to get laid. When entering the world of sex, two words are vital: yes and no. It shouldn't need to be said but it does happen: it is always wrong to spike a drink. Just as consent is a prerequisite to sex, a person should always know what they are drinking. And this not only refers to the illegal use of drugs, such as Rohypnol, to spike drinks, but also to lying about alcohol content. Do not say, "Here's your tropical juice with a shot of vodka" when you've actually ordered the person a "Smash" with six or eight shots in it. It is not okay to order a double without asking or being asked to buy one. A person always has the right to monitor their own drug and alcohol intake. Purposely getting someone wasted so that you can have your way with them is rape. Rape occurs when consent has not been given for sex, or when consent is unable to be given (such as when one partner is paralytically drunk or stoned). Even if you're both naked and one partner pikes at the last minute, you cannot cry, "Not fair, we're past the point of no return" and continue, or demand or pressure for sex. One-night stands may be lusty, sweaty, yummy shagadelics, or pathetically pointless roots from hell, but they should always be a choice.

Drink'n'Dial: picking up the phone — home or mobile — to make calls you will either regret or forget. Most lethally made to an ex when you are drunk, alone and horny.

One-Night Wonderless

After a bad one-night stand, we often wonder why we bothered. A score is a score, and some would say bad sex is always better than no sex. Bad sex has been compared to bad pizza: maybe it tasted bad, and didn't have your favorite bits, but hey, it's pizza! We all love pizza, and pizza, even when it's bad, is still pretty good.

The pizza analogy works if you're a guy who always gets to come. If pizza equals sex, then the cheese is the orgasm: even bad pizza always has cheese for the guy. But for women who have a one-night stand and don't come, who are left swollen, sore and abandoned at the verge, well, it's all a bit like eating a cheeseless bit of dough topped with sausage and sauce. It doesn't even resemble pizza. For these women, bad sex isn't like bad pizza. It's only a bad waste of calories, and you can bet she'll never order from him again.

Sex bomb

You can go home with someone you think has major mojo, but still bomb together in the sack. No explosions of ecstasy, just a downward spiral into the depths of disaster. Not everyone is sexually compatible. Yes, bad sex will eventuate after too much alcohol — it's often short, sloppy and even without orgasm in some cases. But it can also happen that sparks that flew in the bar, without discernible reason, may fizzle in bed. Flirting is a very different game to fucking. There may have been chemistry in the tease, but then in the follow-through fuck, no generation of heat. It can just happen like that.

Most bad one-night stands result from incompatibility, guilt, regret, lack of communication and different ways to rock and roll. The major complaint from the hunters camp is that she just lies there like a wet fish, while the number one complaint from the gatherers camp is that he just humps away missionary style, gets off and rolls over. So, if she's not doing anything at all, and he's not doing anything creative, someone isn't taking the initiative. Hints, anyone? If you are lazy about having a one-night stand, and expect it to all just happen automatically, you probably deserve a shitty shag.

🗨 *"He called out 'Mama.' And not just when he came. Before, too."* — woman, 33

🗨 *"Everything was fine until he lost his erection during intercourse. Over and over he tried. I wanted him to stop trying, but I was at a loss for words. That's never happened to me before. I've been with guys who couldn't get it up, but not during sex. I mean, it went soft, like mid-thrust. But he kept thrusting and pumping for what seemed forever. I wish I could erase the whole experience, it was so awkward. Finally, I faked a small orgasm, hoping he'd get the hint. To this day I can't believe I pretended to actually come with a limp dick inside me."* — woman, 28

"You sleep with a guy once and before you know it he wants to take you to dinner."
— Myers Yori

"She kept asking me if she was too tight, and she was, but I didn't want to say anything to hurt her feelings. It wasn't until I was well and truly inside her that I realised I was in her arse, not her vag. Hey, it was dark, give me a break. I so didn't want to go there, though."
— man, 30

"I went to her place, and as soon as I saw her room, I wanted to get out of there. She turned out to be a dominatrix, and she got so rough that I fled the scene, even before we had sex. She was horrible, not a turn-on at all. And I had bruises that lasted a week to remind me what a wuss I am." — man, 26

"Mine was the classic waking up next to a total stranger, not knowing who he was, and not even remembering the sex, except for vague snippets. And the snippets aren't pretty. One is a blurry recollection of doing a striptease for him to AC/DC. And singing 'You Shook Me All Night Long', holding his cock as the

microphone. It's taken me years to get over the few
memories I do have from that night. And the rest,
I'd rather not know actually." — woman, 31

One-Night Wonderfuls

Sometimes two bodies meet and click. And you remember it always, because it was so amazing. Spontaneously you fall into bed with someone, maybe not even expecting the sex to be good. After all, if you've only known each other a few hours, how well can you connect? But if you're lucky enough, and you've been hit by that divine lightning bolt, then you know a great fuck with someone you hardly know is a sweet gift from the Gods of Pleasure.

"I went home with him and stayed for four days.
We couldn't keep our hands off each other. It was
a perfect mix of physical fucking and talking,
connecting, and complimenting each other. I told
him how much I loved his nipples, his hair, his hands,
and he kissed every square inch of me, and told me
he loved my nose, elbows, the backs of my knees, my
cunt. He made me feel sexy all over. And we kept
telling each other how well our bodies fitted together.
We fucked in every room, in the shower and the bath.
We hardly ate in those four days, really doing little
else other than sleeping and screwing. It was a four-
day orgy for two and it was bliss. I've never seen
him again, and I don't want to. He is my greatest
lover, and I want to always remember him that
way." — woman, 29

"The best one-night-stand fuck I can remember was with a girl who was visiting from out of town. We'd spent all day touring around and finally went back to my place for a drink. When I kissed her and she kissed me back, it started a dance that lasted all night. It was fantastic because we matched each other so well. When I was gentle, she was too, and when she got rough, I followed suit. We really reflected each other's needs well. We moved all around the bed and the room, playing in lots of positions. We had similar body types, so we could do it standing up, sitting, lying, and managed each other's body weight. Plus, she let me fuck her up the arse, which is something I love doing, and not enough girls let me." — man, 32

"I remember the first time I came during intercourse was with a one-night stand, and I was so shocked because it had never happened before, and I came so suddenly that I wasn't prepared for it. I screamed (and I'm usually quiet) and then I laughed. When he realized it was my first one, we shared a nice, almost tender moment. There was no embarrassment and he was sincerely pleased to have been my first lover who gave me an orgasm during sex. I've had lots of great sex since then, but that one night has a special glow around it in my memory, I guess because it was so great physically, and he was so sweet about it all." — woman, 27

Paying with the furry checkbook: when a woman uses sex to make payment rather than cash. A practice employed not only by working girls but by average, "regular" girls too. Most commonly reserved for cabbies: having sex or blowing rather than paying the fare (with the added bonus of getting a quick shag).

🗣 *"I'll never forget her even though I don't remember her name. She taught me how to truly love sex. I've never met a woman who was so comfortable with her body, and who was so open about asking for things, asking me to do something different, or checking with me if I wanted something done differently. But the way she talked and moved and rubbed and asked was so hot. She loved sex, and it showed. We spent a night and a day together and I left wanting to see her again, but she was leaving the next day, home to Europe. I've never felt so honest with a lover, and I barely knew her."* — man, 21

Walk of Shame

I once asked a guy what he thought was the best part of a one-night stand. He told me: the walk home in the morning. It is the delicious, smirking cap-off to a strings-free shag to walk home with puffed chest, a half-hidden proud, satisfied smile, stinking of sex, beer, rum and smoke, hair and clothes rumpled, shirt off, while nodding knowingly to the husbands who've come out to pick up their morning paper, who then look back jealously. For many women, however, this puffed-chest experience is alien territory. Commonly known among women as the walk of shame, the hussy-shuffle home — morning tail tucked in, shoes in hand, make-up-smeared face, hairdo akimbo, bra tucked in handbag — is always too long, too humiliating, even if it's only a block or two. In certain student neighborhoods, balcony cat-calls are commonplace. Hearing calls of "Walk of Shame!" and whispers, even when done jokingly, is the worst, not best, part of a one-night stand. It is in this walk home, or seedy cab ride, that the double standard between male and female slutdom still lingers. Somehow we continue to sustain the idea that a seedy man the morning after is a playboy stud who's done well. Bravo, macho macho-man. And a woman? Ah, the hussy has no publicly proud smirk. It's more a Shakespearean case of, "Get thee home, wench!" (because the nunnery so clearly didn't happen).

But it's after the walk of shame that payback occurs. Males may utter the monosyllabic, "Aw, great mate!" or "Yeah, I've been out. Yup, was a good night" to their hunting mates. Females, however, gather in groups in the kitchen, or on flatmates' beds, tongue wagging over every wag of his tongue on her body the night before; because women don't just spill the beans to each other, they empty the can, spread them around, slice, dice and sauté them.

Home-Court Advantage

* Knowing the way to the bathroom.
* Having your own toothbrush in the morning.
* Fresh underwear at your disposal.
* No walk of shame.
* Knowing where the condoms are kept, including the emergency stash.
* No cabfare required.

* You get to sleep with your own pillow, and on "your" side of the bed.
* Your music selection is at hand.
* You can orgasm as loud as you want, because you know whether your walls are soundproof.
* Your own sheets.

Playing Away Bonus

* Your address is kept a secret, so they can never find you, track you down, spontaneously arrive bearing flowers and condoms, or stalk you.
* You can sneak out and away to the privacy of your own home under the cloak of darkness.
* If you live with flatmates, playing away is essential if you want to avoid the third-degree or post-mortem.
* Anonymity, if you want it. No one ever has to know who you were with, or what you were doing.

Root'n'Scoot Rules

1. Giving out a fake number is appropriate if the sex was shocking.
2. "Darling," "Babe" or "Stud" are dead giveaways that you don't remember their name.
3. It's cool to look in the bathroom for baby oil for a massage, but uncool to spy in private medicine cabinets (unless you're genuinely concerned or alarmed about a red spot, or a fungus ...).
4. If alcohol has been too effective, and "hard" or "wet" aren't happening, for fuck's sake, say something instead of pretending you simply haven't noticed. At least that way you might be able to salvage the situation orally.

5. If you're playing away, try to do it on top of the comforter or duvet, because you don't know who else has been between the sheets, or when they were last washed.
6. Speak up. If you've ever wanted to try something, this is your chance. You'll never see them again.
7. Dodge MAB (morning-after breath) at all cost.
8. Carry condoms with you, and not just for luck or decoration — for use.
9. Faking orgasm because it's all so horribly wrong will only stunt his learning and skill acquisition, and is not helpful in the larger picture; but since you never plan on seeing him again, who cares, it's not your problem, let his next shag deal with it.
10. It is etiquette to be polite to your Sex-Johnny or Sex-Jane afterwards, no matter how bad the sex, but the morning-after post-mortem, held with friends, flatmates and trusted allies, should always give the detailed lowdown, no holds barred. If the sex was either really bad or really good, the "Don't Kiss and Tell" rule does not apply.

Spidersex

flirting and fucking on the web

On the World Wide Web, we can be like spiders, weaving our tangled webs of intrigue and deceit, luring others into our snare, some hoping to mate, others looking to prey.

The Internet was originally designed for military communication, and then extended into the academic world. At the start of the 1990s, the Net became public domain, and has grown exponentially ever since.

A vast majority of Internet users both play and work on the Net. Using the Net for communication is the number one function for most spiders. When chat rooms emerged, it didn't take long for dirty talking to become the most popular genre of chat. People find it erotic to be able to flirt and fuck with virtual strangers around the world. While much of cybersex is about sexy virtual fun, there is an underbelly to the Net which can be dangerous. There are hunters and gatherers on the web, and not all spiders are friendly.

The Internet is the first communication medium that is uncensored and free from private ownership or control. This enables spidersex to be a free-love free-for-all. There's a multitude of sites and chat rooms for every specific fetish, desire, lifestyle and preference. While censors, analysts and do-gooders would love to control the Net, it's obvious that people revel in the freedom. There are hundreds of millions of users, and cybersex is an international phenomenon.

It should surprise no one that cybersex was one of the first industries created by the Internet. With every new technological invention, someone has twisted and tweaked it to turn themselves on: the camera spawned erotic photographs; the phone led to dirty talking and the phone sex industry; movies quickly created erotic films; and the VCR really took off when the adult sex industry started producing porn videos to rent and buy. Even the invention of the car brought about a freedom to bonk in the back seat. The world of sex on the Net is nothing new. What is new about cybersex is the global accessibility, immediate gratification and the privacy and confidentiality it fosters.

When we hop on the Net, we weave in and out of other people's lives and our own fantasies. The Net is the ultimate in escapism. Our fingers tap keyboards in millions of rooms across the globe, as we seek to connect, either for a short private flirt or a prolonged long-distance correspondence affair.

Sex is the most popular keyword searched for on web browsers. By a longshot.

Up to one in three Internet users are estimated to visit an adult site at least once during their Net activities.

Chatting Up

There are chat rooms all over the Net that specialize in non-sexual content, and others that are designed for the orally sexually adventurous. Chat is such a popular aspect of the Net for users, that many sites, no matter what the subject, now have a chat section. You can check out an official band site and meet others to chat about the music. You can look at a techno-tourist site on a particular city or remote location and chat with others who either live there, or have traveled there. There are cyber book-club chat rooms by the thousand. People who suffer from depression or any sort of illness, including sexual difficulty, can find specific support-group chat rooms. If you desire it, experience it or want to know more about it, it's there for you to log in, look up, lurk around, then join in the chat.

"I seek you" chat rooms

Sex is one of the most popular forms of chat. Sites devoted wholly and solely to chat often provide entire rooms for different kinds of chat. You can choose something that grabs you, and then go gab away into the night. The first chat rooms developed as one step up from computer dating. Rather than letting the computer do the matching, the computer simply became the mode for matching. Early sites were based on people connecting out of romance ... the "I seek you" types, but sites such as the popular ICQ (a phonetic representation of "I seek you") now cater to every kind of chatter. As the popularity of chat has increased, cyber flirting has become a pastime in itself, without the goal of actually finding someone to meet in "real life." On sites such as ICQ, identities are kept secret, and users often go by their ICQ number. They meet only in virtual life, not real life.

In any given chat site, there are specific room-boundaries so that people with an interest in virtually-meeting specific types will know who they are chatting to. Many rooms are broken down by age. There are rooms for teens, twenty-, thirty-, forty- and fifty-

I have a computer, a vibrator, and a pizza delivery. So why should I leave my house?

somethings, rooms for gays (in fact, entirely separate sites which are more popular than melting-pot sites), people of different ethnicity and religions, people who want to talk reeeeeally dirty, people looking for romance, and people with specific interests.

If you're interested in chatting with others about a particular subject, such as a book, band or travel destination, it probably wouldn't matter to you whether you're sharing information with a fifty-five-year-old man or a nineteen-year-old lesbian. However, if you're trying to get off by talking cyber dirty, you'd rather talk to someone who interested you, as would most, at least in your fantasy. But the confidentiality of the Net means we never truly know who we are chatting to. To some cyber fuckers, this fantasy element heightens the excitement. The mystery person, or people, chatting to them on their screen could be anyone from anywhere. Getting raunchy with them feels like a safe way to be a naughty slut. To some, it doesn't matter who they're talking to; they take every user at face value, and don't care if their virtual identity is completely different from their real identity. This is probably the best attitude to have if you're interested in being a cyber Casanova. If you're into getting off while you chat cyber sexily, keep it virtual, go with the fantasy, and keep your anonymity. If you're interested in chat to actually take it somewhere off the Net, to make a transition from virtual life to real life, then you need to be more cautious about who you're chatting with and divulging your secrets to.

Pleasure themes and cyber orgies

Some chat sites have specific themes. The most popular ones revolve around bondage and discipline (B&D) fantasies and personalities. Groups meet online and act out their favorite B&D fantasies. Some users may actually be wearing bondage gear while they are typing away, but mostly B&D cybersex is in the realm of fantasy. Other groups log on and choose to act out a group orgy fantasy at a specific location — popular ones tend to have summer and beach themes. The sex-chatters build up the excitement by saying one night what they're each going to "pack" for the trip, and then when they "arrive" on the designated night, they all know what "toys" they have to play with, and they go from there, deep into the group orgy fantasy.

For those who like to fantasize while they masturbate, cybersex elevates the intensity by having a group of others provide elements of the fantasy for them. No matter what the theme or who the users are, cybersex is the ultimate in interactive fantasizing.

Going private

When the chatting gets really intense, you might be invited to have a private chat. A mini-window will usually pop up, or a private line will appear on your screen, inviting you to "go private." You can choose to decline or accept, and it's often in private chats that the computer screens get really steamy.

Sex netiquette

Cybersex has a completely different type of etiquette to normal dating and sexual etiquette. Virtual etiquette, or netiquette, is a separate phenomenon to real etiquette. For example, while it is considered rude in the real world to ask someone's age, in chat, every hour or so at least, someone will ask: A/S/C. This means

Age/Sex Check and most people in the room will respond by typing in their ages and sexes (or those of their alter ego that night). Your basic netiquette rules for cybersex include:

* Watch your tone. Writing in CAPS means YELLING or LOUD. Unless you are in a B&D cybersex chat, as the Master or Mistress, typing in CAPS makes you appear rude.

* Always reply to someone who asks you a direct question (addressing you with your username). Exceptions to this are if you are being stalked, or trying to block someone. Even then, you might get a not-so-warm reception from the rest of the room. You are, after all, in a chat room to talk, so if you do not answer someone, it's considered to be a slight.

* Go with the flow and try to keep up. Chat epitomizes conversation chaos. Do not wait for a lull in the chat to pipe up with an opinion. Blast away on the keyboard. Once you get used to it, you'll be able to follow the strings of conversations, and which lines refer to which conversations, including yours. The cacophony is part of the stimulation.

* Stay with the theme, mood and tone of the room. If you're in a fantasy room, stick with that. If you're in a "vanilla" chat, don't start your chat with "Hello to the room full of wet, horny pussies ^-^ [meow]!" Also, be wary and respectful of the host. The chat host (chat moderator, hired by some sites to maintain appropriate levels of interaction) will boot you from the room if you do not abide by the rules of the room. You will generally be informed of those rules when you sign on to the site. And if you aren't you'll be quickly warned.

* Always say goodbye. Even if you were new, hardly said anything, or spent most of your time in private chat, it is extremely bad netiquette form to abandon a room with no

cheerio. The chorus of byes, TTFNs (Ta Ta For Now) and TTYLs (Talk To You Later) are a chat ritual.

Cyber vocab

When you travel to a foreign country, you have to learn enough of the language to get around, and the same rule applies to the world of chat rooms. The language of chat can be a mystery to "vanillas" and "newbies," and basic knowledge of cyber chat vocabulary (see below) can help you decipher what everyone's talking about and saying to you.

AFK	Away From Keyboard
BAK	Back At Keyboard
A/S/C	Age/Sex Check
A/S/S/C	Age/Sex/State Check
BRB	Be Right Back
BFN	Bye For Now
NC	Nature Calls
TTFN	Ta Ta For Now
TTYL	Talk To You Later
<G>	Grin
<BG>	Big Grin
<EG>	Evil Grin
SS	Sexy Smile
VBS	Very Big Smile
<W>	Wink
CU	See You
CUL8R	See You Later
FAAK	Falling Asleep At Keyboard
LOL	Laugh Out Loud
LSHMSH	Laugh So Hard My Side Hurts
LMAO	Laugh My Ass Off

LTNS	Long Time No See
HTH	Hope This Helps
PIC	Online photo
ISO	In Search Of
SS	So Sorry
VS	Very Sorry
SOH	Sense Of Humor
OMFG	Oh My Fucking God
ROTF	Rolling On The Floor
SOS	SOS/Help
POV	Point Of View
PLS	Please
PPL	People
OIC	Oh, I See!
PC	Private Chat
B4	Before
IMHO	In My Humble Opinion
IDK	I Don't Know
JK	Just Kidding
WB	Write Back
WBS	Write Back Soon
WTG	Way To Go
ITA	I Totally Agree
IRL	In Real Life
RL	Real Life
VL	Virtual Life
Vanilla	An online virgin, or a person who doesn't play sex games or participate in explicit cybersex
Newbie	A person who is new to chat

Lurker	A person signed into a site or chat room who isn't chatting, but simply "lurking" about, as a voyeur or cyber wallflower
Scene	An acted-out B&D fantasy
Collared	A B&D submissive or "slave"
Cyberslut	A chatter who engages in the main room, as well as having multiple simultaneous private chats, or someone who is a serial cyber fucker in the cybersex world — a regular "cybersex player."

Emoticons Icons that represent emotions, facial expressions or body parts. Many chat rooms, email services and messenger programs have menus of colored picture icons to choose from now, but some of the old-fashioned and non-picture emoticons include:

:)	Happy
:(	Sad
;)	Wink
^.^	A Fox
:))	Big Smile
(.) (.)	Breasts
OoOoOo	Orgasm
^_^	Kitty "Meow"
:-O	Surprise
:-D	Laughing
:-P	Sticking Out Tongue
}:-(	Anger
:-#	Censored
:-i	Smoke/Smoker/Smoko
}:->	Devil
(\o/)	Angel

```
\_/\_/        Drinks
(_)? (_)?     Coffee/Tea
@->->->       A Flower
```

Stranger danger

Always engage in safe cybersex and chat to avoid getting tangled up in someone's "web." Chat rooms are fairly safe, and confidential, but the moment you give out your email address, or attach your address to theirs in a messenger program, you can get tangled in a cyber web that's hard to get out of.

The golden rules of safe cybersex are:

* Never give out your personal phone numbers or address.
* Do not give out both your first and last names, and the city you live in.
* Unless you have developed a relationship that you want to take further than the web, do not give out your real name, and even then, use caution and commonsense.
* Use an alter-ego username.
* Create a separate private email account for sexual play on the Net.
* Never use your work email.

Electronic boogaloo — "wanking with one hand," things to bear in mind

1. Most people are either primarily right- or left-handed wankers, but we type with both hands. For the most effective result, wank with your preferred hand, and type with the other.
2. The rhythm and motion of diddling rarely echoes the speed at which we type. Typing and diddling at the same time is a bit like rubbing your tummy and patting your head. It's best to type, then wank while you're waiting for and reading the

response from your lovee. Type, diddle, type, diddle. Keyboard, cock, keyboard, clit.

3. Women: a vibrator can be held against the clit without too much jiggling and will get you to the O while you type quite effectively, and with no one being the wiser.

4. A good tip so you don't come too fast: concentrate on your spelling. If your spelling is way off, people automatically suspect you are either drunk or diddling. And if you're in a sex chat room, diddling is the first suspect. Concentrating on spelling, and focusing on hitting the correct keys, slows the sexual response down and enables you to last longer.

5. Hygiene, Hygiene, Hygiene. Wipe your keyboard down with a soft cloth afterwards. Please, possums. Do this especially if you have lube on your fingers, particularly the natural variety, and if you're not playing on your personal PC.

Virtual Dating

Cybersex is not all dirty chat and web-cam peeping. The dating scene on the web is massive and is an entirely different avenue of sexual expression. There is just as much flirting on the web as there is fucking.

Cyber dating

People meet on the Net in a multitude of ways. There are chat rooms designed specifically for computer dating match-ups, chat rooms for explicit sex talk only, and there are other, non-sexual chat rooms where people with common interests end up flirting and getting together for a private chat.

Two people who connect in a chat room or private chat can take cyber dating to a more intimate level by going on virtual dates together. Using a program such as MSN Messenger, two people can chat while visiting other sites, simultaneously. Virtual daters can arrange to meet at a specific time, send an instant message, and then invite another to visit the same site together. You can go to a museum, visit a rock-band site, travel to sites from various countries, check out dancing sites and videos, download songs, view movie previews, learn to make exotic dishes on cooking sites, learn about historical figures, or visit raunchier sites. You can chat back and forth, sharing insights and banter, as if you were virtually there on a date.

"I met a guy over the Net, in a chat room, and he invited me on a virtual date. I'd never done it before, but I got the impression he had. I was a novice on the Net, and he really opened my eyes about how to surf the Net. We used Instant Messenger, and he would type in a site for me to visit and he would go to it too. We'd then chat as we clicked around, checking different things out. It was much easier to get to know him this way, rather than just chatting and asking questions, because, this way, we had something to talk about in the conversation. He taught me how to download songs and videos, and we would watch and listen, and share our opinions on them. In the end I thought we didn't have enough in common, so I stopped 'seeing' him, but I've since invited a few other people on virtual dates and it's a lot of fun." — Miriam, 33

Cyber dumping

One of the advantages of flirting on the web is the soft landing on rejection. There is no face-to-face rejection where you have to put on a brave front, and take it like a trooper. The flip side of this is it can also make people quite brutal when it comes to cyber dumping. The most common form of e-jection is the virtual disappearing act. The non-response to emails, or the inability to get an email through because they have closed their account, is the same as "he said he'd call and never did." Since you never met them anyway, all you can do is buck up and find someone else to fuck.

🗨 *"I sent this guy a 'Dear John' email. I thought that was decent enough. But when he didn't take the hint and kept emailing me, I stopped using that account and created a new one. He never found me again."*
— Sarah, 27

🗨 *"All I had to do was take her off my Instant Messenger list. She never knew when I was online after that, and she never knew my real email address, so I was in the clear. I'm sure she wondered why I never got back to her, but I was bored of the whole thing and couldn't be bothered explaining it to her. I barely give reasons to my girlfriends in real life about why I dump them. Why should I bother on the Net?"* — Dave, 41

🗨 *"I had the worst time getting rid of a guy. Things got ugly and I had to get mean. I didn't want to stop visiting the chat rooms and sites that we had both been in, so when he kept harassing me, even after I told him I wasn't interested in chatting anymore, I just had to keep ignoring him in chat rooms, and declining to go into a private chat with him. He was*

relentless for about a month, but then he
disappeared. Or he changed his username. God, I
hope I'm not still chatting with him without knowing
it. Shit, I never thought of that." — Celia, 19

Cyber mistakes

To avoid the cyber crash and burn, make sure you keep your head screwed on while you surf and flirt.

Keep your antennae sharp Do not be lured by a false sense of intimacy. Unless you know them in the real world, you have no idea if "Horny Henry" really is thirty-five and a man, or seventeen and a girl. You may be divulging your innermost secrets and desires to someone who isn't who they seem.

Have realistic expectations You are probably not going to find the soul mate of your dreams on the Net. Your Net sexventures are more than likely going to stay on the Net, and won't enter the real world. It's only a tiny minority of people that meet on the Net who go on to actually meet in real life, and an even smaller margin of those go on to have real sex, or even date.

Geography Chances are, your flirtations with people who live far away from you will not go any further than that. If you're on the Net looking for a relationship, stick to your own geographic area. It is highly unlikely that a Net romance is going to end up with one of you moving home and leaving your job. Yes, it does happen, but the chances are as slim as winning Lotto.

Give naivety the boot Be discerning. You don't always have to be nice to everyone you meet. The Net is just as freaky as the real world, if not more so. If you think you're chatting with someone who is a little too left of center for you, stop, and don't let it worry you. Don't be naïve. That guy who claims he has fifty piercings in his penis, and that girl with a fetish for fire, may not be the cyber partner for you.

Cyber stalking To avoid being stalked, beware of Stranger Danger! Be sure to adhere to the basic rules of safe cyber sex (see earlier section, "Stranger Danger"). If you do get trapped, though, sometimes the only way out is to clear your old email, and start a new account. It's a pain, but if you're really being cyber stalked, it's worth it.

Cyberchicks and Cyberdicks

If words aren't your bag and dirty chat doesn't do it for you, there are some ways to play at interactive techno-intercourse. Currently, technology is immature and true virtual sex isn't yet a reality. Virtual sex suits are being designed and will hit the market soon enough, but, like everything else technological, they will be initially expensive and only affordable for the elite. Techno-tactile loving will enable a person to don a virtual sex suit, with stimulators in erogenous zones. The person will then be able to view erotic images while engaging in simulated sex, so that they feel like they're having sex, as well as seeing it. People will be able to program their ideal partner and act out their virtual fantasies.

Even more advanced is the research into prototypes for virtual sex suits that can be controlled by another person, either in the same room, or via the Internet. In this sex suit, a person can be stimulated through the attachments on the suit, whether on the nipples, thighs, hands or genitals, but the power of tactile manipulation through the programming controls is held by a second person. This opens a brave new world for people into B&D. A submissive can put on a sex suit and invite a dominant partner to play with them and stimulate them wherever they please, without them knowing what stimulation is coming next.

Currently, cyberchicks and cyberdicks are on-screen, rather than in suits.

There are cyberchicks and cyberdicks who give the viewer the thrill of having complete power over them. You can double-click on items of their clothing to control their striptease, or choose how your cyber playmate will talk, dress and behave. These images are completely computer-generated, and the sexual thrill is not only in the sexual content, but in the power of programming them to do as you please.

"I'm not a computer nerd at all. I like my sport, I like going to the pub, I work as a laborer. But one of my fantasies is to have virtual-reality sex. I've heard the technology is coming, and that we'll be able to watch porn movies while feeling erotic sensations through probes and things. I don't want that. I like porn the way it is. What I want is to watch a cyber girl, someone like Lara Croft, while wearing virtual-sex gear that makes it seem like I'm having sex with her. I think it'd be fantastic to feel like I'm having sex with a woman who's a woman, but not human. And really actually feel like it's sex. Are they coming out with that technology soon?" — Frank, 33

XXX.Sex.Dot.Cum

Since the moment web cams were invented, people began flashing themselves over the web. There are thousands of strip sites, where viewers can pay to either "spy" on women and men in their bedrooms as they go about their normal routine, pay to watch a strip show at a particular time, or pay to view porn pics. Stripping and streaming web-cam shows are hugely popular, especially among male viewers. The sexual appeal of voyeurism on the Net is not only in seeing live nude girls, but also in the nature of peeping. Men masturbate and get off on watching women, in private, whether they are naked or not, being sexual or not. There are small sites run by individual women, and there are large, funded dormitories where girls live together and every room has a camera. Spying on these girls while they eat, shower, sleep and sometimes masturbate unlocks a web keyhole into the most erotic fantasies of some men.

There are also stripping and streaming sites for women who like to perve on men. They are not quite as common because the demand is higher for women to strip for men. Men are more visually oriented than women, so the market is greater for female strippers.

"I used to subscribe to a site where I could watch three girls in their bedrooms. I felt like a Peeping Tom. I liked it at first, but after a while it got repetitious. It was good when they chatted back, but they didn't reveal very much about themselves so it got boring. I stopped my membership after two months. It was only when I stopped that I realized how many hours I spent viewing that site. If I hadn't stopped, I might've become addicted

to it. I masturbated while I watched them, but after the
first few times, it got old. In terms of visual stimulation
nothing can beat a really hot porn movie. Not even
live girls on the Net." — Mark, 29

Cyber Cheating

The huge phenomenon of cybersex is not, by any stretch of the
imagination, popular among singles alone. Cybersex is not for the
desperate e-nerds who can't get laid in the real world. A large
proportion of cyber fuckers are married folks. Everyone seems to
have an individual opinion about whether e-dultery is a forgivable
offense. People seem to differentiate between actual cheating and
virtual cheating, although the majority of men and women
consider engaging in cybersex without the knowledge of their
partner as cheating. Relationship counselors are only beginning to
treat the damage cybersex can wreak on a marriage or committed
de facto relationship.

Even though most people think cybersex and flirty chat is
harmless fun, because it will never "actually" be realized, the lure
of the web can affect people in their real lives. As cybersex becomes
more appealing or people make sexual and virtual romantic
connections they may experience behavior changes, which can
affect a relationship. People can withdraw from their real
relationships, and reserve their sensuality for their computer
screens. They can find that their alter ego is more interesting and
fun than their own life and personality, and spend more free time
on the Net than with their partner. The excitement of getting it on
with several people at once can make a partner reluctant to break
away from the screen for sex at home with their spouse of ten years.
People can become demanding of their privacy, reclusive and silent.

While a great many people do not consider cybersex cheating in a true sexual, physical sense, they find the transfer of attention, and time, a betrayal. And it's a betrayal some cannot forgive.

Could you forgive your partner if he/she cheated on you in real life?

♠ *"If he was honest with me and admitted it, rather than me finding out on my own, I could consider forgiveness, but it would be difficult."* — woman, 26

♠ *"No way. Sexual infidelity would shatter my trust, and I don't think our marriage would survive something like that."* — woman, 31

♠ *"We have an open marriage, so we don't really have the concept of cheating in our relationship. We have honest communication and talk with each other about having sex with other people."* — man, 29

♠ *"I actually had an affair, and to repair the relationship, we went to counseling. Our relationship is stronger now and I don't think he or I would ever be unfaithful again."* — woman, 28

Could you forgive your partner if he/she cheated on you on the Internet?

♠ *"Not a chance. I've visited those chat rooms myself and I couldn't stand it if my wife was talking to another guy like that. Even if she never acted on it, expressing those*

desires and talking about sex like that is infidelity. I
don't think I could forgive her." — man, 40

🗣 *"I don't really consider it cheating. It's the same as*
him masturbating to porno mags, which he does,
and I don't have a problem with that either. If he
wants to get his rocks off while talking dirty to some
words appearing on a screen from god knows how
far away in the world, well, I'm not really threatened
by that. As long as he stays with me, loves me, and
doesn't stray into some other woman's real bed, I
don't care what he does in those virtual beds."
— woman, 34

🗣 *"This happened to me, and no, I did not forgive him.*
Actually, he wasn't even my partner! He was my cyber
affair, and when I found out he wasn't who he said he
was, I cut it off with him. It all started innocently
enough. We began flirting and sending erotic emails
to each other. They progressed from romantic to quite
hot. We talked about meeting in real life, we talked
about the kinds of sex we wanted to have together, what
we'd do to each other, that kind of thing. When he said
he loved me, and we hadn't even met, I started to get
scared off. That's when I started to think, I'm dealing
with an unbalanced person. Shortly after that, I got an
email from his fiancée! She had suspected he was up to
something on the Net, and broke into his email
account. Not only did I not know he had a fiancée in
real life, but she addressed the email to nine other

women! He was a serial cyberslut who cheated left, right and center. I had to hand it to his fiancée, telling us all about him, and how we had all been played. And she told us she was leaving him, and if we knew what was good for us, we'd leave him too. I certainly did, but I don't know about the other women. His fiancée used his email address, which was a shame, because I would've liked to have emailed her to tell her, "Go girl!" What a gutsy move. I heard from him once after that, desperately trying to get me to come back, but no way. That guy was unforgivable." — Sherry, 28

Cybersex Addiction

With the new phenomenon of cybersex comes the downside: addiction. Some people just can't get enough. The web has lured and trapped them, and they cannot break free from it. Studies into Internet addiction, and particularly cybersex addiction, are only in infantile stages, however the phenomenon of cybersex addiction does seem to be global, and growing.

The temptation of interacting with people, the lure of feeling desired and flirtatious, the appeal of expressing an alter ego, and the wish to escape from one's problems in the real world create an intoxicatingly addictive environment, and the Net quickly snares even the most casual user into spending hours and hours more than they should, or mean to, online.

The Net has been compared to the most powerful of drugs, because of its immediate gratification. It takes seconds to download images, and talking in a chat room is as quick as a flash. It becomes hard to pull away and, for those with a problem, the withdrawal is intense.

Counselors and health workers are only just beginning to comprehend the scope of problems associated with Internet chat and cybersex addiction. People who cannot pull themselves out of the trap of the web become more attached to the virtual world than the real world. Mothers who were supposed to make dinner for the kids at six o'clock can still be typing away at nine o'clock. Partners who were supposed to join their spouse in bed at eleven can still be up in front of the glare of the screen at two in the morning. Relationships can break down as communication in the real world pales in comparison to dot.com flirting. Even single people can find they would rather stay at home and chat to their new affair in Prague or Paraguay than head out with their friends. The seductive appeal of the Net can entrap nearly anyone who's not careful, and the two most common side effects of cybersex addiction are impairment of job performance and destruction of relationships, with both friends and lovers. A new investigation has found that cybersex increases a person's threshold for risk-taking. As the addiction to cybersex deepens, people who normally are clear-headed become greater risk-takers and become more willing to give out personal details and travel to meet strangers alone.

Warning! Warning!

The ten basic warning signs that suggest you may have crossed the line with your online sexual habits, as determined by Dr. Kimberly Young, executive director of the Center for On-Line Addiction, are:

1. Do you routinely spend significant amounts of time in chat rooms and private messaging with the sole purpose of finding cybersex?

2. Do you feel preoccupied with using the Internet to find online sexual partners?
3. Do you frequently use anonymous communication to engage in sexual fantasies not typically carried out in real life?
4. Do you anticipate your next online session with the expectation that you will find sexual arousal or gratification?
5. Do you find that you frequently move from cybersex to phone sex, or even real-life meetings?
6. Do you hide your online interactions from your loved ones?
7. Do you feel guilt or shame about your online activities?
8. Did you accidentally become aroused by cybersex at first, and now find that you actively seek it out when you log on?
9. Do you routinely masturbate while online?
10. Do you feel less investment with your real-life sexual partner, preferring cybersex as a primary form of sexual gratification?

If you answered "yes" to five or more of the ten warning questions, then you may have a problem. Make an appointment with a counselor, or start by visiting the On-Line Addiction site to learn more at www.netaddiction.com.

My Name is _____ and I'm a Cybersex Addict

Dr. Al Cooper of Stanford University in California conducted the largest and most detailed survey of online sex. He calls the sexual nature of the Net the "Dark Side of the Force" and labels cybersex the "crack cocaine of sexual compulsivity." His online study surveyed 9,265 men and women, who admitted to surfing the Net for sexual sites and chats. The study found that at least 1 percent were seriously addicted to online sex, with a psychological obsessive disorder, and needed counseling.

Electronic Lurve

The immediacy of email enables people to use it not only for work, finance, shopping and correspondence, but also to send quick affectionate messages of love. In any form of communication, people will take the opportunity to communicate their feelings, including their sexual feelings.

Cyber pillows

For couples separated by geography, or even couples wanting to send a flirty message during the day, emails can zap and sizzle across the Net at a furious pace. Couples send sexy invitations, hoping to rev each other up to get it on that night, hot words of dirty talk, and loving odes to each other. The more advanced also use web cams to enhance their cyber pillow talk as a way of feeling connected over the Net, and over the miles.

Flirty fuck me forwards

Forwarded emails constitute a large part of the in and out of email. People forward dirty jokes, dirty stories, tips on good porn web sites, dirty greeting cards and e-porn photos. Sexual forwards are estimated to circumnavigate the globe faster and more often than any other type of email. Most of them are not intended to titillate, but are a way of expressing the humorous side of sex. Most forwards are received and sent at work, and to workmates. Businesses have caught on to this and either filter email content, or issue severe warnings to employees who spend their work hours forwarding sexual emails. As fun as some of them are, emails with sexual content can be construed as sexual harassment. Always make sure the recipient will welcome a raunchy forward before you send it.

Kiss and cybertell

If video killed the radio star, then the Internet killed the knight in shining armor. While boys still brag about their conquests in locker rooms and women still spill every detail of previous sexual encounters in bedrooms, kitchens and bathrooms, email is fast becoming an avenue for people to describe and boast about their sexual trysts. While it's not generally etiquette to kiss and tell in any form, few people abide by this law of sexual etiquette anymore. The cyberbrag is flourishing. The kiss and cybertell is common, especially after a one-night stand. Mostly, though, the cybergloat occurs while traveling. Once upon a time, people sent postcards saying, "Having a great time, wish you were here," now travelers, and backpackers especially, seek out the nearest Internet café to send e-notes. A great many of these e-postcards and emails detail the hook-ups of their trip. Because of the confidentiality and ease of communication over the Net, people are saying more and sharing more about their traveling lives, domestic lives, and yes, also their sex lives. They don't call it *hot*mail for nothing.

I Wanna Be A Porn Star!

[the ins and outs of the adult sex industry]

Looking at nude pictures and making naked sexual art has been a human pastime for thousands of years. The ancient Greeks used to view pornographic pictures to cure impotence; ancient temples throughout Asia depict graphic images of sex in every shape and form; and the Romans adorned the walls of their baths and brothels with pornographic frescoes. One wall in a 2,000-year-old thermal bath in Pompeii, known now as the Pleasure Spa, holds not only a myriad of erotic pictures of sexual orgies and couplings, but also the only known artistic representation of cunnilingus in the Roman era. For as long as we've been doing it, we've been watching it and drawing it. And with modern technology, we now also film it.

Today's adult sex industry, from porn to prostitution, reflects our modern sexual tastes, and in many ways, they're not that different from those of our ancient forebears. The oldest profession in the world is still going strong. We not only still pay for sex, we also pay for titillation, teases and trysts. We pay to watch people strip, we pay to have sex with them, we pay to learn how to do it ourselves, we pay to watch others doing it, and we draw, paint and film it all, inside and out. Now, as in ancient times, we like to watch others doing it in groups, anally, orally and in imaginative settings. Why? Because it turns us on. Rules and regulations do, however, vary by country.

The Art of Making a Blue Movie

In Australia, porn film-making is basically non-existent. There are very few adult film industry production companies because there is only a small market to support it. This is mainly because the market and demand for Australian porn is small. Aussie porn films might make money if supported by an overseas market, but the kind of porn made in Australia has little appeal outside of down-under. The censorship regulations in Australia are strict, and the kinds of skin flicks that are allowed to be made here are classified as "soft porn." Overseas, the market for hard-core porn is huge, and Australia's soft porn cannot compete globally. This does not mean Aussies don't love their porn as much as everyone else. They do. The mail-ordering of sex videos is a huge business. Men, women and couples order pornos from every State in the country. The films, though, are mainly imported.

The first porn film industry operated in Buenos Aires, Argentina, from 1904–8, during which time films were sold all across Europe.

Hard-core vs. soft porn

In Australia, soft porn is rated R and can be either ordered via pay television or rented at local video shops. R-rated porn does not show any explicit penetration or oral sex.

VANILLA SEX: the kinds of non-explicit sex shown in R-rated soft-porn movies.

To obtain X-rated porn movies in Australia, you must either go to a sex shop, or order them by mail. X-rated videos can also be ordered over the Internet. As elsewhere, there are serious penalties for the importation of X-rated porn movies that are banned in Australia, so to avoid prosecution or confiscation by customs officials, you should only order videos that regulations allow.

Porn that is banned in Australia includes X-rated movies that feature minors or contain violence. Australia imposes severe punishments on anyone involved in child pornography (as it should do).

Historical Hard-Core Porn

Some of the most explicit erotic prints ever made in Europe were the "Sixteen Positions," engraved in Italy by Marcantonio Raimondi in 1524. Legend has it that the engravings were actually copies of drawings made by Giulio Romano, who drew them on a wall of the Vatican. Raimondi is said to have copied them before they were destroyed by papal censors. Only fragments of Raimondi's original prints still exist today, but the entire set of prints were preserved and repainted by artist Count de Waldeck in 1858. They are representative of one of Western society's earliest controversies over erotic images and censorship.

X-rated porn that is not allowed by law is primarily banned because of violent content. As an example, the types of porn content not allowed in Australian porn, or in any foreign porn within Australia, include any form of explicit or expressive violence — against women or men.

Forbidden acts include, but are not limited to:

Gang rape.

Rape.

Bondage.

Bestiality.

Fetishes or S&M.

Gagging.

Spanking.

Slapping.

Hot wax dribbling on skin.

Guns — in any way shape or form.

Aggressive dirty talk.

Any film imported for distribution in Australia will either have these scenes cut out, or be banned. It is not illegal to own a hard-core porn film, if it was obtained overseas and is private property (provided it is legal, as opposed to illegal child pornography), but the distribution or copying of hard-core porn with any violent content is not allowed. If you are into porn, know the laws in your state or region.

Non-violent erotica

The concern with pornography and violence is a political hot potato. The battle over classifications and censorship regulations is more heated than ever. Most people who watch porn are interested in the sexual content, not the violence. There are, however, those who think the banning of some films has gone too far. People who are into B&D play are not allowed to buy B&D porn films because they are deemed "too violent." The issue over which is more damaging, violence or sexual pornography, is hotly debated, especially as more and more mainstream movies become increasingly violent.

Most people agree, though, that good porn shows good, hot sex, and is not violent in nature. A few years ago, a movement started in Australia to change the porn classification from X to Non-Violent Erotica (NVE). It failed to gain approval. Regardless, NVE is still a good label for Aussies seeking to buy porn, yet wanting to

Moving pictures were first developed in 1895, and shortly after, the first erotic films were made. The original blue movies were filmed through a keyhole to give a spying and peeping perspective and to heighten the thrilling sense of erotic taboo.

Internationally, the pornography industry makes more profit than the music and film industries put together.

make sure the film they are buying is free of any violent content. Learn the rating system in your country before you buy.

GONZO PORN: the rough-around-the-edges style of porn with pure, raw sex, little (no) plot, and shot from the hip, usually using hand-held cameras. The Wham Bam Thank You Ma'am of porn film-making.

MONEY SHOT: also known as the "cum shot," this shot guarantees the film is porn, and that actual, authentic sex is being watched.

Amateurs vs. Professionals

There are two main branches of the porn film industry: the amateurs and the professionals. Amateur films are filmed by "real" couples, rather than paid actors. These couples certainly don't make porn for the money, as there is very little money to be made by acting in amateur porn. Couples interested in making a porn film enjoy sex, exhibitionism, and the thrill of knowing people will watch their fucking on film. All across the world, amateur porn films are very popular, both to make and to buy. Some sex shops have whole sections devoted to amateur sex flicks. Watching one of these films is the ultimate in peeking into someone else's bedroom antics. Very often they have poor cinematography, sets, props and lighting, and little plot; the sole purpose of an amateur blue movie is to watch another couple, or couples, get it on.

"I made a porn movie once. My boyfriend and I used to like to video ourselves when we fucked. It got to the point where we filmed ourselves nearly every time we had sex. And then we would watch them, and get hot together and go again. We never watched other porn, we just watched ourselves. Then one day my boyfriend brought home a porn and when we watched it, we thought the plot part was boring, and that our filming of ourselves was much sexier. So we started talking about the idea of doing a movie. At first we thought of auditioning as a couple for a movie producer, but then we found out how popular amateur porn was, and started talking about doing that. It wasn't until about six months later that we finally got around to doing it. It wasn't that much different than when we normally filmed ourselves, except that we got a friend to hold the camera, instead of using a tripod. We wanted him to get good angles and close-ups of us. If we were going to do it, we wanted to do it right. Having a third person there made me nervous at first, but it ended up making the film way hotter. My boyfriend and I talked dirty to him, and kind of made him part of it, off screen, and the result is that it seems like we're talking to the viewer, and getting it off with the viewer. We sent the video in to an ad we saw at the back of a men's

magazine, and got a small check back. But we didn't
do it for the money. I've kept my own copy of it, but
I've never seen it in a shop. I don't know if it was ever
released or not. But the thought that it might be in
some other state for sale, or in someone else's video
player, gives me a rush of excitement. That was three
years ago, and I've never regretted making the film. I
don't think I'll do it again. It was a one-off
experience. But my boyfriend and I still film each
other for private fun." — Tammy, 28

Professional porn movies are the glossy end of the blue-movie market. From low budget to high glam, there are thousands and thousands of films along the spectrum, for every taste or fancy. You name it, you can find it in porn. From westerns to redone Shakespeare (yes, as in *Midsummer Night's Cream*, for example), dormitory dramas to mysteries; starring white, black, Asian, young, old, gay, straight, bi, fat or skinny people; showing anal, oral, double-entry; geared for a male audience, for female viewers, or couples, the choice is huge.

Boogie Nights

While many people assume that it's men who mainly get off on watching porn, in fact, many women do too. In one study, male and female volunteers were provided with "excitement testers," designed to detect erection in men and vaginal lubrication in women, while they watched porn movies. They were asked to fill out a questionnaire afterwards about how turned on they felt during the film. While men responded that they were immensely turned on, a majority of women answered the questionnaire saying they did not feel excited. Yet the vaginal lubrication tests showed that the majority of women did experience vaginal lubrication during the film. Men get turned on physically and mentally by porn and are aware of it, while only some women are mentally turned on by porn, and others feel physically excited but aren't actually aware that they had become turned on by the images of sex on film.

The sex-research academic journal *The Archives of Sexual Behavior* also reported similar results in a study which found that women get just as turned on by porn as men. So before dismissing porn as a "guy thing" check out the porn flicks made for women and heat yourself up for your own rendition of boogie nights at home.

With the increasing popularity of DVDs, many porn films are now being transferred to DVD, and new films are being made directly onto DVD. There are several benefits to watching a porn DVD as opposed to a video. As with most movies on DVD, porn movies have "bonus tracks." In addition to the film, there are extended raunchy previews of other films, biographies on the stars and additional scenes.

And the winner is ... The awards for pornography products and stars in Australia usually take place at "Sexpo," which is the biggest national sex festival, held in cities around the country. Annabel Chong set the first "world gang-bang record" in 1995 by having sex with 251 men on camera.

Casting couch

If you want to be the next RollerGirl or Dirk Diggler, America is probably your best market. Porn films are occasionally made in

> *"The difference between pornography and erotica is lighting."*
> — Gloria Leonard

Australia, by both foreign and domestic producers, and, when they are, the casting call either occurs by word of mouth (no pun intended) or through a newspaper advertisement. No matter where you are, always be wary of who you audition for, and make sure they are legitimate.

Most legitimate porn film producers will pay for auditions. It's not stellar pay, but it shows professionalism.

"Show Me The Money" If you want to get into the porn industry, for one film or as a career, you sure don't go into it for the money. Few porn stars make very much money. It's the same as prostitution: only the minority at the top end of the scale ever make much money out of sex. And it's hard work. It's not as though you bonk like a bunny, get paid cash and walk away a few hours later. As with any filming, there are cuts, direction and several takes of the same thing, which all takes hours upon hours. Most porn actors get paid per scene — no matter how long that scene might take. And the pay depends on what you are asked to do in the scene. Anal sex and double-entry for women pays higher than straight penis-in-vagina sex or oral sex, for example. Pay in Australia for porn actors can vary between $200 and $1,000 per scene. Unless you are the star of a movie, you might only be in one or two scenes, so you'd have to make a lot of movies to make a living out of porn. Most porn actors do it literally for a "bit on the side"; a bit of money, a bit of sex. Only the big stars make a lot of money, and these days, the biggest money comes from web sites, not films.

Most porn producers look for several things during an audition, including:

* Comfort with nudity and sex.
* Comfort with being filmed.
* Men who look reasonably attractive (women must find them somewhat attractive to sell the film).
* Women who look sexy (although there's a viewing market for every kind of woman, and "sexy" comes in every shape).
* Ability to memorize script lines.
* Acting ability (preferably).
* Ability to fake orgasm — essential.
* Men who get and keep wood, in front of a crew, through cuts and various takes, and must be able to come on command (many men use prostaglandin injections to help stay hard) — essential.

If you do audition for a porn film and get offered the part, you will sign a contract that foregoes your rights to any royalty, profit from or rights to the film. Unless you are a big star, this is standard. In return, though, you have the right to ask for health checks from every partner you will be asked to fuck or suck. Some porn movie directors may insist on the use of condoms until the cum shot, but if not, it is standard practice to ask every actor to provide a current health certificate showing a negative HIV test and clear STI record. Everyone working on a porn movie, including crew, must be over eighteen. Women have more choices than men, and (almost always) are given final say over what they will and won't do in a scene, such as anal sex, or oral sex without a condom. The woman can also choose if she is willing to have the man come on her face, and if not, whether he will then come on her neck, ass, stomach or other body part. This, of course, is all up to negotiation between the director and female actor.

While some pockets of the porn scene are becoming increasingly responsible, there are some porn films that are made with total disregard for health or hygiene. Without editing, one can plainly see a man switching penetration between anal, oral and vaginal, without using a condom, let alone switching condoms, and without washing. This is dangerous sex, not only due to the potential spread of HIV and STIs, but also bacteria from the anal canal to the mouth and vagina. Generally, these films are often either low budget, or use women who are desperate for money or what they perceive as a ticket to freedom or a better life. While a great number of porn films now advocate condom use and safe sex, the market demands hard-core explicit sex acts, and what the market wants, the market gets.

"I tried out for a porn film once, and I was so excited. I'd always wanted to star in one. I wasn't going to be the star, but I was going to get to fuck the female star, and I was really hot for her. I kept getting semi-erections all day, waiting for my scene. Then when I got naked and they called me over, I couldn't do it. I wanted to do it, but the pressure got to me. I couldn't get hard. It was the most embarrassing moment of my life. When I got home, I had sex with my girlfriend no problem, so it must've been the camera thing, and having everyone watch. I just couldn't get it up, as much as I tried. I was so disappointed, I can't tell you. Now I have even more envy for the guys I see in the porn films. Not only do they get to fuck those hot

chicks, but they could do it, and I couldn't. I thought
my friends would make fun of me when they found
out, because I had told them about going out for it,
but they all said I'd gone further with it than they
probably could have. Small consolation, though. As
much as I'd like to, I'll never front up to another
porn audition. I couldn't handle another humiliation
like that. The director was pissed off, the actress was
irritated, and the cameraman was embarrassed for
me. I've never felt like such a fool. That's easily the
most embarrassing moment of my life. And it's not
one I share at parties, let me tell you." — Jeff, 25

"Porn star in training"

Being a porn star and acting like a porn star are two different fantasies. Most people who say, "I want to be a porn star," don't mean they literally want to star in porn films, but rather want to feel like a sex star, a person who is so good at sex, who enjoys it so much, that it feels like they "oughta be in pictures." Popular are T-shirts with "Porn Star in Training" printed on the front, which are being worn by women and men who are pushing the boundaries of taboo. People who buy these T-shirts are flirting with their own sexuality, and playing with their sexual power and confidence.

Modern technology has made it possible for nearly anyone, if they want to, to be a porn star in their own home. While filming oneself having sex was once considered edgy, it's now hardly risqué at all. People love their gadgets and toys, and like to play with them, especially sexually. Taking snapshots, digital video, and home movies of one's private sex-play is more popular than ever before.

"We went for a holiday in LA and found an ad in a magazine for a porn film workshop for porn star hopefuls. We rang and it was cheap and only one day, and my partner and I thought it'd be a laugh, so we went along. It was really cheesy, but it was also interesting. We were taught how to play to the camera, how to give a really hot, turned-on facial expression, and how to fake amazing orgasms. There wasn't too much more to it than that. I think if we really wanted to do a porn movie we would've felt ripped off, but since we did it for a laugh, it was just fun. When we got back, we decided to video ourselves having sex and we had a laugh all over again, giving our steamy looks and faked orgasms to the camera. I'll never show the video to anyone, but I have to say, we make a pretty convincing porn star duo." — Sally, 24

"My wife and I like to film ourselves having sex. We set the camera up on a tripod and go for it. We mainly do it because I like to watch my wife. And we really only film when she is on top, because I can't get enough of her, and I love watching her make love to me. I keep the tapes in a secret place, and whenever she's away, because she travels a lot, I masturbate to the tapes." — Ted, 37

RED LIGHT DISTRICT: refers to a geographic area zoned for prostitution. The

term is thought to come from ancient
Asian prostitution districts where women
used to cover their lanterns with
red cloth to indicate when they were
busy with a client.

BROTHEL: fuckery, birdcage, bordello,
Frenchery, juke, warren, red-lamp house,
boogie joint, fast house, love-you-long-time
hotel, grind joint, hump house, tomcat
house, nookie house, joy house, jump joint,
cake shop, massage parlour, swinging joint,
hook shop, whore shop, by-the-hour house,
flesh house, hotel-de-loose

BROTHEL CLIENT: client, John, trick,
trade, score

Brothels of Old

In ancient Chinese cultures, brothels were ranked according to class and hierarchy. There were separate brothels to cater for underclass men, a mid-ranked class of brothel for soldiers only, and high-class brothels for merchants, artists and high officials. These "high-class entertainment houses" offered not just sex, but also music, dancing, conversation and erotic entertainment. Girls who worked in the high-class brothels were often well educated and talented in dance, music and poetry, as well as erotica.

BROTHEL WORKER: sex worker, prostitute, hooker, Lady, girl, bird, servicer, B-girl, game girl, Charlie, tom

Brothel Bonking

Brothels are places people go to pay to have sex. The controversy surrounding the legalities and regulation of brothels is argued about in hundreds of countries around the world, yet the business of brothels is still going gangbusters in nearly every nation. Mainly, brothels cater to men. The sex workers hired by a particular brothel are almost exclusively women, and nearly all clients are men. In the minority, clients are couples and groups of men and women together.

In Australia, the legality of brothels varies from State to State, but in all States they must be licensed. There are strict regulations that determine who is allowed to run a brothel and where a brothel can be located. Brothels must also adhere to health guidelines. There is a fine (usually $5,000) for not using a condom, and all sex workers must ensure the use of a condom during sex. Each client is provided with fresh towels and a freshly made bed, and the sex worker conducts a health inspection of each client, then invites them to a shower, before any sex takes place. The prices for services, particular girls, particular acts, groups or individuals, and lengths of time, all vary.

"I believe that sex is one of the most beautiful, natural, wholesome things that money can buy."
— Steve Martin

🖤 *"I work in an office with mainly men. It's a stressful job, and we all* work long hours. Most of the men are married, but are hardly ever home. The bosses even have lounges and beds in their offices. Nearly all of the men I work with use sex as stress release. They joke about sex a lot, they flirt with everyone outrageously, and they go to brothels. They go in groups, as often as individually. Once they're there, they don't have sex in groups, but after a long day in the office, they'll say to each other, 'It's that time,' and they'll all get ready to go to one of their two favorite brothels. For them it's about sex release, with no strings, no emotion, no drama, nearly no effort on their part, so they get to unwind. I know all this because I got invited to join them one Friday night. I'm bisexual, and I love sex and was curious, so I went along. They paid for everything, and it must've cost a mint, but to them it was nothing. They do this every week, a few times a week. There were three of them, plus me, and we were there for five hours, and we each had at least three girls each, in private rooms that adjoined. We played in the spa, on the beds, drank champagne, it was powerful, hot and sexy. I could see why they love it. It was a classy place devoted entirely to pleasure. I know none of their wives know anything about this. The girls were sexy, and they weren't subservient or dominatrix types. They seemed like regular girls in for a good time. We all had fun. And I never saw any cash exchange hands, so it didn't seem tawdry or anything. In fact, I think the guys have a tab at the place, or a monthly bill or something. I haven't gone back since then, but I know they have." — Bridget, 26

🗣 *"My family don't know I'm a brothel girl. A few friends do, and I've made friends with some of the girls in here. I alternate between the night shift and day shift. I make more money during the night shift, because we have more clients, but sometimes I need a break, and so I work the day shift. I rarely go straight from client to client during the day shift, so I either watch TV, nap or read. On a really good night I might have ten clients. I usually have them for an hour each, but sometimes it's less. The management here is really good at protecting us, and making sure the client goes on time, if that's all he's paid for. We're not allowed to do drugs on shift, but some girls do. We can drink, if a client buys it for us, but I don't like to drink too much, because I like to stay in control and be with it for another client."* — Tammy, 22*

🗣 *"I've been with gorgeous guys, and some really, really ugly men. I use lube and condoms, so it's not like I have to be turned on to get the job done. It's always nicer to be turned on, but honestly, this is a job. Getting turned on by some cute guy is a rare thing, and only a bonus when it happens. I do have some regulars, and they're always nice to be with because it feels more honest, more of a connection. They tell me about their work and their families. They whinge about their wives and their problems with their kids. With my regulars, it's like I'm an outside counselor, who also does them."* — Christy, 25*

"In between clients, I clean myself up. Some girls use those baby wipe towels to clean themselves, but I don't like the smell. I just use water and a towel. I had a boyfriend, and he knew what I did for a living and he said it didn't bother him. But we broke up about four months ago because I never saw him, because I was always so busy. It wasn't working out anyway. I don't think you can have a good relationship when this is your job. But I don't plan to do this much longer. I'm saving for an overseas holiday, and then I'd like to do either hairdressing or beauty therapy."
— Ruby, 21

Erotic Escorts

Over the years some very famous madams have been scandalously busted for running escort and call-girl services. In the back of any male magazine, or in the Yellow Pages, even in community newspapers, there are scores of ads for escort services.

I'm just a gigolo

Male escorts can be hired for any range of services. Most male escorts are attractive and have good bodies, but the best male escorts have that, plus conversation skills, charm, sensitivity, the ability to listen and the ability to make a woman feel special. Male escorts are not as widely advertised as call girls, but they are popular with the ladies. Escorts can be hired for a date (high school reunions are not uncommon), sexual service, or even non-sexual service. A woman missing a man's company can hire a date to go out to dinner with. It sounds desperate, but the better male escorts are good at being an entertaining companion for the night.

More commonly, gigolos are hired to come over and get jiggy with a woman. He can be hired to deliver a sensual all-over massage, or that plus sex. He's literally at a woman's service, and when booking over the phone, a woman can request any kind of preference for looks, personality, age, body type and sexual act.

*"I was a male escort for two months once, during university. I went on three dates. One was non-sexual, just dinner and talking, and I ran her a bath and shampooed her hair. That's about all we did. She was in her fifties and wanted some company. She was actually really nice. The other two were sexual, and were with women in their forties I would guess, I'm not sure. Both times I went over to the house, had a couple of drinks, danced to some music, and then had sex with them.
I didn't spend the night either time. All my experiences were good. But the money wasn't quite good enough to keep doing it. And it wasn't as easy as I thought. I thought it would be more fun than it was, but when you're a hired sex gun, like I was, you're not there to get your own rocks off, you're there totally for the lady. I found that really one-sided. I'm used to either having a one-night stand, which is all about me, or having sex in a relationship where you're both caring and pleasuring each other. In the end I decided to quit because I wasn't cut out to be an escort." — Dan, 27*

Call girls

Female escorts, like male escorts, come in all types, from sole-trading prostitutes to high-class ladies hired for sexual and non-sexual favors. Men can phone to ask for specific types of ladies, in size, race, education, and for varying sexual and non-sexual activities. Many female escorts cater to businessmen who are traveling and desire companionship or sexual release while away from home. The prices of female escorts range from less than $100 an hour to thousands, depending on which city in the world you are in, and what kind of lady you're after.

Bump and grind: the hip and pelvic thrusting movements that symbolize the striptease were originally borrowed from Arabian belly dancing.

Striptease

Where did the idea for the strip and tease come from? It's such an ingrained part of our sexually titillating culture now that it seems almost silly to ask such an obvious question. In fact, the popularity of striptease originates partly from the Moulin Rouge ...

The French can-can and the American burlesque shows were the two original theatre genres to combine music and dance with erotic unveiling of a woman's body. Strip shows these days have little in common with the can-can and burlesque dancing, except for the stripping part. These days it is most popular in the form of one-on-one contact. Audience members can hire strippers for private shows and lap dances, although the stage show remains very popular too. Strippers widely acknowledge that the secret to a good strip is in the illusion of maintaining eye contact with audience members. Eye contact brings tips.

Anyone can learn the hip moves, eye contact, sultry looks and how to remove clothing sexily for a successful striptease. Keep an eye out in your local paper, or in bookstores that sell quality sexuality books, for workshops on "how to striptease for your man" which are offered throughout the year.

Pin-Ups

Pin-ups are the stars of "girlie magazines." The original pin-ups became popular before World War II, and were poster-size pictures of women who fitted the girl-next-door image. The pin-up girl was meant to look like a man's dream girl, but not one who was out of reach. Unlike pornographic magazine pictures, pin-ups do not show graphic detail of genitalia — no spread-'em shots. Pin-ups are sexy, teasing and titillating, and are usually partially dressed in sexy lingerie, or if they are naked, are posed in a way that reveals only partial nudity.

Pin-ups are still popular today, although the more pornographic centerfold has taken over the dominance of the calendar girl. Men's magazines such as *Playboy* and *Hustler* deliver a range of shots, from retro pin-up poses to as graphically illustrative of a woman's genitalia as is possible to capture on camera.

The new-millennium form of pin-ups and centerfolds are now expressed on the Internet. Women strippers and centerfold stars show themselves in graphic form via web cams, and Net pin-ups show just enough to tease, without actually showing the genitals. Men have been known to ogle their computer screens for hours, straining to see something that is barely, but not quite, being offered for viewing.

Queen of pin-ups

Bettie Page was, and is still, regarded as the queen of pin-ups. Throughout the 1950s, she was the most popular pin-up girl of her time, and continues to be enormously popular today. Bettie Page had long dark hair, a sparkling, warm smile, and was named "The Girl with the Perfect Figure." Bettie had both girl-next-door innocence and a dark, vampy sexuality. Her erotic contradictions won her legions of fans around the world. Her photographs, posters, postcards and centerfolds show her image in everything from a sexy maid's outfit to a beach bombshell and teasing dominatrix. Bettie Page was born in Nashville, Tennessee on April 22, 1923 to a poor family, and began her modeling career when she was discovered while on a walk in Coney Island, New York City, in 1950. She said that she was never embarrassed about posing nude. Even at her first shoot, she felt it came to her naturally. Her easy flirtation with the camera, and her paradoxical sexuality made her an instant celebrity. At the height of her modeling career, Bettie disappeared. Fans, calling themselves "Bettie Scouts," searched for any trace of her, fueling her popularity. Today, Bettie Page lives in privacy with her family, and only maintains intermittent contact with her fans through her official web site. Her image still sells hotly among adoring, devoted fans around the world. Bettie Page is the modern retro-icon of the pin-up girl.

Playboy mogul Hugh Hefner has said about Bettie Page, "She had a saucy innocence that is both contemporary and provocative, and also nostalgic."

Lick 'Ems and Stick 'Ems

[toys, potions, costumes
and other get-ups]

"Sometimes a cigar is just a cigar." — Sigmund Freud.

And sometimes it's not.

Sometimes going south of the border with a Cuban is more about sticking it than smoking it (as made notoriously famous, of course, by Bill and Monica). Sex toys, accessories and aphrodisiacs of every imaginable type have been spicing up sex lives for thousands of years, and the variety is only growing ...

Dildos

Dildos have existed since humans began to experiment with sex. Earliest records of dildos can be traced back to the ancient Babylonians. Most dildos then, as they are now, were in the shape of the penis, though there are some creative substitutes. While they used to be simple insertion objects, today's dildos have capitalized

The term dildo *is thought to derive from the* Italian word diletto, *meaning* delight.

In Siberia, women have masturbated using dildos made from the calf muscle of reindeer.

on modern technology and many of them have battery-operated thrusting bits and parts that wiggle, turn, twist and vibrate.

Dildos are designed to be inserted in the vagina or anus. Many women, however, orgasm through their clit, so like to use a dildo as a go-between, switching stimulation back and forth from honeypot to love button. Both men and women like anal dildos, and they come in sizes varying from pencil-thin to thick and long. Anal dildos come in smooth shapes, as well as devices with small and large balls attached, for the varying stimulation of thick and thin. All anal dildos should have a T-shaped bottom fitting, to prevent them getting sucked up the arse. This does happen, as more than a few emergency-room doctors can attest to.

Letter to the *British Medical Journal*, 30 June 1974

Within the space of a fortnight two patients were admitted through the accident and emergency department "with a painful vibrating umbilicus." Both the patients were ... accustomed to using battery-operated stimulators or vibrators. What had happened was that the vibrators had been lost into the rectum through the anus, apparently at the moment of orgasm. Apart from the vibrating umbilicus, a cylindrical mass could be felt arising from the pelvis and a gentle hum could be heard. The vibrator was removed from one patient easily enough but the other required general anaesthetic.

Source: *The Illustrated Book of Sexual Records*

Dildo Dominance

In the West in the seventeenth century, dildos were manufactured mainly in Italy; in the eighteenth century, the French designs became popular. In the first half of the twentieth century, the best dildos were considered to be those made in Japan — a reputation that still endures in some minds. The dildo has been a popular sex accessory for centuries in the East, but the private use of dildos among couples for sex play did not become popular in the West until after World War II, when American servicemen brought them back from Japan. It didn't take long for their popularity as a lovemaking accessory to spread throughout the rest of the West.

Humdingers

Humdinger: slang for vibrator. The best humdingers are quiet, and hum, rather than buzz loudly. *Hum* is also a euphemism for *cum,* and hints at the word *vibration; dinger* is a play on the word *donger,* which is slang for penis. In a non-sexual context, humdinger refers to the largeness of something. In a sexual context, a humdinger usually refers to a large and powerful super-vibrator, capable of delivering intense orgasms.

The vibrator was invented in 1869, when an American doctor patented the steam-powered massager. It was used in medical practices to treat "female disorders." By 1890, Britain had come up with a portable battery-operated model, and from 1900 there were dozens of styles to choose from, for "medical use." It was

Common modern dildo shapes include: penises, hands, dolphins, dolls and saints. Favorite dildo colors include: peach flesh, brown flesh, black, purple, cream, red and blue.

in Britain and the US in the late nineteenth century, that the advertising of vibrators for "general use" became popular. The ads promised the housewives "relaxation and relief."

It would be a semi-educated guess, but probably 99 percent of the vibrators in the world are bought and used by women. Vibrators are also made for and used by men, but in general, the humdinger is for the horny honey. Vibrators are used in masturbation; in sex therapy, for people who have difficulty reaching orgasm; and during intercourse. A vast majority of women use vibrators during masturbation because they deliver powerful orgasms and a different type of orgasm from those achieved through manual stimulation.

There are four major complaints from women about using vibrators. The noise of some vibrators is hard to disguise, or can

Dildos Through the Ages

Ancient Greek dildos were long and made of leather, and the best were known to come from the town of Miletus. Women used to lubricate their leather dildos with olive oil before inserting them into their vaginas. In the play *Lysistrata*, by Aristophanes, first performed in 413 BC, women characters complained about a lack of "leather comforts" since war had both taken their husbands and stopped trade with Miletus.

The first recommended use of the dildo as a sex aid in China occurred during the reign of Empress Wu Tse-T'ien (1685–1704). Buddhist monks made them and recommended them for satisfying carnal desire. The Empress was presented with her first dildo by her Imperial physician. It came with an attachment so that she could tie it to her ankle. By bending her leg and circling her foot, she could put it inside her, and move it in and out. These dildos were called "live limbs."

Source: *The Illustrated Book of Sexual Records*

interfere in the mood if using them while making love. Some of the more expensive vibrators are quieter, which makes them more popular and worth the expense. The second complaint is that some vibrators are just too damn powerful. The vibration on some of the toys is so strong that it is painful. Third, vibrators can dry the skin. The heavy friction between the vibrating head and a woman's very thin and sensitive tissues around the vulva can dry her out, sometimes in a matter of a few seconds. A buzzing plastic material on a dry button or lips is not pleasant, and can even, in worst-case scenarios, do a little damage. The final and major complaint of women about the humdinger is that it can seem like a too-mechanical way to enjoy the pleasures of human ecstasy. This is especially true for women who like to use a vibrator during intercourse or foreplay. The process of getting hot together with the distant or not-so-distant sound of humming in your ears takes some getting used to.

There are, on the other hand, two major aspects of the vibrator that women applaud. The first is that vibrators are a near-foolproof orgasm guarantee; and the second is that the orgasms experienced from a vibrator are utterly intense. One session with a vibrator can leave a woman exhausted in rapturous contentment.

Vibrators come in every color of the rainbow, and nearly every shape you can imagine. From animals to human organs, rods to orbs, huge turbo missiles to tiny pocket rockets, there are vibrators to fit every female and every fantasy. Male vibrators are often sheaths that fit over the penis or small, rounded vibrating plastic heads which you move over the shaft and glans. Some vibrators are cheap, and some are more expensive than a top-quality Swedish kitchen appliance. Vibrators can be bought in sex shops or, if you prefer, ordered via catalogues or the Internet.

🎤 *"My partner and I use my purple pearl vibrator during sex. In fact, it's the same one we saw on an episode of 'Sex and the City.' So we call it 'Mr. Big' as a joke. But I call my partner 'Mr. Better' so he doesn't think a vibrator is better than him. We use Mr. Big because we like to come together, and we can time it with a vibrator, because it's so easy for me to come with it."* — Wendy, 29

🎤 *"I got a vibrator for my birthday. I was so embarrassed. The card said 'Open in private' but I didn't because I thought it couldn't possibly be anything really, really embarrassing. All my friends knew I had never tried one, and that I'm a bit shy about that sort of thing. I was mortified when I opened it, and tried to hide it, but of course my friends all laughed and wanted to see it. What they don't know is I actually did go home and try it. And I love it! It's my new favorite toy, and I don't go a week without using it. Now that I'm a convert, I think it's a must-have for all women.'* — Lucy, 21

Happy Ring

Also known as the "goat's eyelid," the happy ring was first introduced during the reign of the Mongol emperors in the thirteenth century. After a goat was killed, its eyelids and eyelashes were removed together. They were dried with quick-lime, then steamed in a bamboo basket for at least twelve hours. After several repetitions of this procedure, the eyelids were firm enough to tie around the base of the penis. The attached eyelashes were "ticklers" to stimulate the woman. Modern versions of the happy ring, complete with ticklers, are available, but today they are made of plastic.

Boys' Toys

Cock rings

Cock rings are bands placed around the penis to prolong erection and increase sensation by maintaining the blood flow in the shaft and head of the penis. Cock rings are no modern invention. In ancient China, it was common for men to wear a silver clasp around the base of their penis, and a similar pleasure ring was also popular in ancient Japan. Cock rings today are mainly made out of plastic or leather. Better cock rings are flexible or have a snap-release. If a cock ring is left on too long, damage can occur to the penile tissues and capillaries, or priapism (prolonged, painful erection that won't subside) may result, and treatment involves a trip to the hospital. Always make sure that you can get it off before you put it on.

Penis packing

Modifying the penis to provide better pleasure for women has been an obsession of men through the ages, and across the world. Among the Batak people in Sumatra, Indonesia, men would slit open the head of their penises to insert lumps of stone. It was thought a bumpy head would deliver a smooth ride to the O for their women.

Among Islander and Asian peoples, it was common for men to insert a pearl under the foreskin of their penis or, for a more permanent option, have it sewn into the skin of the glans. This practice is still popular among men today, in the East and the West. The pearl is still the accessory of choice, however, plastic and metal balls, specially made for insertion in this way, are also sometimes used.

"My friend lives in Broome, and her husband had a pearl put into his penis for a while. He took it out after it started to really grow permanently under the skin, because he was afraid of infection. He really only wanted it temporarily. My girlfriend said that even though she didn't notice that much of a difference with it physically during sex, she found the idea of it really erotic. And he loved the feeling it gave him. I don't really want to know much more than that; it's their marriage and that's about as much information as I want. The way she spoke about it was interesting, but never made me think I should go convince my husband to get one. He wouldn't agree to it in a fit, anyway."
— Caroline, 37

Aphrodisiacs Through the Ages

This anonymous sixteenth-century poem from England illustrates some of the foods thought to be aphrodisiacs. We still believe in some of their powers, 500 years later ...

"Good sir if you lack the strengthe
   in your back
And would have a Remediado
Take Eryngo [sea holly] rootes and
   Marybone [marrow bone] tartes
Redde Wine and riche Potato.

An Oyster pie and Lobsters thighe
Hard eggs well drest in Marow
This will ease your backes disease
And make you good
   Cocksparrowe.
An Apricock or an Artichock
Anchovies oyle and Pepper
These to use do not refuse
Twill make your backe the better."

Source: *Sex Watching: Looking into the World of Sexual Behaviour*

Aphrodisiacs

The word *aphrodisiac* is thought to come from the ancient festival of Aphrodisia, the goddess of love, and the Greek word *aphrodisiakos,* relating to sexual intercourse. Some of the earliest love potions and sexual enhancement herbs were traditionally sold and used at this festival.

Crocodile Dundick: In ancient Egypt, the most potent aphrodisiac was powdered crocodile penis.

Natural substances thought to awaken and prolong our sexual response have enticed lovers into erotic taste tests through the ages. Some aphrodisiacs have real merit, and have indeed been shown to spark some sexual arousal, or to at least affect the genitals, physically. Most aphrodisiacs, though, are sexual enhancers purely through the sensual power of suggestion.

Phallic phoods

A great many aphrodisiacs are thought to be erotic because of their phallic shape. Bananas most obviously spring to mind, but there are many more to choose from that can add that extra zing to your rooting recipes.

* Oysters: resemble the vulva, and eating them can be suggestive of eating a woman. They are also reported to give men sexual stamina.

Better Than Fish and Chips

The combination of fish and onions as an aphrodisiac began with the Romans who thought both items were aphrodisiacs. They believed eating them together doubled the chances for a long evening of love. Next time you go to order fish and chips, opt for the fried onions rather than the chips!

Nutty Nookie

Well known by several ancient cultures, pine nuts can be eaten alone, or added to dishes to heighten sexual desire and function. Centuries ago, Arabs used to eat 100 pine nuts before a night of passion. And the ancient Greeks used to mix them with almonds and honey into a paste to increase sexual desire. For a modern twist, try adding pine nuts to a Saturday night meal for you and your lover.

Aboriginal Original

Aged emu eggshell powder has long been valued by Australian Aborigines as a substance for increased sexual rejuvenation and general wellbeing. It has no known adverse side effects and can be used by both men and women.

* Tomatoes: red, juicy, luscious. Early Europeans thought they must be the forbidden fruit, and dubbed them "love apples."
* Lamprey: a phallic-shaped fish, thought to awaken the passion of men.
* Cucumber: not only a phallic symbol from the vegie garden to arouse even the limpest of salads, but was/is also recommended for women as a dildo.
* Ginseng root: phallic in shape, thought to possess a number of aphrodisiac properties.
* Powdered stag horn and rhino horn: while there are ethical debates about their use, powdered rhino horn is still used as an aphrodisiac in some parts of Asia and Africa.
* Mandrake root: resembles both the vagina and penis, and was thought to cure sterility. Modern research indicates it is more effective as an anesthetic.
* Asparagus spears: in theory, good for arousal, but in practice, bad for the odor and taste of semen and vaginal lubrication.
* Cooked okra: thought to be an aphrodisiac and was originally heralded as an erotic substance that resembles vaginal lubrication.
* Eggs and caviar: considered to be aphrodisiacs for both men and women. Their heritage as an aphrodisiac lies in the symbolism of the egg and creation of new life. They were often eaten to cure sterility or prevent barrenness.

Liver-loving diet: in several places, such as the Mediterranean region, the liver was thought to be the seat of all passions, including love. It was believed that the most potent of all aphrodisiacs was the liver of a young person who died in love.

* Anchovies: once opened, they are thought to resemble a vulva, and are regarded as a powerful aphrodisiac
* Cherries and pears: considered aphrodisiac fruits because they contain vitamins A and B, which aid in the production of our sex hormones. Cherries are especially good because they contain zinc, which aids sperm production.

The role of fruit in firing passions and increasing arousal lies in the sexually suggestive shapes, textures and colors they possess, as well as in their sweet taste. The sugar in fruit not only gives energy for lovemaking, but was also thought to create a rush of sweetness to the genitals.

Strawberries are romantic and suggestive, and are also said to increase arousal. Apricots are thought to increase lust while grapes, and the feeding of them to another, have been considered an erotic and powerful aphrodisiac for thousands of years.

Nature's Euphoria

Yohimbine is used as a natural sex aid for men dealing with erectile difficulty (see the Little Boy Blue Lost His Wood chapter). However there are informal reports that taking yohimbine enhances sex drive, and is growing in popularity as a sex drug. Dosages vary, and if you experience profuse sweating or nausea, decrease the dose. First take it on a full stomach to avoid negative side effects. It's always better to consult your naturopath before popping any natural pill, as it might interfere or mix badly with other medications, or other drugs. Do not take it too often as your body can get used to it. Informal studies show yohimbine is more effective than Viagra at helping to produce erections after Saturday night clubbing drug use, but once "The Line" is crossed, there is very little possibility of wood salvation until the next morning.

In some cases, the myth of fruit as aphrodisiacs has been proven to be true by scientific evidence that they are positive, organic sexual enhancers. One study showed oranges increase penile blood flow by 20 percent.

Hot spices for the bedroom

We use the phrase "spice up your sex life" because we've been doing literally that for thousands of years. Spices have been relied on in varying combinations for warming the passions. The five most popular spices for increasing passion and lust are:

1. Powdered licorice root.

2. Nutmeg.

3. Cinnamon.

4. Powdered garlic.

5. Pepper.

Not all aphrodisiacs are designed to work through ingestion. While we mainly think of love potions as concoctions to be eaten or drunk, the natives of the Guianas used to insert the seeds of the mucca-mucca plant directly into the penis to increase sensation by arousing and irritating the urethral tract.

Sow your wild oats: this phrase comes from the fact that wild oats used to be fed to wild horses, and when men noticed that the oats turned the male horses into randy stallions, they began eating oats themselves for their aphrodisiac properties.

Helpful Herbs

Practitioners of natural therapies have been prescribing herbs to aid the sexual drive and response for centuries, and continue to do so today. If you take herbs to boost your waning sex drive, be sure to do

Low fat, high sex: a diet low in fat is your best aphrodisiac, according to health researchers. The lower your body fat, the higher your testosterone levels and sex drive.

so under the guidance of a qualified natural therapist, and always inform them if you are: (a) taking any other medications of any kind; or (b) pregnant or may become pregnant.

Some sexual healing herbs for women Damiana, epimedium (sometimes known as yin–yang), fenugreek (never use if pregnant), fo-ti root (knotweed), alfalfa, anise, saw palmetto, North American black cohosh (powdered), parsley, chasteberry (good for menopausal women and sex drive), Dong Quai, South American quebracho bark, ginger root, licorice, soy, wild yam root (commonly available in cream form; pregnant women should never use it), and fennel.

Some sexual healing herbs for men Ginkgo biloba, ginseng, epimedium (sometimes known as yin–yang), fenugreek (good for erectile difficulty), fo-ti root (knotweed), ashwaganda (from India), South American quebracho bark, barley, celery (especially juiced), ginger root, parsley, peppermint, sarsaparilla (Chinese root), saw palmetto, guarana, wolfberry, yohimbine.

Ginkgo

Used by Chinese herbalists for over 5,000 years, the leaves and nuts of the ginkgo biloba plant contain ginkgolides, which increase general sexual energy and can also improve erectile problems in men. In one American study, 50 percent of the men using ginkgo reported regaining their erections. In another study of men with erectile difficulty due to penile arterial clogging,

78 percent reported sexual function improvement after taking ginkgo over an eighteen-month period.

Ginkgo is one of the best herbs for male sexual function. The only side effect to be aware of is that ginkgo can act as a blood thinner, so should be used with caution by men who are already on an orthodox blood-thinning medication.

Ginseng

Sometimes referred to as the "man's plant," ginseng has properties that make it a stellar sexual healing herb for men. It is the root of the ginseng that is used, and the older the root, the more potent its properties. The oldest roots have been known to sell for tens of thousands of dollars each. There has been a great deal of research into ginseng, but we still don't know much about how it works. It is thought that once ingested, it acts on the body's endocrine system, which in turn affects the sex hormones. Ginseng is taken by men both to increase sex drive and assist with erection. While it is reputed to be a herb mainly for men, there have been reports of women who find it increases their sex drive, too.

Dong Quai

Marketed as "women's ginseng," Dong Quai must be taken correctly to experience its benefits. Dong Quai contains both phyto-oestrogens, chemicals that relax muscles and dilate blood vessels (which is good for blood flow to the genitals during sexual response), and also a substance called safrole. Always avoid purified forms of Dong Quai because safrole in its pure form has been linked to cancer. In an extracted form as a capsule or powder, though, Dong Quai is an effective herb for the stimulation of sexual drive in women. It can alleviate the symptoms of menopause and also increase vaginal lubrication.

The famous aphrodisiac "Spanish Fly," technically known as Lytta vesicatoria, is made from the dried and crushed cantharidine beetle. Cantharidine is a poisonous and potentially lethal substance.

Horny goat weed

Mixed anecdotal reports range from "Fantastic! I've never felt so horny," to "It didn't do a thing — it must only work on goats." If your horny factor has been a little low, give it a try, but be advised, it doesn't help everyone!

Tribulus terrestris

Reports indicate that this herb, also known as puncture vine, cat head, caltrop or gokharu, boosts libido in much the same way as testosterone replacement therapy. It has been shown to increase sex drive successfully in both men and women. The root and fruit of the plant are dried and used in powder and capsule form. Visit your local health food store or naturopath for dosage information.

Note: It also works as a diuretic, so be warned! And if you suffer from chronic urinary tract infections, check with your naturopath before taking this supplement.

Vita-loving

Vitamins A, E and B are reputed to be aphrodisiacs, however any vitamin that makes you feel healthier will positively affect your sex drive. Singly, no vitamin will maintain your sexual health, but boosting up on A, E and B, within reason, certainly couldn't hurt.

There's anecdotal evidence to support the claim that the vitamin supplement L-Arginine boosts sex drive in both men and women.

Romance me with chocolate

Chocolate is a famous aphrodisiac, not only because of its traditional association with dating, but because it is rich in phenylethylamine (PEA). PEA is a chemical that mimics the inner biological feelings of lust and post-sex afterglow.

In its alcoholic form, PEA has the fragrance of rosewater. It could be that the tradition of men appearing with roses and chocolates prior to a date had some original biochemical foundation.

When asked what she wore to bed, Marilyn Monroe famously replied, "At night, I don't wear anything, except a few drops of Chanel No 5."

Perfumes

Perfume and cologne are strongly marketed as come-hither sexy scents. We like to smell nice for ourselves, and for others. Scents we add to our skin are meant to mimic the chemistry of natural scents; they are designed to make us appealing and attractive to others. Perfume has long played a central part in the art of seduction. How someone smells is often one of the first things we notice, and can ignite the seduction game. Pleasant, sensual smells lure us closer to another and engage our body language, flirtations, fantasies, and desires. People like to wear fragrances that smell like flowers (the attraction of nature), as well as animals (the attraction of sex). Scents that were considered to be the original animal sexuality fragrances included musk, ambergris and civet, which came from deer, whales and the civet cat. These scents gained popularity in the eighteenth century. Most perfumes manufactured around the world today are varying mixes of both floral and animal scents.

The first modern eau de toilette was made in 1370, and was called Eau d'Hongrie. It came with a guarantee of successful seduction and was made especially for Elisabeth of Hungary. When she was 72, she put some on and, legend has it, the King of Poland fell instantly in love with her.

The basic role of perfume is to awaken and excite the erogenous mind. It's been working for centuries and still works well today; it's a global billion-dollar industry. When applying perfume and cologne to your skin, in the hope (or guarantee) of scoring sensual sweetness with your lover, there are a few things to keep in mind. Perfume should not be rubbed on, but applied and allowed to settle on the skin itself. The better perfumes and colognes are potent, so it's not necessary to marinate yourself in them: a little goes a long way. Cheaper perfumes should be put on sparingly, or the alcohol content can smell stronger than the scent. The scent of some perfumes can be quite strong and can last on the skin for a long period of time, so think before you apply. If you put perfume on your neck, will your lover get a mouthful of perfume-laced skin later? Many lovers like only to smell your sexy perfume scent, not taste it.

❧ *"On special occasions, when we are celebrating and dressing up, and I know the evening will end in sex, I take a lot of time to get ready. I shave and pluck everything in sight. I go at my skin with a loofah and moisturize every inch. And I shampoo and condition my pubic hair so it feels soft and smells nice. I put perfume in those odd*

Perfume Box

Natural body odor has been regarded as the most potent of sexual scents throughout human history. Even though the French produce much of the world's most famous perfumes, they also find the body's natural scent sexual, and call it *la cassolette*, slang for perfume box.

places where he can smell it, but probably won't kiss. Places like my ankles, feet, hair, back and hips. If I do put perfume on the backs of my knees or neck, I mention it. He's never complained about tasting my perfume, but one time he kissed me back and the taste even in my mouth was so strong, from then on I thought I'd better be more considerate about how much I put on and where." — Lily, 28

Love Potion Number Nine

Bees do it. So do wasps, moths and mammals. It is well known that many animals use special odors, known as pheromones, as a sexual signalling mechanism to let males know when females are ready to mate. Whether humans give off a come-hither aroma has been a subject of great debate.

There are actually two different types of pheromones:

Signalling pheromones have an immediate, sexually enticing effect. Equivalent to the mythic Love Potion Number Nine, there is no evidence (yet) that humans give off this type of pheromone.

Releaser pheromones have a much slower effect and only work after prolonged exposure. This second type has been shown to exist in humans.

Both Napoleon and his wife, Josephine, found musk perfumes erotic, but most of all, Napoleon loved Josephine's natural smell. He once wrote to her, "I'll be arriving in Paris tomorrow. Don't bathe."

Scientists have discovered that there is a chemical pheromone in men that exudes from the apocrine glands in the armpits and genital area. A study has shown that women either smell or absorb this pheromone in men's natural body odor during intimate sexual contact, and that it makes women sexually healthy. The study showed that women who have sex with a man at least once a week have normal-length menstrual cycles, milder menopause and are more fertile, as compared to women who are celibate or having irregular sex.

Women possess pheromones too. In fact, unlike the "male essence," which requires direct contact to have an impact, the "female essence" can disperse across a room. At present, research indicates that this aromatic female pheromone works more on other women, than men. Studies involving experimental trials show women can be highly sensitive to pheromones. The classic example is menstrual synchronization. Studies of women who live together show that after time, their menstrual cycles will shift until they are within a few days of each other. The prime suspect for this occurrence is the female pheromone.

Scientists and perfume companies are still working on harnessing the male and female pheromone essences. Love Potion Number Nine may very well become a reality one of these days.

Dressing Up, or Down

Lingerie

Lingerie comes in both top-end and bottom-end ranges. You can spend a fortune on something jewel-encrusted, or very little on some cheap material laced with bright feathers and lace. Whether your desire is trashy sex-worker chic, or ooh la la French fashion, there are styles for every man and every woman. Dressing vaginas in pajamas to inflame the desire of a lover is one of the most common sexual seduction practices engaged in by women. Just prior to Valentine's Day, sales for lingerie soar through the roof. Both men and women buy lingerie, and many lingerie shop attendants are trained to help male customers through the maze of styles, shapes and sizes.

Fancy dress

If role-playing is your fancy, there are get-ups for every fantasy. The most popular costumes for sex play are uniforms, for both men and women, but sexual dress certainly doesn't end there. There are fairy outfits for women and sexy genie get-ups for men who want to grant their partner their every wish, and wicked-witch fashions for those who want to deny them. Leather and B&D outfits are also very popular, as are superheroes and masquerade-ball designs.

There are also numerous styles of novelty lingerie, from jungle G-strings with banana cock pouches for men, to G-strings for

*According to Ayurvedic medicine, the sexual center of a woman is her lower stomach. Rubbing essential oils of sandalwood, jasmine and neroli on the lower belly is thought to awaken passion. (**Caution**: check with a naturopath before using essential oils when pregnant.)*

women with cunnilingus instructions written on the front brief followed by "enter here" and a graphic of a downward arrow. These are available in sex shops and novelty shops, and can make for good gag-gifts on nights you want to prime your lover into having fun in the sack.

🗣 *"The funniest story I ever heard was about a couple who tried a role-play for the first time. They rented Batman and Batgirl outfits from a costume shop, and he tied her to the bed. He apparently climbed up onto the dresser to 'fly' at her on the bed, but slipped and hit his head on the edge of the bed, blacking out. It was only when the neighbors heard the woman screaming, that they were discovered, in a very compromising position. I'm sure they and the neighbors never saw each other in quite the same way again!"* — Jane, 34

Love Spells

Men and women have been using love spells for seduction for centuries. Love magic tends to involve the acquiring of some personal object or body part, such as a hair or ribbon, and imbuing it with one's desire. For example, a Scottish love spell required the lovee to draw a circle of his or her own blood on a wafer, eat half of it, then somehow feed the other half to their desired lover. The joint taking of the food and blood was thought to make the desired fall in love with the hopeful one.

Motion Lotion

Lube, maybe more than any other accessory, is a crucial bonking ingredient. Not every woman gets wet enough on her own to make sex comfortable, and even women who do have times during the month when they are drier. The amount of natural vaginal lubricant a woman produces sometimes is not a reflection of how turned on she is, but of her body type. Dry, chafing sex is bad sex, and keeping a pack of lube handy prevents any discomfort. Lube is also a critical ingredient for anal sex. Water-based lube is the best choice because oil-based lubricants destroy latex and make condoms unsafe. Specialty sex shops sell lube in varying flavors, which can scent your sex as you rub against each

Number one color of lingerie women prefer to wear: black. Number one color men prefer to see women wear: red.

other. If the wet, sliding friction of cock in vag or dick in arse really heats you up, lube should be the first accessory to reach for. After playing slip'n'slide with each other's bits, the only debate afterwards is who should sleep in the wet spot.

Monkeying Around

The bonobos, also called pygmy chimpanzees, are remarkably close to humans in their genetic make-up. The genitals of female bonobos are rotated forwards, as they are in human females, which facilitates face-to-face sex, rather than the traditional animal rear-entry style. The Bonobos have sex every day, and often. They do it facing each other, and demonstrate feelings of love. They often have sex while looking deeply into each other's eyes and spend long periods French kissing. Bonobos not only have a lot of sex, they do it in all different kinds of ways. They are notorious sexual experimenters, and often tease and play games during seduction, foreplay and intercourse.

Humans also like to play when having sex. Do not underestimate the power of laughter to light your sexual flame and teases and tickles to turn you on.

To fire up foreplay, couples can engage in a variety of games. Strip poker is a favorite, but there are many others to choose from.

Share and share alike

Remember the rule you learned as a child, and share your toys. Whether playing with traditional sex toys, or blazing your own trail with creative toys like feathers, fruit, chocolate sauce, ice cubes, honey and blindfolds, give each other a fair turn (unless, of course, you're playing a B&D game).

Getting wet

Taking a cold shower is legendary for the "abort launch" of the sexual mission. Those who have had to make a premature departure from the launch pad without flying up to the Land of Sex jump in a cold shower to cool those sexual engines. There are ways, though, to use the shower to steam up, rather than cool down. A hot, relaxing bath for two is always a successful way to connect together. Showers for two can be great for a quickie. For those who want to use water to get wet'n'wild, here are some potential techniques:

* Drip water on their skin. If you're in a hot bath, drip cold water to alter the sensation.
* Lather up a soft loofah and massage your partner all over.
* Massage their feet with slippery bath gel.
* Shampoo their hair, above and below.
* Pour a jug of water over them slowly, from top to tail.
* Make love in a sauna to really sweat things up. Research indicates that sweating rids the body of stores of stress hormones, making us more relaxed and increasing sex drive.
* Sit in the bath, have your partner close their eyes, then write sexual messages and draw sexy pictures on their back, and see if they can guess what you're hinting at.
* Add lavender oil to the bath. Studies show men find this scent erotic.

Inspector Gadget

Buy an array of sex accessories, or find them around the house. You can gather foods, scarves, vibrators, and things that have differing sensations, such as fur, scratchy lace, lotion, hot wax and massage oil that heats as you rub it. Invite your partner up to the "Inspection Room" and explain to them that their mission, should they choose to accept it, is to be the "test dummy" for the inspection and approval of these items as sex toys. You can tie them up or blindfold them if you wish, and experiment with each accessory, asking them to describe what they are feeling and if it makes the get-it-on grade.

Art for sex's sake

Body decorating does not have to be in the form of permanent tattoos. You can buy water-based body paint to draw on each other. The feel of the brush lightly playing against your skin will excite you as much as the attention. You can draw art that starts up top and winds itself down below. You can also dip your brush in chocolate sauce as you begin to paint the thighs, and work your way into the area of artistic and sexual inspiration. Then say, "Damn, that's not what I meant to draw," and erase it by licking it off.

Praise you

Toss the sex toys to one side for a change and use your mouth, tongue and mind for sexual play. Praise your lover with descriptions. Start with *Who:* describe who you love, and everything about them. *What:* describe the things you love most about them. *When:* describe the times that stand out in memory as your most exciting sexual times. *Where:* describe where you love making love with them, and where you'd love to do it in the future. *Why:* describe why you stay with them, and why you think they are the lover of lovers for you. *How:* describe how you are about to make love to them. Then do it.

Gourmet lovers' basket

Pack a lovers' picnic basket for a feast of sexual pleasures. Find a hideaway, or if the weather is bad, plan a bedroom picnic. Add sexy, phallic foods to hint at pleasures to come and create an erotic vibe. Light the area with candles for mood lighting, and if you're outdoors with mosquitoes buzzing about, citronella candles work a treat to keep them at bay. For dessert, after some passionfruit, make your own passion. Your lover will enjoy the attention and romance and give you an O for effort.

Wicked wick

To prolong sex play, light a candle and make out while it burns. Try to make foreplay last as long as the candle, and go for broke when the wick burns out.

Flashlight relay

Play in the dark with a flashlight. Take turns each lighting one area of your own body. The rule is that each lit body part must be caressed for two minutes, before passing the torch to your partner.

Bedside box of delights

To really delight her box, create a real box, filled with sex toys and keep it near the bedside for easy and spontaneous access. You can either surprise her by presenting her with an accessory to play with, or treat the box as a lucky dip. Blindfold her and ask her to dip into the box, to choose something that feels promising. Then delight her body with that accessory. Remember to share toys and take turns.

Many of history's composers have been famous muses for love, as well as famous lovers. It is said that Mozart is an example of the passion–music link: he was a man who, in his time, inspired a great deal of love, and made even more of it.

A castrato was a man with immense singing ability, who was castrated before puberty to preserve his high-octave soprano range. Many women revered and worshipped castratos — the music gods of their time. They were able to sing like a god, but not love like a man.

What a pearler . . .

Take a pearl necklace (real ones are best) and wrap it either around your hand, or around the shaft of your partner's penis. Using a rotating, basket-weaving motion with both your hands, twist and slide the pearls up and down the shaft, and over the glans. The collective motion of the individual smooth and firm pearls gives the man a sensation unlike any other. Put your grandmother's pearls to good use, and do a pearl job instead of a hand job.

Hand me a sex toy

Your hands have over 72,000 nerve endings, and make excellent sensation receptor tools. Maximize their erotic sensation by highlighting the touch sensation, and decreasing your other sensations, such as sight and sound. Silently, with your eyes closed, caress each other and focus on the pleasures of your hands as they both give and receive sensual touch.

The Music of Love

Music moves the soul, so when we are aching for our souls to intertwine, we often play music to spark passion, romance the heart and provide the background ambience to lovemaking. Music has been an integral part of love and lovemaking for centuries, and both melodies and lyrics have melted the hearts of lovers around the world.

Poems of courtly love have been sung and set to music for thousands of years. In ancient times, men primarily serenaded women to show their love and devotion. Today, both women and men serenade each other.

Today, the range of music that opens our hearts, and our bedroom doors, is immeasurable. Everyone has a different idea of the best tune to bonk to. Nearly everyone agrees, though, that if they happened to be the last man and woman on earth charged with repopulating the world, music would be on their list of survival gear.

Troubadours were minstrels, poets and composers, mainly from Provence, France, who were famous during the eleventh to thirteenth centuries for writing the ballads of courtly love of their time.

🎤 *"I don't think you can get more romantic than opera. The passion of opera makes me want to jump into bed to express my own passion."* — Kay, 40

🎤 *"My favorite lovemaking music is my boyfriend. He plays guitar, and I love it when he sings and plays for me. I feel so much love for him, and when he plays for me, it makes me want to be as close as I can to him. I want to make love especially when he plays his own songs. He is an amazingly expressive guitarist and singer, and making love is an extension of how we feel after we've shared his music."* — Christine, 24

🗣 *"The best music to make love to would have to be ambient, moody jazz. Not that crazy inaccessible jazz, and not the big-band stuff, but play me something with groove and a bit of sax, and I'm yours."* — Tim, 29

🗣 *"Even if they have a bad voice, any kind of singing for my benefit, like serenading or even karaoke, wins me over. It's the combination of music, vulnerability and feeling that makes me open my heart and want to kiss them."* — Sarah, 32

🗣 *"The top sex-music of all time has to be anything by Marvin Gaye, or Barry White. Hands down, no question."* — Ed, 30

Have you ever used an unusual sex accessory in your lovemaking?

🗣 *"I decorated my girlfriend's body with pieces of fruit, added whipped cream and ate her up like a delicious fruit salad."* — man, 30

🗣 *"When we got engaged, one of our presents was a 'his and hers' vibrator set. We've had a lot of fun with*

*that. Until then, I didn't even know there were
vibrators made for men!"* — woman, 27

*"This will sound strange, and it developed quite by
accident one night. My husband and I used to talk
dirty to each other over the baby monitor while I was
nursing in the middle of the night. Now that our child
is older, we don't do that anymore."* — woman, 32

*"One time my partner and I were inspired to try
dribbling hot wax on each other. All we could find,
though, were drip-less candles and the whole thing
turned out to be a hysterical disaster!"* — man, 33

Nude Twister, Anyone?

[*playing with positions in*
a hot'n'heavy session]

SEX: fuck, do it, the Discovery Channel,
nookie, get a bit, bonk, the business,
horizontal hula, horizontal dancing,
get laid, do the nasty, sow one's oats,
roll in the hay, get a thrill, the you-know-
what, sportfucking, rock'n'roll, head down
Lover's Lane, visit Cupid's Alley, flesh
beating, go *au naturel,* get some tail, bang,
ride, ram, screw, tango, slap skins, spear the
hairy doughnut, root, do the mattress mambo,
nail, throw a leg over, rumble,
whoop it up, tumble, work it, the wet'n'wild,
get in the saddle, shake the sheets, rumple
the bed, get busy, hide the sausage, prong,
do the shaft, get serviced, get rude, get one's
cookies off, get one's rocks off,
get off, park one's shoes under the bed,

**doing it doggy-style, body bumping,
hump, get some pink, shag, do the Adam and
Eve, go belly to belly, to couple,
bunny humping, make it, bump'n'grind,
score, go all the way**

**NOONER: a fuck during a
noon lunch-break**

FUNCH: a fuck after lunch

Trust, honesty, fun, devotion, humor, communication, yadda yadda yadda. Granted, they are all important qualities to a good relationship. But the power and role of sex should not be underestimated in the health of a good relationship. Sexual satisfaction, through orgasms, connection, experimentation, variety, and giving and taking is really one of the secret ingredients to making love last. If you become one of those partners who say, "Well, there are other things to my relationship than having good sex," your relationship has not only gone off its passionate boil, it's got slow death written all over it. Sex is a lifelong love affair, and good sex has been described by some as 90 percent of the success of a good relationship. I might not go quite that far, but it's pretty damn important. So do it — often and well.

> *"Love is not the dying moan of a distant violin — it's the triumphant twang of a bedspring."*
> — SJ Perlman

How We Do It

* Number of adults who prefer the missionary position: 6 in 10
* Number of adults who prefer the woman-on-top position: 1 in 4
* Number who prefer to do it with the lights off: 6 in 10
* Those who prefer sex with their spouse over doing it with anyone else: 8 out of 10

Pussy-tions

Whether you're in for a marathon or a sprint, to feel a spiritual connection, to make love, to re-enact the Kamasutra, or just have a plain ol' bonk, there are positions to suit every couple, for every occasion.

Missionary

As a standard Western society bonking position for yonks, little description of the missionary position is required. The benefit is face-to-face contact, intimacy and the opportunity for a full-body-rocking hug. It is a good position for conception, because with deep thrusting, the semen is deposited towards the cervix, and doesn't spill out (because if the woman stays lying down, the sperm don't have to swim against gravity, as in the woman-on-top and sitting positions). The downsides are that the man must support his weight on his arms, so he can tire easily, leading to shorter intercourse duration; and there is little contact with the clitoris, so it is one of the most difficult positions for women to come in.

A popular variation on the missionary position, known as the CAT, is the coital alignment technique. This technique still uses the man-on-top position, but the man "rides high" on the

The woman-on-top position is one of the most common sexual positions depicted in art in the ancient world, such as seen in the reliefs painted by the very ancient cultures of Mesopotamia.

woman, creating contact and friction with the woman's clitoris. For detailed how-to information, see the Energizer Bunny chapter.

The term "missionary position" is thought to derive from amused South Pacific Islanders who were visited by Christian missionaries. The missionaries did not approve of the multiple sexual positions that the Islanders engaged in, and prescribed the man-on-top position as the Christian, and therefore the only natural, acceptable way to have sex.

In some parts of conservative Italy, the missionary position is so highly regarded, it is known as the "angelic position."

Ride him, cowgirl

The woman-on-top position is favored by men and women around the world. In one European survey of men and women between their late teens and mid-thirties, the woman-on-top position was listed as the favorite for both sexes.

There are a great number of variations to the woman-on-top position. The woman can face the man, or have her back to him. She can squat, kneel upright, kneel tilting forward, sit or lie on the man. The woman has the freedom in this position to control her movements, and unless lying completely on the man, her clitoris is exposed for manual stimulation to help her come. The majority of women who have trouble coming during intercourse use this position to learn how. And for others, it's the preferred position to get to the Second Coming.

In this position the woman has the ability to control the rhythms and also the types of penetrative motions. A woman who is fucking on top should not just think her role is simply to pump up and down on the man. Sure, it's going to get him to come, but it's little more than a "vag job," and like a routine hand job, it's not very creative and doesn't use the full potential of the sexual power and pleasure that's at your disposal in this position. In addition to pumping up and down on your man's cock, you can sit on him firmly, so that his dick is all the way inside you, and tilt your pelvis from side to side (picture a slow hula dancer). With each upward tilt, contract your pelvic floor muscles (like your Kegel exercises — see Peckers, Boobs and Blast Off! chapter). You can also rotate your hips from front to back. Many women like to contract their pelvic floor muscles on the back rotation, and this is sometimes referred to as "milking the cock." For women who are confident in their abilities on top, put everything together and "go around the world": rotate your hips in a circular motion (clockwise, counter-clockwise, both, whatever floats your boat).

There are three main benefits of contracting your pelvic floor muscles: 1) it feels fantastic for him; 2) it increases the muscle tension in your genital area, leading to a better chance of orgasm; and 3) the firm grip you keep with your muscles ensures he's not going to slip out — you've got him in your grasp.

The women who do not like this position very often state they don't like it because they are intimidated by it: What if he doesn't like the way I fuck? What if I slip? What if I can't get our rhythms right?

Women, please know that there's very little you can do wrong in this position, except cause injury (which is easily prevented). The first thing you've got going for you is that nearly all men love this position, no matter what you do. It's a nice change of pace for him and he can lie back and enjoy the stimulation without doing most of the work. A lot of men also have domination fantasies so they're keen to get under you. If you maintain a positive body image and feel sexy, even better: he's going to find this a huge turn-on. With practice, the woman-on-top position easily becomes a favorite among couples. It gives the intimacy of face-to-face contact, clit stimulation, and the woman can control the pace so that she comes before him.

Women should bear in mind that they are in control. Do not be bullied into rhythms that are not comfortable. You are riding his cock and you get to ride it how you like. Sure, you can compromise and adjust movements and rhythms to suit him too, but they should always be comfortable with you. If you feel you are bump'n'grinding away at an uncomfortable pace or in an awkward position, the chances are much greater that his dick is going to slip out, and if you slam your pelvis down on him by accident, you can cause some serious pain (to you both, but especially to him).

You are the star of the show. So next time you're on top for your "giddy up," look down at him and show him the pleasure on your face. He's got a front-seat view of his favorite show — you.

Spooning

Many couples like the near full body contact the side-to-side position brings, as well as the freedom of movement for both partners. There are several main variations to the side-to-side position. There is "spooning," in which the couple lies side to side, with the man behind. Her clit is exposed for stimulation by the man, or she can do it herself. A couple can also go for it facing each other, for added intimacy. A third variation is having the woman lie on her side, legs spread in a kind of wide scissors-style or, alternatively, with one leg bent or lifted up, and the man facing her straight on. Her straight bottom leg is between his two legs, while the other one is drawn up against her. This gives a slightly different sensation, as he is penetrating her like the missionary position, but she is twisted slightly sideways from him.

"I love the side-to-side position. We generally do it facing each other, and it's great because it's intimate, but we are supporting our own body weight. We like it a lot for shallow, teasing penetration." — Amy, 27

Head down bum up

A variation on the man-on-top and woman-on-top positions is to do it on the side of the bed, with the bottom partner bent backwards off the bed, so their head is below the rest of their body. The blood rushing to the head creates an altered mind–body sensation that can heighten orgasm.

Lap dancing

Technically a variation of the woman-on-top position, the sitting position is another popular bonking basic. There are a number of variations to the lap-dance sit-fuck. A less personal ride is when the woman has her back facing her partner and rides on his lap while he sits on a chair or on a bed. In bed, it's usually easiest if the man's legs are spread straight out in front of him, and she kneels over him and sits. She can also sit on his legs, but this leaves maneuvering a somewhat difficult task. Sitting on him with her back to him on a chair can give her greater movement. This sometimes takes practice, though, unless there is another chair or edge of something to hold onto with your hands. If there isn't you can brace yourself with your arms against his hips or legs.

More commonly, the more intimate sitting position is initiated face to face. Many couples enjoy wrapping their arms and legs around each other for greater intimacy, and for the stimulation of skin-on-skin touch. It's a great position for kissing while you do it, and you can keep on rocking together till you get your rocks off. This position has been popular for centuries and a variation from Arabia, called "pounding the spot," is explained below.

Pounding the spot

The *dok el arz*, which means "pounding the spot," is an ancient

Arabian position designed for both clitoral stimulation and deep penetration. The man is in the sitting position with his legs stretched out in front of him. The woman straddles and sits on top of him and crosses her legs behind his back. She guides his penis into her, and then leans forward and wraps her arms around his neck. He wraps his arms around her waist, and helps to guide her up and down and rock backwards and forwards. She can gain clitoral stimulation through contact with his pubic bone, but if that isn't enough (or it doesn't "line up" correctly), he or she can use one hand for manual stimulation.

Lie back and enjoy the ride

There are two more advanced positions which involve lying down. One starts with the couple sitting face to face, and then the man and woman each pull apart and lie backwards stretching their legs out, so that the body of each partner is between the other's legs (while still staying joined at the genitals with the penis in vag). It's not intimate, but it's a position some couples like for variety.

Another lying position starts with the woman on top, with her back facing the man. Then she lies back on his chest, and stretches her legs out. It's easy for the man's penis to slip out in this position, so a rocking motion is better than any thrusting.

"Discovery Channel" style

More crassly known as "doggy-style," or otherwise referred to as "rear-entry," the Discovery Channel style takes its name from the well-known natural history TV channel that often features sex in the wild. Many women don't like the rear-entry position because they feel subordinated and miss the affectionate intimacy of being face-to-face, but actually, rear-entry sex is as natural a position as there is. Doing it like they do on the Discovery Channel is doing it rear-entry.

Rear-entry is physically satisfying for both the man and the woman. The man has control over rhythm, motion and depth. It also enables a man to have deep penetration, and he can experiment with long or shallow strokes in and out of the vag. The woman, since she basically just receives his dick in her, can play with her clit to come over and over. For the women who like to use a vibrator during sex to come in multiplicity, this is an ideal position.

🗣 *"I never liked rear-entry until I met my husband. He doesn't make me feel dirty about doing it that way, and never makes me feel I'm just a sex object to him. It's great because he presented me with a mirror one time and told me to put it on the ground between my legs and play with it until I could get a good view of him sliding in and out of me. It's so hot watching him entering me as we're doing it."* — Fran, 32

Standing ovation

Not the most popular position, but a good one for a quickie, and a practical one, sometimes, for alfresco (outdoor/in public) sex. The success of the standing position lies in muscle strength and control, access, balance, grip and height adjustment (if necessary). One option is to twist the horizontal man-on-top position to the vertical, and for the woman to wrap her legs around his hips and hang on for the ride. If you thought your man came quickly holding his own weight up, watch his Speedy Gonzales-ness if he's holding both your weights. But for the he-men out there, give it a go. Some people love it. And it's not a position that needs to be held for long. The sex might start standing, and progress to sitting, for example. (Members of the "Mile-High Club" who have done it in airplane restrooms or WCs can attest to this.)

The other standing option is for the man and woman to each stand and support their own weights. If each partner is a similar height, you are at a distinct advantage. For the shorter partner, Dr. Alex Comfort, author of *The Joy of Sex*, and *The New Joy of Sex*, suggests the shorter partner (usually the woman) stands on two Manhattan phone books. I would suggest something handy to reach out and grab, or fling a leg on, for balance is even more important (and if you're doing it in the shower, you'll wreck your phone books). You do need to adjust your heights to match somehow. Women also might find that if they bend their legs in a slight plié (bent knees out to the sides, keeping a straight back), tilting their pelvis forwards and let him do all the thrusting, it will aid the whole process. For those who can't manage this position, don't worry, you are not alone. And for those who do: a standing ovation to you.

Least common sexual position, according to a study by Dr. Alfred Kinsey: standing up.

Verging on the Ridiculous

Experimenting with different positions can be intimidating and nerve-wracking, and it's easy to feel inadequate. It's far, far better to get a couple of positions down pat, and really make them sing, than to get messy with dozens. People have been trying to find new and different ways to fuck for literally ages. Most variations reflect only subtle shifts in body angles, or a different placement of an arm or leg. Or, for example, one category might be woman-on-top, but another, completely different position might be "woman on top, using vibrator." The addition of props and toys is the icing on the cake. Learn to bake the cake first. Stick to your basics and get saucy and sexpertly confident with those first, before you start

Third Time Lucky

Try something new at least three times.

The first time you'll be worrying about knocking elbows, knees and doing it "right." The second time you'll be trying to make it work for you — milking its potential. But the third time's the winner, and you'll be able to relax and go with the flow as it will feel more familiar to you.

going Kamasutra krazy. After all, some of the variations on sexual positions that you hear about are truly verging on the ridiculous.

For example, in Fiji, the "flying fox" position would only be possible for acrobats, and maybe not even then. In this position, the couple hang from a beam and do it. In your dreams, mate!

And: in the sixteenth century, writer Sheikh Nefzawi described the following position:

Step one: the woman lies down, and the man sits on her chest (okay, so far).

Step two: the man grips her hips and bends over her (beginning to get suspicious and wondering what on earth the next step could possibly be).

Step three: the man keeps bending until he can slot the woman's vagina over his penis (okay, you've lost me).

Of course, right after this, Sheikh Nefzawi added: "This position, as you perceive, is very fatiguing and difficult to attain. I even believe that the only realisation of it exists in words." (Source: *Sex and Spirit: Ecstasy, Ritual and Taboo*)

Leave the ridiculous rooting to others and get brilliant at the bonking basics for your bag of tricks.

Fucking Pear-Shaped

If your sex life has gone pear-shaped, you're not alone. Just as our sex drives go up and down, so do our sex lives. The killers of a good sex life (other than not doing it) include boredom, faking pleasure, feeling pain and acrobatic attempts. If you're bored, don't keep doing the same old thing. Either take a break from sex and come back to it freshly inspired, or enter a brave new world and try something alternative (check out the Sexperimenting chapter). If you're faking pleasure, stop, talk and fix the problem. If you're having painful sex, visit your doctor. Sex should feel good, not bad. And if you're trying too many acrobatic attempts and way-out positions, take it down a notch. In some positions you need to be careful you don't injure yourself or your partner. You can break a penis (see Peckers, Boobs and Blast Off! chapter), you can strain a muscle, and/or you can inadvertently twist something; it's nude twister that's supposed to be pleasing to your soul, not harmful to your body.

30 percent of men and 18 percent of women name the act of intercourse as the best part of sex.

Source: Sex Life Survey, *Courier-Mail* 2001

Mood Lighting

Couples differ about whether they like to do it with the lights on or off. Sex shops (and other "regular" shops) sell light bulbs in different colors which can create different moods in the bedroom. If there is a body image or shyness issue, try a darker red light bulb, throw a scarf over the lampshade, or do it by candlelight.

Scatter fresh rose petals on the bed and over your bodies before you make love (especially on the skin that comes into contact with your partner, like bellies and thighs). As your bodies create friction and heat and you become sweaty, the petals will crush between you and the fragrance will sweeten your sex.

Naked or Dressed for the Occasion

Fucking naked or doing it dressed is a completely individual affair. Certainly naked is the most common option for couples, but a bit of dress-up doesn't go astray, either. Costumes and props are popular for S&M and B&D, and also for fantasy role-playing, of which uniforms are the most common (especially maid, nurse and school uniforms — old habits and desires die hard). But it's also quite common to hike up the skirt, reveal the crotchless panties and have a quickie. And some couples love the rushed "we can't wait" frenzied bonk before leaving for a party: having sex with a man in his suit, pants zipped down, while your good black pants are twirling around one leg, and your breasts are jiggling in your best slinky going-out top.

Playing and Plunging

There are different strokes for different folks. And different strokes for different sex. There are many motions to the bump and grind, and couples can experiment to figure out what suits them best. Some couples like to tease each other with short, shallow thrusting, before deep, long penetration. Similarly varying rhythms can arouse different sensations and create multiple moods for fucking. From the crazy, wild, sweat-producing quick in and out, to the slow, meditative dance for two, penis-in-vag action can be as different as you want to make it. Every different stroke in and out of the vag creates varying levels of arousal in men and women: women often like a fair amount of shallow penetration because the outer one-third of the vagina has the most nerve endings; and men may need to slow down at times to maintain ejaculatory control. As well, there are differing angles from which to penetrate the vag. Straightforward is not the only way. You can angle the penis in or rotate your hips, so while it's in the vag, the penis moves in a circular motion around the sensitive outer rim.

Having a big dick isn't enough, especially if you don't know how to play it. Being a good lover is not just about pumping your giant rod in and out; the motion bit is the key bit. Truly. If you don't believe me, believe Helen:

🗣 *"Last year I had two lovers at once. I had a young hottie who had a great body and a huge cock. But he didn't know what to do with it. He just pumped away at me until he got off. It was such a disappointment. I dumped him for my other lover, who I'm still with. He hasn't got the greatest body, and he has an average dick, but good god, does he know how to use it and get me panting for more."* — Helen, 27

Pumping, Rocking, Pounding, Grinding

Certain positions require specific thrusting styles. The sitting position with the woman facing the man, for example, is more successful with a rocking and grinding pelvic motion, rather than pumping in and out. Couples can play and work out their preferences but, in general, if a woman wants to come during intercourse without manual/self/vibrator stimulation of the clitoris, there needs to be direct, constant body contact and friction on the clit. This is best achieved by keeping contact between the man's pelvis and her clitoris. Some positions are better for this than others, and the coital alignment technique is one of the more popular ones, as is woman on top. While women may love the sensation of a hard cock sliding in and out of them, unless her G-spot is ultra-sensitive and he's hitting it exactly right (which is uncommon), a slapping-skin pounding motion is not going to deliver the big O. For him, he may prefer to pump, but for her, it's go the grind.

Boudoir Banter

A great many couples like to talk and make sounds while they're bonking. There is an entire chapter on talking dirty, but in addition to getting nasty and raw with their boudoir banter, couples also like to give direction when things aren't quite working for them. Bear in mind that sugar will get you further than spice in this particular bedroom area. Barking orders not only throws ice-cold water on the flames of passion, but it doesn't improve the situation or right the wrong technique. The key to your bedroom vocab is to be specific: "Don't do that" and "No, not like that" are about as unhelpful as you can get.

Think of it like you are giving directions to someone who's driving. You don't say, "Get in the car, turn the engine on, and just drive straight until you get there." You have to use words like: left, right, up, down, around, circle, faster, slower, and, of course, the beauties are, "You're nearly there" and "Don't stop!"

What is good sex?

🗣 *"Good sex is magic. It's like when you see a fantastic magic trick and it stuns you. You don't want to analyze it and figure it out, you just want to ponder its mystery."* — Lynne, 60

🗣 *"Good sex is having sex with the same person for years. Knowing exactly what they like, when they know you inside and out, when the commitment of two bodies echoes the commitment of two lives."* — Alan, 58

🗣 *"Good sex is like when you have a really good meal: you sit back, completely satisfied, and want for nothing else."* — Gene, 37

🗣 *"Good sex is any sex. I'm single, and beggars can't be choosers."* — Barbara, 28

🗣 *"Good sex is when I feel bonded with my partner, like we're sharing not just our bodies, but our hearts. And great sex is when I have all that, and I come."* — Elizabeth, 26

ANAL SEX: arsefuck, go in the back door, do it Greek-style, browning, bumfuck, buttfuck, fudge pack, go up the dirt road, plug, pack, buy the ring, access all areas

Access All Areas

While most people think anal sex is a practice more common for gay men, there are, in fact, a lot of straight men and women who enjoy it. It actually rates in the top ten (straight) male fantasies.

The anal region is connected to the vagina and penis by nerve roots. The anus itself is filled with nerve endings that also make anal intercourse pleasurable. Most women rate anal intercourse as their least favorite sexual act, however, there are a minority of women who genuinely get off by being fucked up the arse. A number of men, as well, like to have a woman use a dildo to penetrate them up their back doors. And for other couples, anal sex isn't as much about pleasure as it is about sexual curiosity and a desire to know all parts of their lover's body.

For the beginner, anal sex can be scary and painful, as well as exciting. The most common mistake couples make when trying it for the first time is to ram the dick up the arse in one forceful thrust. This usually has the woman screaming with shock and pain, not pleasure. The first time you try anal sex, depending on how tight or comfortable the woman is, the goal might not be full anal intercourse. The key is to go slowly and adjust with each centimeter of entry. The couple should be in a position where the man has controlled access to penetration, but the woman also feels some control. This includes both rear-entry, as well as the sitting position, with the woman's back to the man. Both the woman and the man should be active participants in guiding the penis in, and partners should talk, and check with each other that it feels okay. A man can play with his penis around the anus before penetration to stimulate the area and get her aroused. He should then try to penetrate, literally one centimeter or half a centimeter at a time, stopping frequently to allow the woman to adjust to being "filled" in her anal canal. The woman may also want to use relaxation and breathing techniques (slow, steady, deep breaths) to help relax all the muscles in her body. If she's nervous, her body is bound to be tense, and that area is already tight enough without consciously squeezing it tighter in anxiety.

If it doesn't work, try not to feel a sense of failure. Many women like to please their man and are curious about trying anal sex, but it's not for everyone.

If you're with a new partner, or regularly use condoms as your contraceptive method, always use a lubricated condom. Anal sex is a high-risk behavior for the transmission of HIV, and the lubrication aids the entry, especially the first time. Always put a new condom on (or thoroughly wash the penis) if you switch from anal to vaginal intercourse, to prevent the spread of bacteria to the vagina.

"Nope. Never tried it. Don't want to. That area has a permanent 'Do Not Enter' sign." — Maggie, 25

"I love anal sex, and I've initiated a number of women into it, and most of them have liked it. I always go slowly, and I hate hearing stories of women who've been practically ripped open by guys who are too rough. If it's done right, it's the best." — William, 30

"I've tried it a couple of times. I don't mind it. It's something I do for my boyfriend because I know he

*likes it. I much prefer regular sex, but I'd rather put
out than deny him, and then find out he's gone
elsewhere to get it."* — Joanne, 26

*"I tried it once, totally fucking off my head on drugs.
I don't remember any of it, but holy shit, I was so
sore the next day. I could hardly walk!"* — *Kathy, 23*

Sport Sex

If you ever needed a persuasive reason to work out, this is it:
keeping fit increases your sexual prowess. Healthy muscles and a
fit cardiovascular system keep the blood flowing effectively in
your body, including to your genitals. The endorphin rush your
body experiences after exercise can also raise sex hormones and
rev you up to get you in the mood for a second, more sexual,
hot'n'sweaty session.

Exercise has been proven to increase body image. Women and
men surveyed after attending the gym reported finding their
body sexier on the way out than on the way in. And a healthy
body image increases desire. Especially for women: women who
feel comfortable with their body and feel like a sex-kitten are
more attractive to their partners. There is nothing sexier than a
woman who knows she's sexy, and uses it.

Post-Coital Etiquette

What's In
* Saying thank you.
* Asking, not assuming, to stay the night (in casual encounters).
* Kissing.

The Three "Rules" of Lovemaking

US sex therapist Dr. Jude Cotter maintains that a multitude of problems could be avoided if we all followed three simple rules for intercourse.

1. Women first

The woman should be encouraged to reach orgasm before the man. A man requires a recovery time after ejaculation before being able to have a "repeat performance" whereas a woman needs no such recovery time. She may orgasm again without needing a rest. As Dr. Cotter states, "When the guy is done, he's done — it's all over." Allowing the woman to orgasm first enables both partners to be sexually satisfied without the pressure of timing simultaneous orgasm or wondering if they both came.

2. She decides when it's time for penetration, not him

According to Dr. Cotter, the woman should determine when penetration should take place because the only one who knows for certain when she's ready is the woman. Dr. Cotter explains that the male sexual response is like a light bulb: turn it on and it's hot almost instantly; turn it off and it's cold within a matter of seconds. Female sexual response is more like an iron: turn it on, and then wait, and wait, and wait for it to heat up. After you turn it off, you wait until it cools down.

3. It should always be the woman who guides her partner's penis in

The woman should control how rapidly things proceed to climax, and allowing her to guide him in is just another way to make sure this happens. The more active the woman is in participating in intercourse, the more likely that both partners will finish each fully sexually satisfied.

Source: *The Practical Encyclopedia of Sex and Healing*

NOTE: These "rules" are simple guidelines and are not meant to be followed strictly. They may or may not be applicable to your sex life.

Things That Go Bump In The Night

In one survey of sexual desires, the one that topped the list for men was to be able to have sex with their partner during the night while half asleep. The desire to reach over and silently bonk during the night may interrupt sleep, but there's never been a better reason to be woken up in the middle of the night.

* Staying naked.
* Paying compliments.

What's Out
* Smoking.
* Apologizing.
* Rolling over within ten minutes of orgasm.
* Using your partner's toothbrush without asking.
* Farting under the sheets.

Sexperimenting

[*it's a fine line between pleasure and pain*]

Sexual experimentation is as old as sex itself. Humans have been trying to work out how to get off in assorted saucy and sordid ways since their first orgasm. If it feels good this way, perhaps it'll feel good *that* way. Tie me up, tie me down. Slide on that rubber. Those shoes look sexy. Steal that riding crop from the stables and sneak it into my bedroom. When "wine me, dine me" got to be old hat, "whip me and hot wax drip me" became a new vogue. Peep shows and creep shows. There is no limit to what turns us on and gets us off, save the limit of our imagination.

S&M: sadism and masochism, sadie and maisie, sado-maso

THE PASSIVE PERSON IN S&M OR ANAL SEX: bottom, submissive

THE DOMINANT PERSON IN S&M OR
ANAL SEX: top, dominatrix, master/mistress

S&M

Sadism and masochism are two separate sexual practices. They are often linked, as reflected in the term sadomasochism, but they developed out of distinctly singular desires.

Sadism

Sadism, commonly thought of as a sexual perversion, is the giving of pain to others to feel sexual pleasure. The term sadism was coined from the name of the world's most famous sadist pioneer: Marquis Donatien Alphonse François de Sade. The Marquis de Sade was an aristocratic Parisian who lived from 1740 to 1814, and is still considered an inspiring sadist nearly 200 years later. While many S&M purists regard de Sade technically as a sadomasochist, because he enjoyed both giving and receiving pain, most sadists agree that de Sade was the pioneer who brought sadism to the fore in sexual philosophy and experimentation. There are two contrasting beliefs about de Sade. One view is that he was simply a dark, twisted sex fiend, while others regard him as the "divine Marquis."

De Sade viewed people as sex objects and treated them as such. In fact, he treated his sex objects very badly and was arrested more than once for brutal abuse of women. The Marquis de Sade's life revolved around one single dominant theme: performed cruelty of every kind for the purpose of sexual excitement and pleasure. When he wasn't engaged in cruel sex, he wrote about it. His most famous works translated into English, include *Justine*, *The Story of Juliette* and *120 Days of Sodom*. During his life, all of de

Sade's works were banned. He primarily wrote his definitive works on sadism and sexual cruelty over the twenty-seven years he spent in prison for his various sexual crimes. The imposed abstinence that prison forced upon him reportedly inspired him to write about such acts and characters in great depth and detail. His works glorified violence against women and children, and *120 Days of Sodom* was not released to the public until 1904, nearly 100 years after his death.

Masochism

Masochism is the other side of the sado-maso coin and, like sadism, true masochism is considered a sexual aberration. Masochism refers to the need to feel pain in order to feel sexual pleasure. Pure masochists are unable to orgasm or feel any sexual pleasure without a dimension of pain involved. It is more common for masochists today, though, to use the sensation of pain to enhance and stimulate the sensation of pleasure.

The term masochism was named after the Austrian writer Leopold Ritter von Sacher-Masoch. He lived from 1836 to 1895 and was married to Wanda, who was his dominator. Wanda became such a predominant part of Sacher-Masoch's writings that she is still the object of many masochists' fantasies, over 100 years later. The relationship between Leopold and Wanda was complex, and

Fire and Ice

In your bondage games, play with keeping it hot and cold. Varying temperatures heightens your sensitivity to sensations because your blood vessels expand and contract. So heat up with wax and smacks, then pleasurably torture with ice.

Sacher-Masoch had several requirements to ensure that Wanda excited his sexual masochistic pleasures. He even had her sign a sexual masochistic contract obliging her to obey his masochistic fantasies. The most famous of Sacher-Masoch's masochistic obsessions was to have Wanda dominate him while wearing fur. In fact, fur was a fetish of his, and his most famous work is titled *Venus in Furs*. When Leopold and Wanda divorced, he was disappointed to find out that there was nothing special about Wanda after all: any fur-wearing dominatrix could get him off.

Most true masochists have a desire to be dominated, but total powerlessness is not part of the game. Masochists can be control freaks, and often like to carefully outline and orchestrate the exact ingredients of pain that will give them pleasure. It is in this way a masochist can manipulate his or her dominatrix. Leopold held control over Wanda and his own excitement even while being dominated and in receipt of severe pain. We see remnants of this seeming paradox in today's S&M/B&D scene when a customer hires a dominatrix for the first time. The master or mistress will usually ask what the submissive's preferences are, which will be described by them, often in great detail, before any control is handed over. Many submissives like to be dominated, but on their terms.

Sacher-Masoch was teased horribly by the press because he was so open in his writings about his masochistic erotic-pain fantasies and practices. Many newspaper caricature artists illustrated his stories to make fun of him. Sacher-Masoch not only described masochistic pain fantasies, but also detailed the element of masochism that is less common, although still practiced today, humiliation. Severe humiliation included acts such as being forced to drink the urine from Wanda's chamber pot. Today, verbal humiliation is more common than forced acts of gross humiliation, but the latter are not unheard of.

The relationship between sadists and masochists is complex, and in its truest form, never works out. For example, a pure sadistic dominator hates their submissive, and a pure masochistic submissive despises their dominator, as the hate is essential to the pleasure associated with the infliction and receipt of the pain. If a dominating woman really hates a submissive man, she will leave him eventually; and if she doesn't really hate him, the submissive man will leave her for someone who will. It's very complicated and explains why the majority of sadists and masochists today are not strictly S&M-ers, but rather play at the S&M games.

S&M today

Often when one reads about S&M today, the phrase seen is S&M & B&D. Bondage and domination (B&D) are expressions of the desires behind sadism and masochism. Most people who are into S&M are really acting out bondage and domination practices. True sadists and masochists exist, but public expressions of it like those of de Sade and Sacher-Masoch are mostly a thing of the past. People who call themselves sadists and masochists are generally expressing their sexual identities as pain givers or receivers in the

*Q. What's
the difference
between erotic
sex and
kinky sex?
A. During
erotic sex you
use a feather,
during kinky
sex you use the
whole chicken.*

B&D world. The minority of true sadists and masochists who cross the lines of legal sexual expression are treated by sex therapists.

B&D

This refers either to bondage and domination, or bondage and discipline. The most common form of bondage is the tying up of a lover, however any type of restraint is regarded as bondage. Discipline revolves around the acting out of a fantasy of being punished or humiliated; domination is the act of dominating another, or experiencing domination, usually in sex play where one person is tied up and at the mercy of another.

B&D covers a spectrum of behaviors and intensities. Some couples spice up their sex life by engaging in a little bondage: using his ties and taking turns tying one another to the bedposts, for example, or maybe even buying a pair of handcuffs at a sex shop and playing with those on the odd occasion. That's amateur bondage, and huge numbers of couples like to play at it. Serious bondage involves more complex props, scenarios and situations. The same applies to domination and discipline. Some people play at spanking and whipping for a one-off or for the excitement, not really to cause any pain. Others use domination and discipline in serious sex games, where clamps, clips, paddles, gags, blindfolds and chains are used, sometimes to cause agonizing pain. For some, B&D is a way of life, a serious alternative for sexual pleasure; it's their sexual norm, not an adventure for extra titillation.

B&D is really an extension of erotic fantasy: the feeling of being dominated or disciplined is thrilling because of the illusion of the loss of power, rather than any actual loss of real control. In B&D sex games, the submissive and dominant partners both agree on boundaries and "safe words" to stop the game if it goes too far. The sex play is always consensual. Role-playing is a major aspect of B&D sex play. Very often role-played B&D fantasies include the headmistress and the naughty school student, big bad cop and prisoner, and doctor and nurse. B&D appeals to people who are into darker sexual erotica; it allows them to indulge their taboo fantasies. People who want to act out their dirtiest, most dominating or submissive secret fantasies often find B&D is their preferred option.

If you're interested in trying B&D for the first time, there are some key points to bear in mind to help make your initial exploratory experience more pleasurable. The three basic B&D "rules" are to Stop, Look, and Listen.

Stop The very first thing you need to establish before you start playing at B&D games are the boundaries that you and your partner agree to adhere to. Couples often work out a "safe word" to mean

---

Sexperimenting Accessories

A poll of favorite sex accessories Down Under reveals that the average person loves their sexperimentation:

Vibrator, costumes, whips, chains, paddles, camera, video camera, music, fireplace, blindfolds, scarves, candles, condoms, lube, whipped cream, honey, chocolate sauce (the food list is endless), masks, wax, nipple clamps, handcuffs, ankle cuffs, G-strings, any leather gear, full-body rubber suit, crotchless panties, edible underwear, dildos, massage oil, incense.

"Stop." A popular word is *red* (as in red light), because often people accidentally call out "No" or "Stop" during sexual pleasures when they don't actually mean "Stop." A word like *red* is rarely an automatic sexual-reflex word, and is a clear message to the dominator to either stop or slow down. Alternatively, if B&D is being performed in a loud S&M club, couples can use hand signals such as one finger held up equals "Okay," but two fingers up equals "Stop." If there are certain behaviors that don't interest you, such as verbal humiliation or spanking, those should be discussed with your partner before getting into it. Similarly, talk about your fantasies so your partner knows not only what you don't want, but what you do want.

Look If you plan to use props, be sure to look them over before playing with them. Serious B&D toys are designed to maximize bondage, and pain. Any props with clamps should have release clasps. Whips and paddles should be felt over to make sure they don't have any unintended sharp points. Be sure you have the key for anything that locks. Never restrain anyone too tightly, and it's best to use only one type of restraint at a time, if it's your first time. It's a good idea to use one simple prop for your first time, and then work up to other more sophisticated toys. Beginners should stay away from any neck restraints, gags or hoods. (For details of the use of chastity belts in B&D sex play, see the chapter Been There, *Not* Doing That.)

Listen Always start slowly and listen to your partner's wants and needs. B&D should be intense, but also erotic, pleasurable and fun. Use softer toys before getting hard core, and try spanking before whipping or wax dripping. You and your partner may want to work up to higher levels of pain and discipline, but go slow, and stay tuned in to each other. Always stay loving, attentive and respectful of each other, and stick to what was negotiated at the beginning. B&D, every step of the way, should always be consensual.

🗣 *"I dated a B&D master once. I didn't know that's what he was into when we first met. He actually worked at a club, it wasn't just a hobby. He knew I wasn't into that, and he respected that. He was one of the most respectful, attentive lovers I've ever had. And he loved foreplay. His interest in B&D made him really sensual, because he was into starting slowly, and concentrating on the sensations of touch, and the feel of skin. He opened my eyes to sensuality in a lot of ways I had never imagined."* — Sara, 28

🗣 *"My husband and I are right into the B&D scene. We met at a club and hit it off (no pun intended). He's the submissive and I'm the dominatrix. We shop for outfits together and like to experiment with all kinds of fantasies. It keeps our sex life interesting. If the girls at work ever found out we were into that scene, I'm sure they'd be shocked. They think I'm a prude, but little do they know!"* — Rachel, 34

Keeping up with the Joneses

Swinging hit its heyday in the 1970s, and is still a popular pastime in subgroups and suburbs around the world. Swinging can take place both privately and publicly. Couples can get together for private swinging parties, where both large and small groups of couples gather at one person's house for group orgies, or to pair off with other people's spouses — musical sex partners, if you will. Naturally, jealousy is a predominant emotion that needs to be attended to. One partner might only be swinging to indulge their spouse's fantasy, and can find it difficult watching as their spouse makes it with another person. Only the most open-minded of people in open marriages can make swinging work as an ongoing practice.

More commonly, swinging takes place as an experimentation in swinging clubs. There are establishments that cater for people who are interested in engaging in random, anonymous group sex. In most of these clubs, the etiquette is to allow females to choose male partners. It is not etiquette for a man to approach a woman. In this sense, swinging clubs are somewhat liberated, and allow women to feel safe and comfortable. Not everyone who goes to a swinging club goes to fuck. Some go to be wallflower voyeurs. Entry into a swinging club is generally always by couple only, not for singles (it is, after all, a club for the spirit of togetherness, not for flagrant get-your-rocks-off voyeurism for desperate singles). Many swinging parties require little more than a few mattresses in the center of a room, and some music. The couples then talk, pair off, or triple and quadruple off, and go for O. The fancier swinging clubs, though, provide spas, themed rooms and a cocktail bar.

FLAGRANTE DELICTO: refers to the advanced stages of foreplay, and in certain situations is the point at which a woman might venture up and ask to join in for group intercourse and oral sex.

Ménage à Trois

The French phrase *ménage à trois* more aptly refers to a three-way relationship, although in the last decade or so, it has come to be synonymous with threesome sex. The typical fantasy is one man and two women, however, many women fantasize about getting it on with two guys at once. Very often, when couples agree to have a threesome, it is to act out the fantasy of one of the partners. Other times, a couple invite a friend or random stranger for some spice and variety. Couples often advertise in the sexual ads in papers and mags for a semi-regular third sex-wheel.

Jealousy can arise from having a threesome, and many a couple have split after trying it. While one might assume men get more jealous of seeing their woman with another lover, informal surveys indicate that it is more often women who cannot cope with their jealous feelings.

"I had a threesome once. I went over to my friend's house for dinner, as a housewarming, because she had just moved in with her boyfriend. We drank quite a bit of wine, and while we were sitting in the lounge, all listening to music, we just started touching and massaging each other. Before I knew it, we were all naked and having oral and manual sex. It's all a bit blurry in my memory, but I remember thinking the whole thing was very sexy." — Samantha, 24

🗣 *"My wife and I regularly have threesomes. We first*
tried it because I mentioned I wanted to see what it
was like. And our first experience was with a friend
that my wife chose. I always let her choose. Mostly we
do it with another woman, but sometimes she chooses
a guy, and while it's not as fun for me, it's okay. It's
exciting having a third person to play with, and since
my wife and I both enjoy it and accept it, why not?"
— Tim, 31

<u>Rubdown</u>

Mutual masturbation may seem to some to be quite tame sexual
experimentation, however a vast majority of couples spend their
entire relationship getting each other off with their genitals and
mouths through oral sex and intercourse without ever doing the job
together with their hands. Watching your partner masturbate
themselves can teach you a great deal about how they like to be
pleasured. You can take turns, or do it together. If you feel self-
conscious, try having a bath together. You can sit at different ends of
the tub, and reach down and pleasure yourselves. It's not so obvious
under water, and while you might not come, at least the first time it's
great foreplay. You can then either do it in the tub, or hop out and
have slippery sex on the bathroom floor, or in the bedroom.

🗣 *"I had never masturbated in front of anyone before,*
until I met my current boyfriend. He said he liked to
masturbate himself while watching me do myself, so
I agreed to try it. I was completely self-conscious the
first time and I didn't come. But I did learn a lot

about what he likes by watching him. Now we masturbate together quite often. At least once a month. We agree to do it especially on nights when we've both had a big day and are tired, and we don't have the energy to have a long session, but want the connection and release of orgasm." — Ingrid, 36

Knuckle-Down Loving

Anal eroticism is not contained to penetrative anal sex, rimming, or even fingering. Fisting is a lesser known and practised anal turn-on, and is more common among gay men, though others have been known to try it, and like it. Fisting is exactly what it sounds like: plunging the whole hand up that anal canal. If dick in arse isn't your thing, and is uncomfortable, it's probably best to leave this particular practice off your "might try one day" list.

"I was with a guy who was really arse-centerd, unlike me. I like a nice, smooth chest and a big cock, honey. He stuck two fingers up me, and when I didn't object, which was only because I was being polite, mind you, he asked if he could stick his whole hand up there. Oh my goodness, thank god he asked, because I would've got the shock of my life if he'd just gone ahead and done it. Of course I said no. I'm not into that kind of thing." — Stuart, 27

Restif de la Bretonne (1734–1806) was renowned for his public admission of having a fully fledged shoe fetish. Shoe fetishism is sometimes referred to as "restifism" as a result.

Fetish

Shoes are the number-one fetish object, closely followed by rubber and leather. Straight men make up the vast majority of fetishists — it's not nearly as common for women to be into fetishes. True fetishists are rare. In the purest form of fetishism, a man cannot experience sexual excitement, or orgasm, unless the fetish object is present. If a man has a fetish for feathers, for example, he will not be able to become aroused, experience an erection or come unless he is touching a feather or being stimulated with a feather. This pure form of fetishism is a sexual abnormality.

Far more popular is the adoption of fetish objects for sexual enhancement. These fetishes become sex accessories: they heighten and intensify pleasure, but are not absolutely necessary to get turned on. One develops a preference for a sexual fetish through sexual conditioning, usually in childhood or adolescence. A boy can become repeatedly aroused while touching a particular object and develop a fetish for that object, in which he associates sexual thrill and excitement. It's also possible to adopt a fetish object as an adult, but in these cases the fetish objects are more likely to be horny preferences, not absolute requirements. Most people who say they have a fetish actually just find that a particular object or substance makes them really horny. You can experiment with various toys to play with, and you might find one excites you more than most. This is normal, not abnormal fetishism, and you can then reserve this fetish for those occasions you want to have "blow your socks off and hand me that shoe" fantastic fucking.

> *"There is no unhappier creature on earth than a fetishist who yearns for a woman's shoe and has to embrace the whole woman."*
> — Klaus Kraus

"I had an unusual client once. He had a fetish for fur, and traced it back to masturbating on his mother's fur coat as a boy. He loved the feel of fur and while he could become aroused without it, he complained that his erections weren't as strong when he wasn't in contact with fur, and his orgasms weren't as intense. He had recently married a woman who was a vegetarian and strictly unsupportive of the killing of any animals, and especially having any fur in the house. Deprogramming his sexual fetish was unsuccessful, and in the end counseling enabled the couple to compromise on making love with fake-fur accessories." — sex therapist

> *Fetish: comes from the Greek word* facere, *meaning to fascinate.*
>
> Source: *The Sex Chronicles*

Alfresco Sex

Doing what comes naturally out in nature is a sexperimentation that isn't particularly wild, given that so many couples do it. The thrill of alfresco sex is in the change of scenery and in the potential of perhaps being discovered. Having a roll in the hay is a centuries-old sexual pastime: until the seventeenth century, it was common for young couples to be encouraged to bonk in fields to increase fertility. Now our hay-rolling adventures are less about fertility and more about alfresco fucking. Usually in the back of a shaggin' wagon.

Alfresco sex: having a sexual encounter either outdoors, or in public. In one German study, "in an elevator" topped the list of venues couples would most like to have alfresco sex, in reality or fantasy. Number of adults who have had sex alfresco: 1 in 3.

Where's the wildest place you've had sex?

🗣 *"In the loo of a nightclub with a queue of people waiting and listening."* — woman, 22

🗣 *"At the beach, after the pubs shut. At the time we thought no one could see us — we thought we were under the cloak of darkness, but the next night, when we walked by the spot, we saw we were in front of the light of a surf club, and anyone passing by could've seen us. I'm glad I didn't know that at the time!"* — man, 25

🗣 *"Out in the open, against the side of the car in one of those public rest stops on the side of the highway. The RTA (Roads and Traffic Authority) tells us to Stop, Revive, Survive and it revived me alright."* — man, 29

🗣 *"In an elevator. Actually, it wasn't sex. I was standing in front of him, and I reached back and put my hand down his pants and started to give him a hand job on our way up to my apartment. There were two other people in the lift. It was so erotic."* — woman, 28

🗣 *"In the back seat of a limo. I know it's stereotypical, but it was hot. I barely knew the girls, there were two, and it was like all my Christmases had come at once."* — man, 23

🗣 *"In one of those rock pools at the beach. There were only a few other people in the pool, it was dark, and it just looked like we were hugging. I think. I hope."* — woman, 33

🗣 *"One night I picked a secret spot in a remote park, spread out a romantic picnic, and dessert was me. It was great, but I did end up getting my knees scraped on a few rocks."* — woman, 26

"I don't mind where people make love, so long as they don't do it in the street and frighten the horses." — Mrs. Patrick Campbell

Peep Shows

A voyeur leers, ogles, peeps, peeks and spies. A true voyeur only gets sexually excited by spying secretly, without the object of their admiration knowing of their presence. In 95 percent of cases, the voyeur spies on strangers. But if you want to add a little voyeurism to spice up your sex life, you can create a situation of voyeurism on your own. If your partner is busy working at home, and not paying you attention, you can surreptitiously do a little strip show in their peripheral vision to distract them. Their gaze will quickly switch from that quarterly report to you. Some couples also find watching strip shows, porn or even spying on neighbors together

> ## Peeping Tom
>
> Tom was a tailor in the eleventh century who peeped at Lady Godiva as she rode naked on her horse through the streets of Coventry. What was Lady Godiva doing riding naked? Legend has it her husband promised tax relief to the people of Coventry if she did it. She did, and ever since Tom peeped, voyeurism has become joked and gasped about, and the term "Peeping Tom" is now synonymous with "voyeur."

erotically exciting. The act of spying on people while they are fucking generally arouses the sexual response in both partners, although men are more stimulated than women by visual erotica (though this is a general rule only; many women get completely wet and horny from a little peeping at porn).

More often than not, a little voyeurism goes a long way to steaming up the windows.

🗣 *"My partner loves to watch me undress, and he finds it even more exciting if he hasn't asked me to undress for him. So every once in awhile, I take the remote off him, switch the telly off, put on some music, and strip for him. It never fails to excite him, and we always have great sex when our foreplay starts with my striptease. He says sitting back and watching me get slowly naked is his biggest turn on."* — Anna, 34

Showing Off

While voyeurs lustily try to spy on sex, other show-offs desire to be unashamedly and blatantly ogled while doing it. While a true exhibitionist is your man-in-raincoat-but-naked-underneath flasher, who exposes himself for a shock reaction and the sexual excitement it produces, exhibitionists are also people who like to have sex and be watched while they do it.

Some exhibitionists are content to have the "viewer" be a camera, and get off on being filmed while they bonk — wanna-be porn stars, or, ahem, "Big Brother" contestants. Others go to couples and swingers clubs to do it and be watched. And still others go crazy sexually and try to find very public places to have alfresco sex where they know they will be seen or spied on.

If you suspect you are a sexual show-off, give it whirl; you might find it's as saucy as it sounds.

🗣 *"We live near a university, and across the street is an apartment block, full of student housing. I'm not sure if anyone ever spies on us, but I like to imagine someone does. My partner and I have sex with the curtains open sometimes, and just the fantasy that someone is spying on us and masturbating to our lovemaking is enough to send me over the edge. I always come during sex when we do it within full view of the neighborhood."* — Kate, 29

Addicted to Sex

As people increasingly experiment with sex, they often find themselves having more sex: variation brings curiosity, desire and burning urges to do it in ever more new ways. Sex therapists field concerns from people who find themselves having sex more than they ever have before, and who are worried that they may be developing a sex addiction. In the vast majority of cases,

What Is _Not_ Sex Addiction

* Liking one-night stands.
* Fear of intimacy or commitment (that's another issue).

* Having a lot of lovers.
* Making a living as a sex worker.
* Loving sex.

couples are just having lots of great sex; they are not addicted. There does exist such a thing as sex addiction, though, and if someone suffers from the incessant need to have sex, they should see a therapist.

In the growing field of addiction studies, sexual addiction is a primary topic of research. Celebrities have claimed to be under the spell of the dark side of the force, aka sex addiction, to explain their bed-hopping scandals, and there are a multitude of Sex Addicts Anonymous groups around the globe. As with any addiction, sex addiction takes many forms, from the subtle problem to the severe disorder. Sexual addiction is thought to stem from childhood neglect. Some neglected children develop a need to please others, to feel fulfilled and approved through the desire of others, and satisfaction is only gained through fulfilling that desire to please. In adolescence, this need to please and be pleased can take on a sexual context, and by adulthood, a full addiction to sexual need, sexual pleasure and desire can develop.

Sex addicts get a high or buzz from serial sexual conquests, in which they feel the need to please others and themselves, and so manipulate as many situations as possible into a sexual encounter. Sex addicts fear intimacy but really crave love, and since this is a paradox, they can only be helped through psychological help and support. The steps to recover from sex addiction are similar to the process for other addictions, which include acknowledging the problem; deciding to break the cycle of meaningless, manipulated sex; accepting personal flaws and motivations with regard to sex; and accepting professional help.

Sex with Substance

[*doing it with drugs*]

Drugs and sex combine to form a radical paradox: while drugs can be exciting, relaxing or awakening to the mind, to a sense of perceived "otherness," they are positively, no bones about it, deadening to our sexual response (and, it should go without saying, illegal, dangerous and potentially lethal, especially in large amounts, or over long periods of time). Scientific experts in drug use and abuse tell of damage to the heart, brain, liver, lungs and blood vessels; scientific sexologists tell of impotence, permanent painful erections, inability to come and decreased sex drive. And yet, non-scientific, experienced drug-sex bunnies who fuck on all different highs, regularly tell of surges of warm feelings, tingling skin sensations, rushes of blood to the head and genitals, and increased excitement, arousal and orgasm.

So who is right and who is wrong? I did some field research and discovered that they're all right.

Remember the old ads? This is your brain: egg. This is your brain on drugs: egg frying in hot skillet. Well, this is sex: ooooo, mmmmm, yeah yeah yeah! This is sex on drugs: oooooooooo, mmmmmmmmmmmmmmmmmmmmmmmm, OOOOOOOOOOO,

From Good Time to Flatline!

Most drugs are addictive and can lead to a serious decline in personal health and lifestyle. They also, more often than not, lead to the destruction of relationships. Even though the use of drugs with sex might be thousands of years old, the effects of drug use, whether casual or constant, has been, can be, and is still today, devastating on personal health, sexual response, sexual decisions and relationships. Some couples take drugs together, but experience very different responses (one can be good, another can be bad) and this can lead to sexual and relationship rifts. It is also important to trust the source of any drug — there are serious repercussions to obtaining drugs when you are not sure of the content of the pill, liquid or powder. It's a good idea to experiment with sex, but it's a bad idea to experiment with drugs. If you're looking for good sex, a healthy body, a consciously aware, pleasurable sexual response, and a sane relationship, drugs are never the way to go!

MMMMMMMMMMMMMMMMMMMMMM, YEAH! YEAH! YEAH! Repeat. And, this is sex on too many drugs: ———flatline———. Drugs may positively alter your sex experience or perception of intimacy once or twice (or maybe a bit more than that), but as an ongoing habit (and it doesn't take much to form a habit with many drugs) your body will begin to choose drugs over sex and then you're not just a junkie. You're a celibate junkie.

Done well, sober sex beats the pants off drug sex any day. The best lovemaking, with true, deep connection and make-the-earth-move orgasms, is accomplished with all senses sharpened, an intense focus on each other, and with only natural lust, desire, passion and love chemicals rushing through the brain and body. Adding an assortment of other chemicals to your body changes your sex experience, but doesn't necessarily make it better. Even shit sober sex is always better than shit drug sex: sober, you only have to come down from the disappointment of a lame shag; on drugs, it's shit to the power of ten magnified, because not only are you dealing with the crushing blow of a bad bonk, but to top off the experience you have to deal with the depression after you come down from your high, which can make everything feel and seem much worse.

ALCOHOL: drink, plonk, booze, grog, piss, vino, brew, brewski, poison, nectar of the gods

Boozy Bonking

Fermented brew is fucking's foreplay. Has been for centuries, and still is today. A drink or two revs the sexual engine out of neutral and into va va voom. The effectiveness of alcohol on lubricating our sexual interest is well documented and well experienced. The art of seduction nearly always includes a bottle of bubbly. Or, less romantically, buy her a "Cocksucker" shot and then she may well want to become one later in the night. Swig a "Slow Steady Screw up Against the Wall" and that starts to become a rather appealing idea. In the world of clubbing and pubbing, knocking back a few often increases the

Initiates into the ancient cult of the fertility goddess Demeter drank a potion called kykeon, which was thought to contain a mixture of ingredients that produced an effect similar to LSD. Once drunk, the resulting hallucinations were thought to be acts of ritual sex.

chances that you won't get knocked back for sex. The majority of one-night stands are facilitated by the lube and lure of grog. Whether it be two strangers across a room, or two old-marrieds across a dining table, having a few drinks gets people in the mood for lurve. They talk more, flirt more, feel more confident and their inhibitions decrease. This paves the way to the bedroom (or hotel room, kitchen table, back seat of the car . . .).

The line

Most people, whether their boozy bonk was a one-night stand or a relationship root, will acknowledge that there exists "The Line" with alcohol and sex. A few drinks can be great to get some interest going, to increase confidence and willingness to experiment, but once you cross The Line, all function south of the border seriously heads south. The pecker will not face north, no matter how much effort you put into it. He's down for the count. End of show, all flirt, no fuck. And, for the lady: lubing her sex brain with booze often means there is no lube happening anywhere else in the body. She won't get wet for anything, not even to break the longest sex drought she's ever had. It's all tease and no tussle; the mouth may have said green light, but the vag screams red light.

If systems haven't completely shut down and are still "go" for launch, the journey of the boozy bonk can be messy and hardly worth the trip. Not only is sloppy sex inattentive and plain bad, grogged-up groping does very little to ignite the sex response.

Alcohol actually acts as a depressant on the central nervous system, which decreases libido and sexual response. The depressed system is slower to respond to internal and external sexual signals, if able to respond at all. Men can experience total erection loss, or only a partial erection; women can experience no or little vaginal lubrication, resulting in painful sex. Both men and women find it harder to come (even if they're feeling quite randy, the alcohol still shuts the system down, regardless). Chronic abuse of alcohol leads not only to liver damage, but also hormonal imbalances that can make erection for men and orgasm for women a thing of the past. If you have the occasional boozy bonk, it's really no big deal (and it really is no big deal without orgasm). But if you're on the piss (drunk) a lot, or all the time, it's absolute poison for your sex life. As Shakespeare said, alcohol "provokes the desire, but it takes away the performance."

"I always feel more eager for sex when I'm drunk, but it's never as good. The whole thing feels more sloppy, and I feel ready to go, ready to come, but it rarely happens. It's like a sexual dead feeling — nothing happening down there. If I do orgasm, it's never as good. But when I'm drunk I can be louder and I think my hearing and touch is better. And I'll try new things, be less shy about it. Afterwards there's never that nice feeling, or cuddling. I just want to roll over and pass out. And morning sex is usually out — we both stink and feel like hell." — Amy, 19

"I have sex drunk because I get horny when I've been drinking, but I prefer to have sex without being drunk." — Michael, 31

CANNABIS: marijuana, pot, weed, grass, dope,
Mary Jane, hash, herb, reefer, the happy
chemical, THC, ganja, smoke, bong stuffing,
hubbly bubbly ingredient

Doing it with Mary Jane

Having a bong and a bonk has grown in popularity with every passing decade. While public health educators worry over the increase of pot use among adolescents and young adults, the trend of smoking and screwing isn't stopping. Pot is not widely heralded as a "sex drug," as a drug specifically taken to enhance sexual experience, although reports indicate that getting high does heighten the experience of getting off.

People who smoke a joint before having a sexual joyride say the experience of intimacy and touch is enhanced and intensified by being high. Few people report better or stronger orgasms, or better sex performance. What they do say is that their sensory perception of sex is altered: their skin is more sensitive, their awareness of their body and their partner is heightened, and they feel more able to relax and enjoy sex. Some people report feeling horny after smoking pot, while others don't crave sex but chips, chocolate and cookies. A lot of people also say sex lasts longer, but pot messes with the brain's perception of time, so what feels like an hour may only be twenty minutes.

Apart from perception, physiologically, pot is bad for the body and bad for the sexual response. Studies show marijuana use slows the body's reflexes and decreases sensation. One's ability to take in, assimilate and react to stimuli (including sexual stimulation) is compromised. Your head may feel like it's swimming in desire and sexual sensation, but your body is not computing it. Getting stoned does not help your body get its rocks off. Ability to increase pleasure to orgasm in both men and women is hampered, especially with regular pot use. If you only eat hash cookies, this doesn't apply as much, but smoking pot is also bad for blood flow to the genitals. Smoking affects the small capillaries and arteries to the penis and vaginal areas. Smoking also decreases testosterone and sperm count in men, and badly affects fertility in women. Quit smoking pot if you're trying to get pregnant. Do not, however, use pot smoking as a birth control method: there were lots of unplanned babies born in the sixties to pot-smoking hippies. Occasional pot use is not going to stuff up your sexual response, but if you're having any trouble reaching orgasm and you're a regular pot smoker (or hash-cookie eater), look no further than the bottom of your bong to find your rooting problem.

"It's easier for me to initiate sex, or feel like having sex, when I'm stoned, but my energy level for sex is really low. It's nice to lie back and have someone get me off while I'm stoned, so I can concentrate on my body and how it feels, but to actually make love is not as physically good when I'm stoned. My orgasms are usually pretty weak, and I guess I'm more into me and my pleasure than I am into my partner, what she's feeling, or what I'm doing to help her get off." — Tim, 28

ECSTASY: E, eccy, pill, Elizabeth, partytime, love drug, sex drug, pleasure pill, happy pill, EX, X, hug drug, party biscuit, party biccy, biccy

Ecstasy

Sexual ecstasy as easy as popping a pill? Taking an E to deliver the big O is a growing trend, especially among groups of younger people. Known for its pleasure potential, ecstasy is touted as a first-class sex drug. The high experienced on ecstasy includes feelings of euphoria, confidence, trust in others, warmth and wellbeing. Ecstasy users tell of a heightened sense of touch and of connection, and a dramatic increase in their desire for sex. During sex, one's sense of sensuality, and erotic body-to-body and body–mind connections are at an all-time high, and can be extremely intense.

There are few long-term studies investigating potential long-ranging side effects of the drug, and this includes effects on the sexual response after prolonged use. Current research indicates ecstasy affects the nervous system, brain and hormonal systems, all of which are critical to sexual response, so it is likely to have negative and harmful long-term effects on the body's sexual response and function, such as erectile dysfunction, vaginal dryness and inability to orgasm.

Because ecstasy induces feelings of pleasure and sexuality, care should be taken when popping an E. In addition to the dangers and harmful side effects of the drug, such as depression, flashbacks, anxiety, nausea, loss of appetite and overwhelming thirst, ecstasy also decreases one's ability to determine sexual red flags. The feelings of warmth, sexuality and trust can lead (girls, especially) to dangerous situations, such as date rape, or engaging in sexual acts without consent. If you are going to take a drug that enhances feelings of sexual desire it is always best to take it with a trusted lover or friends who look out for one another.

B*E* Sure

Ecstasy is potentially lethal, and there have been accidental deaths across the globe by people who were only casual, or one-off users of E. Be sure ... absolutely sure ... of your drug source, so that you are confident of what you are taking. E is one of the most common "tweaked" drugs, meaning you might think you're buying pure ecstasy, but in fact, purchasing a combination of ecstasy and other amphetamines in one pill. Be very careful! For your sexual response, but more importantly, your health. The side effects of ecstasy are not to fool around with: be aware of dehydration, overdose and heart failure. Never mix E with other drugs. If you are considering using E for a sexual experience, check out the literature on ecstasy on the net, or at your local drug information centre.

"I've had some amazing sexual experiences on ecstasy. It's just one of those magic drugs where I feel both uninhibited and alert. It's way better sex than drunk sex, which just doesn't even compare. I love everything when I've had an E. I love my partner, my body, his body, my sensuality, having sex. I'm just happy, and I feel connected, deeply connected, to my partner. The sex feels fucking fantastic, and it really is an intense experience where I feel like our souls are mixing and making love together." — Janelle, 26

Candy flipping: taking a combination of ecstasy and acid to produce feelings of euphoric sexual energy while on a trip.

🗣 *"I don't take ecstasy anymore because I couldn't deal with the come-downs, and I really felt it was fucking with my body. But the one thing I miss about taking it is the sex. The sex was great, better than great. Every inch of my body would get turned on, and the whole act felt pleasurable, not just orgasm."* — Chris, 29

🗣 *"I don't know why they call it ecstasy because there's nothing ecstatic about it, as far as I'm concerned. I was so out of it when I tried it that I only had a vague idea I was even having sex. I certainly didn't come, or even get close. I'd much rather have sex sober."* — Pam, 22

GHB (GAMMA HYDROXY BUTYRATE): grievous bodily harm, easy lay, vita-G, somatomax, gamma 10, bedtime scoop, energy drink

Bedtime Scoop

GHB is one of the more dangerous of the street drugs. It is often sold as "liquid ecstasy." It's taken for its euphoric effect on the body and mind, but its resemblance to ecstasy is minimal.

Dosage is the key with this drug: if too much is taken, euphoria can be replaced by sudden sleep or abrupt unconsciousness. The difference between a dose and an overdose is minuscule, so playing with this drug, especially when you know little about it, is not recommended. Officially, GHB is a medical anesthetic which depresses the central nervous system. Since it is a depressant, its effect on the sexual response system is negative rather than positive. In fact, the effect of the drug does not last long, and is pointless as a sex drug. In high doses, or with the wrong mixtures, GHB can be poisonous to the body, resulting in vomiting, slow respiration and seizures. GHB is not a drug to fuck around with, and do not mix it with alcohol.

SPECIAL K (KETAMINE HYDROCHLORIDE): ket, K, breakfast cereal, vitamin K, ketalar, Kit Kat, cat valium

Animal Sex

Special K is a fast-acting general anesthetic used mainly in veterinary medicine as an animal tranquilizer. In the human world, it's a popular club drug. It induces a feeling of relaxation and causes changes in sensory perceptions, including sight, space, time, color, movement and hearing. Some people experience disassociative episodes and "waking dreams" with vivid color changes and the sense of mind–body separation. Special K can temporarily take away all sensory perception and motor skills, a state known as a "K hole." The come-down from Special K can be strong and seedy.

Sexually, Special K can induce feelings of desire and connection, however these last only as long as the drug and often people feel way too fucked up and out of mind and body for sex. The appeal of sex on Special K, for some, though, lies in the out-of-body experience and sense of orgasm during altered sensory perception.

🎤 *"I got a blowjob at a club after I'd had a pill and some ket and the whole experience was literally mind-blowing. As the pleasure increased, so did my sense of color. It was all bright, and I felt like the rays of color were wrapping around my body. Like, sex sober is one-dimensional and this experience was three-dimensional. I felt separate from my body, but I felt pleasure throughout my whole body and mind. It was like going from Kansas to the Land of Oz. It was that trip-the-light-fantastic. I was completely fucked. In fact, for a while I thought it was a dream, but it was real. I think. Oz, it was totally Oz. That's the best way I can put it."* — Max, 31

"Ket is so not a sex drug. You get so out of it, in another world, that sex isn't even a consideration. Your body becomes separated from your mind, so what's the point? You don't come, you don't connect with your partner. You're way too messed up to enjoy doing it." — Bas, 28

Do not mix Special K with alcohol as it can induce severe nausea and vomiting. As popular as it is, mixing Special K with other drugs, especially cocaine, can overload the toxicity of the body, resulting in overdose effects that may require emergency attention.

HEROIN: smack, H, hammer, dope, go slow, horse, Harry Dope

SPEED BALL: when heroin is mixed with coke or amphetamines.

Getting Down

Heroin is a semi-synthetic opiate derived from morphine, which is extracted from the opium poppy. Whether snorted, smoked, swallowed, shot up or taken as a suppository, heroin produces feelings of relaxation and ease, and senses of floating, feeling carefree and connection with others. It is also a dangerously addictive drug and can utterly destroy a person's health and lifestyle.

Generally, heroin's effect of reducing cares and worries also reduces any strong drive, including sex drive. Heroin is a central nervous system depressant, so it also seriously messes with the ability to have an orgasm. This is particularly frustrating to some because heroin produces feelings of connection and increases the desire to be intimate. However, when this desire for intimacy is translated into sexual intimacy, the sex drive has usually plummeted, and the sexual response goes on hiatus. For this reason heroin is not considered a sexual drug.

With prolonged use of heroin, any desire for sex goes out the window and is replaced by a sense of passivity and the desire for another hit. Junkies very often have active sex lives, not because they are horny, but because sex often becomes payment, or partial payment, for their habit. As a sex drug, heroin is a very effective anaphrodisiac. The more you take it, the less you want to have sex.

"I tried heroin with my boyfriend because I wanted to know what it was like. I felt really sick at first, but when that passed, I felt really relaxed and pretty happy. It's true what they say; it felt like I didn't have a care in the world. My boyfriend and I cuddled together but we didn't have sex. We didn't feel like it.

It wasn't like, 'We can't be bothered,' it was more like,
'We feel good just like this, this is enough for us.'
I can see how people can get hooked on it." — Peta, 19

"Heroin is an anti-sex drug. I'm a recovering addict,
and I can tell you, when I was doing heroin, I never
wanted to have sex. Heroin is a fucked-up drug, no
one should do it. It's bad for your whole life. I lost
everything, my sex drive included." — Heather, 33

Optional opiates

There is a family of legal and illegal pain relief drugs which also come from the opium poppy, such as morphine and codeine. Synthetic analgesic drugs include Demerol, Methadone, Percocet, Percodan and Vicodin, among others. These drugs are opiates that act similarly to heroin in the system, in that they produce feelings of relaxation, drowsiness, mental clouding, pain relief and comfort. People also tend to take drugs in combinations. After a few drinks, they'll take a popper, or smoke a spliff. Others may feel too wired from an upper, so they swallow a sleeping pill or two. Drugs, in any combination, can be seriously dangerous. And combining drugs only worsens your sexual response and function. Bottom line: none of them are good for your sex drive, function or life.

High Heaven

Popular club drugs as well as rooting drugs are those that send you up rather than down. Drugs that inject the body with an "all systems go!" signal incite a (temporary) awakening of the sexual response.

COCAINE: coke, ok-y-dokeys, Charlie, Charles, snort, powder my nose, white powder, Snow White, rock

The fairytale of Snow White

Cocaine is a drug renowned for its ability to give a sense of euphoria, insight, alertness, distorted perception, power and confidence. The quality of the high completely depends on the quality of the drug, the dose, and any other drugs in one's system at the time of taking it. Like heroin, it can be smoked, snorted, shot up or taken as a suppository.

Sigmund Freud was the first modern-age researcher to note the sexual effect of cocaine. A powerful sex drug, cocaine can affect the sexual response in both radically good and devastatingly bad ways. Cocaine stimulates the body's production of the brain chemical dopamine, a neurotransmitter that acts like a natural body aphrodisiac, increasing both sexual desire and performance. Using cocaine in small amounts can increase sexual desire and stimulate sexual activity and performance. However, used repeatedly or in large doses, cocaine actually depletes the body's stores of dopamine and it is burned up so fast that the body doesn't have the time it needs to manufacture more of it. When this line is crossed, the first thing to fly out the window is sexual performance, and sexual desire isn't far behind it. Coke can increase sexual desire, sensuality and performance in the very short term, but in the long term, sayonara sexual function.

Cocaine is an immediately addictive drug that has devastated millions of lives. The cons of taking cocaine as a sexually experimental drug, in terms of lifestyle, health, and relationships far outweigh any pros to it. Sober sex is always better than sex on drugs. And that's the truthful bottom line from anyone who's had a lot of sex, or a lot of coke.

"I had never tried coke, and one night, after being at a fashion show, I tried some with a friend in the toilets. I know what it's like being out-of-control drunk, but once I added coke I felt clearer and much, much hornier. When I got home to my husband we had frenzied sex. It felt great, but I haven't tried cocaine since then." — Belinda, 25

"I must be the only person, but I don't really notice a difference with sex on coke. I'm horny when I'm sober, and I'm horny when I've had cocaine. I didn't think my orgasm was any better when I was on coke. When I take coke, it's got nothing to do with getting laid or having better sex." — Rob, 30

"When I tried having sex on coke, I was so wired that my attention span was shot. I didn't enjoy it because I couldn't focus. And because I was high, I forgot to insist on using a condom, so then afterwards I got an intense, horrible panic attack about HIV and diseases. I really freaked. The whole experience is one I'd rather forget, actually." — Bree, 27

POPPERS: bullet, Jac blaster, heart on, aroma of man, locker room, rush

Poppers

Commonly known as poppers, volatile nitrates such as amyl nitrate and butyl nitrate are regarded as the true aphrodisiacs in the drug sex world. Called "poppers" because they used to be (and sometimes still are) given out in glass ampoules that made a popping sound when snapped open, after the "popper" was opened the vapors inside were inhaled. Now, poppers are usually inhaled from a glass vial with a screw-top, so there's no popping sound. These drugs should not be injected as they can become toxic when absorbed by the body in this way. Also, avoid contact with skin, as they can lead to serious burns.

As a sex drug, poppers play with sensory perception, enhancing sounds — especially music — rhythm, movement, warmth and also lights and colors. Sexual desire can increase as can feelings of sensuality. While most drugs decrease the sexual response, poppers, like cocaine, can increase and heighten it. Users of poppers tell of an increase in the sexual sensations they feel on their skin and a sense of letting go, connection, bliss and lust. If inhaled during sex, right before orgasm, poppers can heighten the experience of orgasm, as well as make it last longer. Overuse can lead to erectile dysfunction and vaginal dryness.

Poppers are also used for heightening anal sex pleasure. These drugs automatically relax some muscle fibres in the body, including the muscles around the rectum, making anal sex easier and more pleasurable.

AMPHETAMINES: uppers, pep pills, bumblebees, hearts, black beauties, bennies, dexies, co-pilots

Stimulates

Amphetamines are central nervous system drugs, like speed, which were once routinely used for the treatment of obesity, hyperactivity and narcolepsy. Their effect on the body is a stimulated high, similar to that of cocaine, but without the same intense sexual effect. They give increased energy, which in some sexual situations can be beneficial, but they will not help sexual performance or function.

METHCATHINONE: kat, bathtabspeed, speed, wild cat, mulka, the C, cadillac express, ephedrine

Speed

Methcathinone, or speed as it is commonly known, is a synthetic drug that was made by a college student from old records that revealed the formula. It is basic to make and contains ingredients including asthma and cold medications, paint solvent, paint thinner and car battery acid. It is a serious drug that can be snorted, smoked or shot up, and is highly addictive. Its effects are stimulating like cocaine, but it interferes with rather than stimulates the sexual response. Users report feelings of restlessness, tremors, fits and headaches; they are hardly in the mood for sex. And if they do have sex, they can be distracted, paranoid and anxious. First-time or early users report a feeling of euphoria, but this can quickly be replaced by delusions and anxiety. Sexual function rapidly becomes impaired as addiction sets in.

Shagadelic, Yeah Baby

"Shrooms" come in various species and are renowned for their psychedelic effects. Usually eaten, or drunk in a tea, shrooms can produce both mild and strong hallucinations.

All psychedelic drugs, including acid, can produce a variety of feelings, sensations and hallucinations. From mild mental relaxation to way-out trips, the inducement of sexual desire and sensation can be highly individual. To some, the idea of sex is repulsive, to others, the energy for sex isn't there, while for others, sex improves a trip or relaxation sensation. Depending on dose, drug and interaction with other drugs in the body, the sexual response may function, or it may be completely shut off. Hallucinogenic drugs are highly experimental and sex is not the goal for most people who take these drugs.

**ROHYPNOL (BENZODIAZEPINE): ruffies,
roofies, roches, rophes, la roche, rib,
Mexican valium, rope, R2, stupefi,
forget drug, date-rape drug**

Rough Sex

Rohypnol has become famous in recent times for being the date-rape drug. It is known as the "forget drug" because users usually do not remember anything from when they were under its influence. It magnifies the effects of alcohol, Special K and nitrous oxide. It decreases motor skills and inhibitions. No one is capable of consenting to sex when under the influence of Rohypnol because they are so out of it. It is never okay to drop any kind of drug into someone's drink without their consent.

One of the beauties of fucking lies in two people sharing a physical and emotional, maybe even spiritual, experience together, and whether that is shared soberly, intensely, passionately, or spinning off their dial, whirling through the trippy sensations in stereo, consent is the crucial key, not only to good sex, but to legal sex.

Love Drug Number One

Despite being designed and marketed as a sex aid drug for erectile difficulty, Viagra is now also popular as a sex drug. The section on Viagra in the Little Boy Blue Lost his Wood chapter outlines exactly why it does not do very much for men, unless they suffer from chronic, clinical erectile dysfunction. Trials are still being conducted on Viagra's effectiveness for women, but again, it is believed only to be helpful to women who have sexual difficulty. Viagra is a sex aid, not a sex enhancer.

But regardless of science, from Ibiza to India, and from the top of swanky uptown to the belly of the underground rave, the little blue pill is popularly popped. Porn stars and escort service workers take it to ensure action and performance, body-builders take it to counteract the effects of steroids, and club-goers take it to enhance the effect of Special K, GHB and ecstasy, or to help them get it up if they're too stoned or drunk (which is quite a different thing altogether from clinical erectile difficulty). Research has not proved that Viagra is beneficial in any of these circumstances. It's just another substance for the poor ol' liver to cope with at the end of the weekend.

Herbal Highs

There are also a number of "herbal high" concoctions sold — in shops, on the Net, and in clubs. Meant to be safe, these herbal highs vary in dose, effectiveness and side effects. Some of them do nothing at all; they are like a placebo. Others do what they say, as in produce a sense of wellbeing, but on such a subtle level that it's probably not the "high" you were after when you bought the product. Others can make you sick, negatively interact with alcohol and drugs or any medications you might be on, or can raise your heart rate and blood pressure. Be wary of any herbal product that promotes a "high" that does not list its ingredients on the packaging. Even though many are legal to buy, that does not always mean they are safe. Most herbal highs produce feelings of being very awake or alert, maybe even some happiness, but they will not enhance your sexual function or expression. If you are after a natural aphrodisiac, see the list in the Lick 'Ems and Stick 'Ems chapter.

"I took one of those natural high pills at a club because I was too chicken to take ecstasy, and I still am. I wanted to feel a sexy high, but I didn't want to risk dying or whatever from a pill. I did feel a difference — my heart raced and I felt kind of wired, but I didn't feel warm or sexual or horny. I think I got ripped off. But my friend who took another brand said hers was great and she felt really uninhibited after taking it. I might try one of those sometime."
— Jessica, 18

The Yawn Effect

While most antidepressant drugs decrease sexual drive and function, one drug, Clomipramine, actually has an unusual sexual side effect: producing an orgasm every time a yawn is experienced. While this effect only seems to occur in 5 percent of cases, it is thoroughly enjoyed by nearly all who experience it. One woman was able to produce orgasms by deliberately yawning, and another man found himself yawning and coming so much he wore a condom at all times to save embarrassment. Some found the orgasm a treatment for depression as much as the drug.

Smokin' Sex

The post-coital cigarette may be a cherished romantic ritual (at least in the movies), but the truth is smoking is about as unsexy as you can get. In addition to giving you bad breath, smoking has some serious sexual health consequences (not to mention being linked with lung cancer and heart disease).

Smoking is harmful to the reproductive systems in both men and women. In women, smoking can cause decreased fertility rates by causing damage to the fallopian tubes. In pregnant women, those who smoke are more likely to give birth before their babies have reached full term.

For women smokers on the pill, the risk of circulatory problems such as heart attack, stroke and thrombosis are increased, especially for women over 35.

In men, studies reveal that smoking significantly decreases the number and liveliness of sperm. One study found that men who smoke were twice as likely to have low sperm densities than men who don't smoke.

Studies also indicate a link between smoking and erectile difficulty — it is one of the causes of peripheral vascular disease (damage to small arteries like the ones that supply the penis).

Smoking also increases the risk of cancer of the cervix in women, and cancer of the penis in men.

So if damage to your lungs isn't enough incentive to quit, next time you light up, think of the damage to your sex life and maybe then you'll want to kick the habit.

Cosmic Orgasms

sex and the mind-body-spirit connection

Have you ever rolled over to your side of the bed in the afterglow of sex and wondered, "Isn't there more to it than this?" Have you thought it's not about the earth moving or whether bells ring, but more about a body-and-soul connection, but you're just not getting it? If so, it turns out you're not alone. Thousands of couples are turning to ancient and cosmic sexual teachings to reinvigorate their modern, hectic, stressed-out relationships; they are tuning in and turning on to them to rediscover the art of making love.

TANTRICKING: making love Tantra-style

TANTRIKA: a person who is into Tantra and Tantricking

Tantra

In the wake of escalating divorce rates and troubled relationships, couples are anxious to find ways to live happily ever after. Satisfying sex is an integral part of any successful relationship but varying sexual positions and sex toys will only take you so far.

Many couples searching for a more intimate and lasting connection are finding the answer in Tantric sex. They learn how to enhance their love and sustain sexual passion for a lifetime together.

There are many misconceptions about Tantric sex. Some think it has something to do with free-love cults and orgies; some believe it's a sort of New Age sex therapy; while others believe it's just about new sexual positions. In fact, Tantra is an Eastern science of spiritual enlightenment that has been around since the seventh century.

Derived from the Sanskrit word meaning to weave or expand, Tantra honors the sacred union of the male and female energies that create life. Tantra emerged out of a rebellion against the prevailing Hindu beliefs of the time that sexuality had to be denied in order to achieve enlightenment. While there are many descriptions of the origins of Tantra, it was essentially born out of the philosophies of the union of the Hindu god Shiva, the embodiment of pure consciousness, and the goddess Shakti, the embodiment of pure energy.

Margo Anand, author of *The Art of Sexual Ecstasy*, explains that by uniting sexually and spiritually with Shiva, Shakti created the universe. Tantra, then, views the creation of the world as an "erotic act of love." With this emphasis on creation and fusion, Tantra includes sexuality as a doorway to human ecstasy and enlightenment.

Not since ancient times has the idea of the joining of sex with spirituality been so popular. The tradition of Tantra fosters such connections by viewing sexual love as a sacrament: it offers a path to understanding yourself and deepening the relationship with your beloved.

How do you do Tantric sex?

Slowly, it seems.

Tantric sex techniques allow the man to slow down during intercourse and direct his sexual energy through gradual, controlled thrusting. This enables the woman to use techniques such as vaginal tensing and flexing, which build up and release her sexual energy.

"The health of sex and sensuality lies in the personal, in that ancient, ever-new feeling of unselfish bonding that can create a new relationship, a new life, or a new society."
— George Leonard

While intercourse usually lasts an average of ten to fifteen minutes, it's not unusual for those who practice Tantric sex to go on for one or two hours. Some refer to this long Tantric lovemaking as "Tantricking."

There's a great deal more to Tantric sex than simply making a marathon of your lovemaking, though. With an emphasis on connection between lovers, there are many exercises designed to help couples to relax and "be in the moment" while they are making love.

Being aware and fully present during any lovemaking session is a tenet of Tantric sex. For the woman who has mentally constructed the shopping list during intercourse, or the man who has fantasised about the quarterly financial reports to

As dusty as those ancient Tantra texts may be, Tantric sex is fast becoming the latest "must try" phenomenon. In one US survey of 14 to 25 year olds, Tantric sex topped the list of things they'd most like to learn.

delay orgasm, there are good reasons for discovering Tantric sex.

There are many avenues for learning to incorporate Tantric sex into your life. There are how-to guide books and videos available at your local bookstores and libraries. For a truly comprehensive and clear understanding of Tantric sex, though, a workshop is the best option.

Tantric sex workshops are not full of writhing, naked couples chanting while having sex in a circle. Most reputable Tantric sex practitioners and teachers assure students that there is no nudity or sexual activity in their workshops. While some may think "Aw shucks!," the reality is that Tantra is best learned in a comfortable, non-threatening, supportive environment; not one that boasts titillation and confronting nudity.

So what can you expect to gain from Tantric sex? There are sexual, personal, interpersonal, health and spiritual benefits. People who practice Tantric sex, or "Tantrikas," as they are known, claim to have greater intimacy with their partners and a deeper understanding of themselves and their spirituality, not to mention better sex lives.

Tantric sex uses many breathing exercises which stimulate and cleanse the lymphatic system, improve sexual tone and fitness, and balance the male and female energies in the body.

In some Tantric sex workshops, participants may learn the art of sexual Tantric breathing. While that may sound wild, it's an ancient technique that helps direct and transform your kundalini, or sexual energy, into a loving spiritual meditation. Tantrikas say this technique enables couples to prolong intercourse and can also prevent premature ejaculation in men.

The full-body orgasm

With its benefits of longer intercourse, prolonging orgasm and assisting multiple orgasms in women, Tantric sex shouldn't need many more selling points. But there's an extra bonus — *the full-body orgasm*.

By learning the proper steps and techniques from a Tantric sex teacher, Tantrikas are able to channel their kundalini throughout their entire body, flood their brain with orgasmic sensations and perpetuate this ecstatic state for minutes or for over an hour. They do this by opening their chakras — the body's energy centres, located at the base of the spine, the genitals, the stomach, the throat, the forehead and the crown of the head. Tantrikas say this ecstasy is a hypersensitive state of being, the fusion of body, mind, heart and spirit.

As mind-blowing as a genital orgasm may feel, it pales in comparison to the full-body version. And unlike the garden-variety genital orgasm, the full-body orgasm can last more than an hour. Learning this technique, sometimes referred to as "riding the wave of bliss," may take time and application, but is worth the effort.

Couples who have tried Tantric sex say that longer-lasting sex leads to longer-lasting relationships. Studies show couples are struggling to fulfil their exceedingly high expectations of sex, reinforced by the media and movies, in their own bedrooms: she doesn't have multiple orgasms, he can't last for hours, or they can't come together every time. A survey in the US found 85 percent of respondents believe "perfect sex" exists, yet only 38 percent of men and 45 percent of women reported being "very satisfied" with their own sex lives.

Tantric sex teaches couples to enjoy each other and discard the notions of goals and performance in sex. It is about taking time out to be together, incorporating ritual and romance in lovemaking and honoring the love you share. The time spent having sex is really time spent making love.

Tantra is appealing to many because it offers couples a way to reconnect with their hearts and minds as well as their bodies. So next time you feel a little blue about your relationship or ho-hum about your sex life, think about those Tantrikas experiencing the bliss of a full-body orgasm and go learn how to get yourself some pill-free ecstasy.

Mmmmm

One Tantric practice involves performing "ritual sex" in a ceremony known as the "Five Ms," or *pancamakara*. The first four Ms involve the taking of wine and foods believed to hold aphrodisiac qualities. These are madya (wine), matsya (fish), mamsa (meat) and mudra (parched grain). The final step involves the ritual sex, known as *maithuna,* and focuses more on the art of transformation than the act of sex. Maithuna is about attaining higher pleasure: while the body experiences physical pleasure, the actual goal is to experience a transcendental bliss through the pleasure. True Tantrikas do not experience the physical pleasure of sex as man and woman, but as aspects of higher divinities — as gods (Shiva) and goddesses (Devis). Often, a man may have ritual sex with many women in one night of

Jewel in the Lotus

Mantras are often chanted or spoken during Tantric sex to echo the divine fundamental energy vibration of the universe and to awaken sexual energy in the body. The most famous and most common mantra in Tantric sex is "Om mani padme hum." *Mani* means jewel or thunderbolt (male penis), *padme* means in the lotus (vulva and vagina) and *hum* equates to the highest form of enlightenment. The mantra sums up Tantric sex as a way to bliss and transformation.

maithuna. In ancient times, some Tantricking men might have had maithuna with over 100 women in one night, although it is important to note that this didn't always include intercourse: he might have only touched some women. Other Tantrikas sometimes smoke ganga (cannabis) prior to maithuna, but this is only to glimpse potential transcendental ecstasy, not for the pleasure of a smoke.

Maithuna may sound like a gorging orgy: a feast, some wine, some smoke, and sex with lots of people, but again, the true emphasis is not on the sexual pleasure, but on the connection and transformation achieved through performing specific ritual acts. Often Tantrikas who perform maithuna are coached by a guru, even during the act of intercourse. The guru directs the Tantrikas through recommended subtle positions, meditations and visualisations to help the couple transfer their sexual energies between them. Men are trained not to ejaculate, and women are encouraged to orgasm, sometimes in multiplicity. Ritual sex is not about wild, frantic thrusting, in fact, couples are encouraged to move only a little; the goal is the exchange and experience of transcendental energy and enlightenment, not copulation.

Cunnilingus was encouraged between men and women to enhance a man's yin energy, and also between women to balance yin energy. Fellatio was seen as beneficial only if the man did not ejaculate. It was believed the penis could absorb some female saliva during fellatio.

Afterwards, the vaginal lubrication, known as *rajas,* is collected from the woman's genitals with a leaf, mixed in with a bowl of water and presented to the gods as an offering. Once this ceremony is complete, the man then drinks the bowl of water, completing the circle of coupled energy transformation.

Paying homage to the hard-on

The center of many Hindu ceremonies is the offering of food, gifts, ornaments, flowers, coins and the like, to the gods. In Tantra, this principle is also important, but it is the body that is worshipped. The body, in Tantra, is regarded as the icon of cosmic sexuality, and in ancient practices the most common form of worship was of the penis. Honoring the penis was most commonly performed by anointing and rubbing it with either scented oil or butter. Worship of the divinity in the body was also done through intercourse: some Tantric sex was performed as an act of body worship, in which the erect penis was honored at the altar of the vagina, and the ejaculate served as the sacrificial oil.

Kundalini

In Tantra, one's kundalini, or sexual energy, is believed to stay dormant at the base of the spine, like a coiled serpent, until it is awakened. From there, it spreads up through the spine to the top of the head, through the body's chakras (energy centers). Meditation, touch and visualization are all used to awaken and stimulate the flow of kundalini.

An example of Tantric lovemaking to kindle kundalini might start with creating a sacred space for sex by lighting candles, strewing the bed and floor with petals, lighting incense and playing music. A couple might take a bath together, or take turns bathing each other, shampooing their hair, giving a scalp massage, then rubbing each other with scented oil. This would be followed by some meditation, alternate nostril breathing, placing your hand over the heart of your partner, sitting still, and doing Tantric yantras (visualizations). Chanting or humming some mantras might take place while each partner visualizes himself/herself as the divine god/goddess. The woman then usually starts by lying down to the right of the man, and he initiates sex by kissing, licking and stroking her whole body, working from her toes to her head (in the direction kundalini flows). The woman then responds by doing the same to the man. She then places herself on the left side of the man for intercourse, and the couple might move into various positions and continue making love for hours, until experiencing a body, mind and soul orgasm, and transcendental bliss.

Taoism

In the sixth century BC, Lao Tzu collected the principles of Taoism, which had been flourishing in the form of folk wisdom, and put them down in the *Tao Te Ching*. The "Tao," or the way, is the ultimate reality and is expressed through energy which is constantly in flux, in which opposites balance and merge in harmony. In all things there is the yin (female) and the yang (male) and the flow of energy between them is known as ch'i. Ch'i is the same life-force

Taoist master Wu-hsien described a woman's saliva as her "jade spring" and believed it was highly beneficial to men who drank it. Adhering to his promotion of "Libation of the Three Peaks" (drinking a woman's saliva, vaginal secretions and breast milk), it is said minister Chang Ts'ang, who lived in the time of 200 BC, died at over 180 years old. Oral sex was very Tao.

energy that flows in the human body. The philosophy of Taoism teaches people to live within the flux of changing energy: to cultivate harmony, moderation and flexibility.

The Tao of sex

The sexual theories of Taoism (the Tao of sex) formally became a part of Taoism in the fifth century AD, when Taoism became an official religion. The sexual theories of Taoism date back to the very earliest Chinese occult sects. Meditation was the foremost means to get close to the Tao, and sexual exercises were the second. Taoists believe that a man's yang force is like fire: it burns brightly, but quickly burns out. A woman's yin energy is like the sea: it is slow to move, but vast. The Taoist sex manuals recommended that to attain balance, a man must absorb the yin energy of his partner by stimulating her vaginal secretions and bringing her to orgasm, without releasing any of his yang through ejaculation. Ejaculation was permitted only when necessary and a number of ancient and modern Taoist sex guides recommend ways of learning how not to release the valuable yang energy.

One method for coitus interruptus, or not coming, suggested gnashing one's teeth, and pressing firmly down on the perineum behind the scrotum, while breathing deeply. With practice, the control over ejaculation could be learned by men, and they would be able to make love numerous times and with numerous women, increasing their yin energy.

To the Taoists good sex was a tonic. It was a form of medicine recommended to cure diseases of both the body and the spirit, and was believed possibly to make one immortal.

Master of the way of sex

A master of the Tao of sex was Tung-hsuan. A physician in seventh century AD, he believed that sexual intercourse had to establish even rhythms just as the seasons and heaven and earth had their own natural rhythms. In his book, *Tung-hsuan-tzu*, he describes a variety of thrusting techniques for men and suggests that they all be used. He categorized nine different types of thrusting, recommending that a man thrust nine times into a woman one way, then nine times the second way, etc., until he had experienced all nine styles, and achieved eighty-one thrusts. Based in numerology, nine is a powerful number, and eighty-one represents the ultimate yang. There were many prescriptions of varying numbered thrusts and styles of intercourse to cure many ills. Maybe next time you say, "Sorry, honey, I have a headache," the solution might not be in popping a pill, but in pumping away eighty-one times.

Tibetan Mysticism

Tibetan Buddhism regards Buddha as possessing both male and female elements. This is often depicted in pictures of Bodhisattvas, beings who have attained enlightenment, but choose to remain in the earth-world as teachers, protectors and saviors. Often the Bodhisattvas are male, and shown in art with female consorts, very often in the act of intercourse. They are the representation of the union of male, female, enlightenment and earth. The female consort represents power and wisdom, while the male represents enlightenment. The female consorts of the Bodhisattvas are the highest form of the *dakini*. A dakini is a powerful female, either human or demonic, who has the ability and knowledge to initiate a man into the secrets of Tantric magic. Men would go to nearly any length to obtain these sexual and philosophical secrets, including rape. The transfer of this knowledge was always through intercourse, either real or symbolic, depending on whether the dakini was human or spiritual.

Today, in some Buddhist sects in Tibet and Nepal, to ritually obtain esoteric or Tantric knowledge, a statue of a dakini is placed in the lap of a man, as a symbolic gesture of intercourse.

Wicked Sex

Witchcraft began to rise in popularity at the end of the seventeenth century, and some estimates claim there are many hundreds of thousands of active witches in the world today. The occult has a number of divergent groups, from small, self-formed groups to the widely recognized Wiccan religion. The guiding principle of most occult groups is taken from an ancient Latin translation of the *Emerald Tablet of Hermes Trismegistus*, which states, "That which is above is like that which is below and that which is below is like that which is above, to achieve the wonders of one thing." The essential meaning behind this, and the occult, is that the earth, heaven, nature and humanity are linked and on a continuum. Human wishes, desires, emotions and drives can influence and be used to change the universe. The more intense the drive or desire, the more powerful the result. It is believed the sexual drive is one of our more potent drives, and can be used in rituals to influence or bring about change in people, in nature and in specific situations. Some spells are not just about adding wart of toad and eye of newt to the cauldron. Some involve far more sexual aspects in their spell rituals.

There have been many influences on the occult, from older religions such as Cabbalism and Gnosticism, Tantra and Taoism, as well as key influential founders of sects, such as Aleister Crowley, a sexual extrovert who was known as "the wickedest man in the world." Aleister Crowley called himself the "Great Beast" and had an insatiable sexual appetite. He was a magician who lived between 1875 and 1947 and became involved in sex magic and the occult. Crowley invented a number of potions and rituals. One of his most famous inventions was a ritual called the *Liber Samekh,* in which the person recites the names of supernatural beings while masturbating to climax. The purpose of this ritual was metaphoric intercourse with the demons, as a way of releasing the demons and angels that lie in the individual unconscious, projecting them into the universe, and transforming this resulting force from divine creativity to personal power. The end result of this ritual is for every spirit and spell to become obedient to the person's desires. Humanity and nature influence each other, using the power of sexual drive.

Crowley was also commissioned by Gerald Gardner, author of *Witchcraft Today*, to invent some witch-cult rituals for use in their occult practice. There were a number of rituals which incorporated nudity, sexual intercourse, masturbation and flagellation. Soon after, though, splinter sects formed and many current witchcraft rituals have done away with the sexuality component.

These days, practical magic has little to do with sexual rituals. But the belief that sexual drives, creative forces and our emotional and physical human sexuality are fundamental forces reflected in the universe remains a core tenet of the occult.

Many witches earn a part-time living recommending spells and reading the tarot for others. In one survey, the topic of love was the number one request for spells, and most frequently asked question to the tarot cards.

Erotica Worship
Ancient sex manuals

Turning to books to turn up the heat in one's sex life is an old, tried-and-true custom. For thousands of years manuals on the art of making love have been popular. The most famous sex manual is the Kamasutra. Sutras were texts designed to state complex ideas in the briefest, most succinct way. All sutra texts are meant to be read alongside an adjoining commentary. The most popular commentary to the Kamasutra is the Jayamangala, which elaborates on the positions and techniques in greater detail, so that readers may understand the complex nature of each sexual technique. While most modern readers flick through the Kamasutra for the pictures, the most valuable information is in the commentary.

Kama is the term used by Hindus to refer to any form of pleasure that can be attained through the senses (not just sex). Kama, along with other objectives, such as duty and responsibility, are aims of Hindus for living a good life. The Kamasutra (text guide to achieving kama) is no simple, basic sex manual. It was written in India between the third and fifth centuries and comprises seven books in total. Only the second book in the Kamasutra is devoted to sex and physical love. The other six books cover topics ranging from courtship and marriage to philosophies of love and life, even to techniques on carrying out a successful affair and methods for breaking into a harem.

The author of the world's most famous sex book, *Vatsyayana*, was a sage who was a lifelong celibate. (If you don't do it, at least write about it.) His specific writing about sex was a phenomenal study into the intricate details of sexuality; he chronicled thousands of positions and techniques, and classified and coded as many sexual techniques and physical attributes as there are known to humans. For example, he classified nine different ways of moving the penis inside the vagina, and eight stages of oral sex. He also contradicted the prevailing wisdom by stating women did indeed experience orgasm (some people at the time thought there was no such thing), and recommended that a man ensure his lovers came and were satisfied before satisfying himself.

As the Kamasutra became popular, other medieval sex books began to flourish. One of the more popular ones, the *Secret Doctrine of Love's Delight*, or *Koka Shastra* as it came to be known, borrowed heavily from the Kamasutra, but used far more flowery and descriptive language, providing more information without needing an accompanying commentary. As times became more conservative, practical guides for young lovers, as was the Kamasutra, started to become replaced by marriage guides. These sex manuals focused more on learning to please one partner over a lifetime, rather than general bonking. Boredom prevention became a focus in these marriage–sex manuals. In the fifteenth century, the most famous of these was released, and is known as the *Ananga Ranga*. The author, Kalyana Malla, believed adultery was caused by boredom and the desire for varied pleasures, so he wrote the first definitive guide on spicing up your sex life with your spouse, to ensure neither partner would be tempted into extra-marital naughtiness. Unlike the Kamasutra which is straight sex information, the *Ananga Ranga* peppers its sex information with some psychology, astrology and palmistry.

For lovers around the world, both the Kamasutra and *Ananga Ranga* continue to be hot-selling sex manuals today.

Holy Willy

The god Shiva is often worshipped by honoring the Shiva-linga: the representation of the phallus of Shiva. There are two contrasting accounts of how the phallus came to be the primarily honored part of Shiva. One story tells of Shiva wandering around as an ascetic, dancing naked with an erection, when the wives of some sages became entranced and fell in love with him. Their husbands became jealous and placed a curse on Shiva to make his penis fall off. But Shiva's great penis immediately became a powerful fire that no one could put out, and Shiva only put it out when the sages promised to worship it.

The second story tells of a time when Shiva was making love with his consort, Parvati. While they were having sex, some gods

Love Temples

In ancient India, temples often featured sexual imagery in the form of erotic sculptures. The most explicit sexual images decorated the exterior of the temples. These images showed couples in the throes of ecstatic intercourse, and in varying positions — a sculptural Kamasutra of sorts.

The most abstract and sacred of sexual sculptures, called yonis and lingas, were reserved for inside Love temples, and they represented and honored images of the vaginas and phalluses of gods and goddesses.

came to visit. When they refused to stop making love because visitors had arrived, the gods became incensed and cursed them. They died intertwined and Shiva announced that his new shape was the linga (phallus) and Parvati's was the yoni (vagina). They are often worshipped together in the shape of a yoni-linga. Together, forever.

Making Love

Whether couples are into experimenting with Tantric principles, love spells and potions concocted by witches, honoring themselves and their love through honoring a yoni-linga, or reading the Kamasutra, the desire to merge sex with love is as strong as it ever was. Couples may want information on how to do it better, but fundamentally, the desire for sex is the desire for connection. Having sex can be a physical fuck, it can be fun, wet, wild and horny. Making love is on a different plane altogether. Making love is an emotional journey, a soul connection, a shared, passionate experience that binds two people. Couples who make love aren't looking for a bonk to get their rocks off; they experience sex as an external, physical expression of their deepest, innermost feelings for each other.

What's the difference between having sex and making love?

🗣 *"Having sex is about me and my body, my pleasure. Making love is about sharing my soul with a partner."* — Chris, 25

🗣 *"When I have sex, I just like to fuck. When I'm making love, I'm not only inviting someone into my body, but into my heart."* — Marie, 29

🗣 *"When my wife and I have sex, we have a lot of fun, and we love to experiment. When we take time for each other and make love, it's like we connect, open ourselves to each other, lock gazes and don't let go."* — Matthew, 29

🗣 *"Making love isn't even about sex. It's totally different. Yes, it's two bodies joining together in pleasure, but the pleasure is given through lips and eyes, and feelings and words, not through a penis and a clitoris."* — Anna, 27

🗣 *"There aren't words to describe making love. That's why it's called that. How do you describe love? How do you describe making love? It's personal, it's what you feel, how you share and give, that's what makes it so amazing and special. Each person makes love their own unique way, and if someone makes love with me, I treasure it."* — John, 30

Been There, *Not* Doing That

[not having sex, new-found
celibacy and wearing
the chastity belt]

When faced with the question, "To bonk or not to bonk?," there
are some who go the latter route and choose Not To Bonk.

Not having sex doesn't mean denying your sexuality, which
also incorporates who you are, your desires and your values.
Sexuality is an integral part of us, and we are sexual beings from
the cradle to the grave, whether we're actively engaging in
pashing, petting, canoodling, diddling or shagging ... or not.
When we choose to bonk, and whether we choose to bonk, is
private and sacred.

Not Having Sex

In our ever-modernizing and ultra-sexual world, virgins seem to
be anomalies, and adult virgins are thought to be at least a little
odd or throwbacks to eras gone by. This is how it seems because
our culture is bombarded with titillating sexual images and
messages screaming "Everyone Is Doing It, So You Should Too."

But in reality, there are millions of virgins in the world, and millions of adults who continue to choose Not To Bonk.

The reasons not to have sex are many. Mainly those who choose not to have sex do so out of a desire to stay true to their personal values. The value to not have sex may stem from religious beliefs, romantic beliefs, or a promise made, to family, a future partner, or one's self. There are "promise" campaigns, such as "True Love Waits," which mainly focus on teens, but are also keen to have adults join their sexual-purity legions. Each person pledges to stay a virgin until marriage and that sex shall wait for true love. This is not everyone's cup of tea, but for people who want to spend their lives making love, rather than fucking frequently and casually, it can be an appealing option.

Temptation Island

No man is an island, and those who choose to remain sexually abstinent live in a sexually provocative world, filled with daily temptations. It's not easy to play the gatekeeper role, to constantly say no to sex. Virgins vigilantly fight temptation; it's not as if the decision to abstain from sex automatically shuts the sexual response system down. Virgins still get very horny!

Not all virgins abstain from all sexual behavior. There are still a number of ways to get your rocks off without technically popping the cherry . . .

Outercourse If intercourse is out of the question, outercourse might be an outlet for your sexual desires or frustrations. Depending on how far you're willing to compromise on total abstinence, outercourse includes a range of sexual behaviors without actually doing "it." Kissing is usually a fave among virgins, teens and adults alike. Kissing ignites the sexual response, whether you want to go there or not, and the resulting sexual feelings you have can be very pleasurable — some proponents of complete abstinence would argue that even kissing is too pleasurable, too tempting.

Before giving the whole kissing and physical pleasure thing a miss, though, be aware that there are side detours on the pleasure path that you can take, detour paths that lead to different pleasures and connections other than intercourse. To some, anything other than holding hands is either risky, or too much of a compromise. Others aren't so conservative and engage in some sexual behaviors, both to express their feelings and to connect with their partner in some sexual way, without having intercourse, which is often viewed as the culminating step to be undertaken only with a lifelong mate, or deep love.

Some of the sexual expressions that can be pleasurable in outercourse include kissing, necking, body massages, hand jobs, mutual masturbation, oral sex and dry humping, though this can be a little painful for both men and women if it goes on for hours and if orgasm is not experienced.

"Are there still virgins? One is tempted to answer no. There are only girls who have not yet crossed the line, because they want to preserve their market value ... call them virgins if you wish, these travellers in transit."
— Françoise Giroux

Thigh-high humping For the more risqué, those who are teetering on the verge of virginity, dry humping can be taken a step further, and done naked. Sometimes called mock-fucking, thigh humping is done exactly how it sounds. It's screwing naked, but with penis in between thighs, rather than penis in vagina. It's most effectively done in the side-to-side position, as this allows the man better maneuverability. It's also wise to either wet the penis with saliva or lube, and/or lube the inner thighs of the woman for better friction and sensation. In the side-to-side position, the woman's clitoris is well exposed to touch, so she can come as well as him. While thigh humping can feel like risk-free sex, be careful not to let the man ejaculate too close to her vaginal entrance, to avoid any chance of pregnancy or STI transmission. For those couples who are abstaining only from penis-in-vagina sex, this can be a connecting, bonding way to make love together.

Milking the jugs This sexual act is similar to thigh humping, except instead of placing the penis between the thighs to fuck, the penis is placed between the breasts. Unless the woman masturbates herself while doing this, titty fucking is mainly a way for guys to get off. It's often not very intimate because the man is raised up above the woman, making face-to-face contact difficult. Titty fucking, or breast bonking, can be done in a variety of positions, and a little experimentation can tell you which position is most comfortable for you. It can be done side to side, man on top, or even woman on top, although this is usually less successful. Lube the cleavage and penis well so there is no chafing and to increase sensation. Women with breasts of any size can titty fuck with their man; it's not just for girls with big bazooms. In fact, because breasts are so fleshy, most men like to have the woman use her hands to press her boobs together for a tighter sensation. When the man comes, the woman will be presented with a pearl necklace (when a man ejaculates on a woman's neck). Many couples like to watch; they find it erotic to look down at his penis sliding in and out of her sexy cleavage. Women can also partially close one fist over the top of the cleavage, to provide further sensation for the glans of the penis, every time it slides through the top and into her hand. Men appreciate this extra bonus to titty fucking.

You are the master

If any sexual expression is a compromise of your sexual values, but you still want to experience sexual pleasure and get to know your body and sexual response, masturbation may be something you can consider. There is little research on the masturbation habits of virgins, but informal inquiries reveal that girl teens who are virgins are less likely to masturbate than boys. Often teen boys who do not engage in sex do still regularly masturbate. The opposite seems to be true for celibate adults. In terms of adults who abstain from sex, it is the women who masturbate more often than men. This may be because adult men who choose not to have sex are swimming against the tide of their peers, fighting the machismo pressure to act like a man by humping everything in sight, so they are unwilling to spark any kind of sexual temptation, even on their own. Women's sexuality is often kept more private, and the adult pressure to have sex is more subtle. As a result, adult women may feel more comfortable releasing their sexual energy through masturbation, without fear that it may send them over the horny edge and hurtling fast-forward into the need to go out and do it with someone.

Our sexual response is not like a bike that gets rusty in the driveway, or a battery that dies because you haven't used it. Your sexual body hums away, whether you use it or not. Whether or not you're abstinent, men experience erections, women get clitoral erections, and both can experience spontaneous nocturnal orgasms. The body sings its own sexual tune, even if you don't turn it on. So, it's perfectly fine to let it sit in neutral until you're ready to roar.

Benefits of "doing a Britney"

There are health, social and personal advantages to "doing a Britney," rather than doing "it." Singer Britney Spears inspired thousands of girls to stay virgins, simply by admitting she was one. Such is the power of role models. But sticking to the decision to abstain from intercourse in the face of temptation takes more motivation than listening to the words of a role model, especially when said virgin role model releases a single called "I'm Not So Innocent." Many women and men, young and old, find there are benefits to abstinence that make the commitment to say No a lot easier. Some of the benefits of being abstinent from sex include:

* Next to no risk of HIV or STI transmission, or pregnancy.
* Economics: it's cheaper not having to pay for condoms and birth control.
* You know your partner is into you, rather than getting into your pants.
* No guilt over regretted root'n'scoots.
* Can make you more focused because you're not being distracted by sex all the time.
* You don't lie to your parents about whether you've done it.
* You can't "all the way" cheat on your partner, because you don't go "all the way."

Vestal Virgins

Vesta was the Roman goddess of the hearth and was attended to by six virgins because she was so virtuous and sacred. Vesta's representation was a flame, and her sacred fire was tended by her virgin priestess attendants, called the Vestal Virgins. The Vestal Virgins worshipped and took care of this sacred fire to ensure Vesta's health and care of Rome. In 216 BC, when Rome experienced military defeat, it was not the army that was blamed, but two of the Vestal Virgins.

Vestal Virgins were chosen to attend to the fire of Vesta between the ages of six and ten, and their vows committed them to thirty years of service to Vesta and to virginity. Vestal Virgins who broke this commitment were buried alive.

Source: *Sex and Spirit: Ecstasy, Ritual and Taboo*

* Pride in discipline, and in keeping a promise.
* Increased self-esteem and self-empowerment.
* The time you might spend chasing sex and having sex is time you can spend on other things.
* You really get to know each other by talking together. Instead of diddling and making out, you have more deep and meaningfuls into the night.
* Alternative health practitioners say you conserve vital body energy by abstaining from orgasm.
* You stand out from the crowd as a person who caters to no one and no temptation.
* You get to know yourself and what you want, before sharing yourself completely with another.
* You are admired, and deserve to be, for the strength of your convictions.
* You develop killer kissing skills.

Confession of a 24-year-old virgin

"Since as far back as I can remember, I've always wanted to have sex for the first time with someone special. I want to be in love and be loved when I first experience sex. It's not like I ever planned to remain a virgin until twenty-four. I never thought in terms of numbers or age. And it's not that I haven't come close, either. I nearly did it when I was seventeen, but backed off at the last minute. It felt like I would just be doing it to do it, to fit in, and I realized that I really didn't want to have sex for the sake of my friends. I want to do it for me. I smoke, drink and swear. I dress sexy, for me, and I don't go to church or listen to Christian rock. Not that I think I have to prove myself as cool, because I think virginity isn't cool. I don't think of virginity as either cool or not cool; it's not a public thing, it's totally private and has nothing to do with 'coolness.' I see it as a positive, not a negative. I get so many people assuming I must be some conservative prude, just because I haven't had sex. There are a few reasons I haven't had sex. First, I'm not ready to have kids, and pregnancy can happen even with the best birth-control methods. But that's not even the real reason, that's only the quick answer. I think sex is a beautiful thing, one of the most beautiful things that two people can share. And the way we are made, our bodies, for man and woman to fit together so perfectly, literally designed to be fused together in pleasure, I feel that it's a special enough thing to reserve for only the most special person, closest to me. And bottom line, I'm twenty-four, and I haven't found him yet. I've got lots of girlfriends who are my age and older, and they're not married either. They have sex, but they're not satisfied by it, because they, too, are looking for a soul mate who will fulfill them, please them, share with

them. I'm looking for the same as them, but just not compromising on my sexual values in the meantime. And I think everyone should know that virgins feel just as many sexual impulses, and get as hot and turned on as non-virgins. And I'm not a 'Just Say No' girl. I've done a lot of sexual things, because I don't think it's wrong to act on your sexual feelings. If some people think because I've given hand jobs, let a guy bring me to orgasm, and so forth, that, well, I'm not a virgin, then they can think what they like. It's not that I want to stay 'pure' or whatever that's all about. I don't abstain from intercourse out of some chaste connotation, or whatever. I simply reserve a special place in my heart for that ultimate sexual sharing, and I want to be in love when I do it. Not only the first time, either. I want to feel love every time I have sex in my life. I don't want to spend my time with my partner fucking meaninglessly. I want to make love. And so I'm still a virgin at twenty-four. Is that really so hard to imagine? It seems perfectly normal to me."
— Tiffany, 24

The Romans and Greeks had two definitions of virginity: virgo intacta *referred to an "untouched" virgin who had never had sex;* virgo *referred to an unmarried, independent woman. Historians believe this confusion may explain many ancient accounts of "virgin births."*

New-Found Celibacy

Born-again virgins are people who have rediscovered sexual abstinence, even though they've already previously sacrificed

Enlightened Choice

Ancient ascetics in religions such as Hinduism, Jainism and Christianity used to deny themselves pleasure in programs of self-discipline and self-denial, designed to achieve higher spiritual goals. Sacrifices included celibacy, fasting, seclusion and poverty. In many countries and spiritual cultural groups around the world, followers still practice these self-denials in the name of enlightenment.

their virginity. People who choose to be abstinent after already experiencing sex, who enjoy a so-called "secondary virginity," do so for a variety of reasons. Sometimes it's a cultural reason: someone might convert to a religion or lifestyle that preaches sexual abstinence, and some of these include established and alternative spiritual groups. Contrary to popular perceptions, not every new-fangled religious cult preaches free love; some preach discipline through celibacy, and often recommend periods of abstinence, a voluntary sacrifice of sex, to attain spiritual and personal learning.

"I took up yoga about ten years ago, and about five years ago, I trained to become a yoga teacher. I also studied some alternative health, and gradually, it wasn't planned or anything, I simply stopped having sex. It seemed natural to me, not to do it, and I always try to listen to my body and mind. My mind rebels sometimes, and I get tempted, but for the most part, celibacy is a natural lifestyle for me. I don't know that I'll always be celibate, but it's been terrific for my spiritual being, my health and clarity of

mind. I think it makes me a better yoga teacher, because I practice the type of discipline I teach." — Melinda, 32

Reluctant celibates

Not everyone who has new-found celibacy found it by choice. There are more reluctant celibates out there than care to be named. Roam through any bar in any city and you'll find men and women who haven't been getting any, and it hasn't been for lack of wanting. There are thousands of men and women, in every town, county, state, and capital city, who are single, looking and not scoring. These unsuccessful hunters and gatherers are reluctant celibates and will continue to prowl until they finally pull.

In the Trobriand Islands, a person can "reclaim" their virginity after a period of mourning for a previous partner. After the appropriate length of time the person is considered a virgin again.

People often joke about sexual frustration. It's funny to say "I'm sexually frustrated" if you haven't had sex in two weeks and you're horny. It usually gets you a laugh, some anxiety is released and, in the right audience, maybe even a sympathy fuck. But admitting you're sexually frustrated after being reluctantly celibate for a year or two is one of the last remaining sexual taboos in our society. Just like many people don't feel comfortable dining out alone, people also don't like to admit that they haven't been able to get laid and it's making them sexually frustrated. Chosen celibacy is one lifestyle, but being celibate for months and years on end, when it's not your chosen lifestyle, can feel like a solitary confinement sentence and it can sometimes wear down a person's spirit, self-confidence and joie de vivre.

Urban Myth

Chewing mindlessly or distractedly on ice cubes, cracking your knuckles or chewing your lip means you are sexually frustrated. The only sure-fire way to tell if a person is sexually frustrated is if they scream out, "Fucking hell, I'm so sexually frustrated, I'd bonk the next bloke to come through that door!" Then, and only then, if they start chewing on an ice cube, should you assume it means sexual frustration.

It is difficult to survey the invisible population of sexually frustrated men and women, primarily because of the shyness and embarrassment that accompanies it. People do not like to admit that they haven't been able, for whatever reason, to fulfil one of our most basic needs. Health professionals and MDs can "prescribe" masturbation for sexual frustration release, but the kind of sexual frustration that builds up over years, when a person desires the touch and experience of bonking with another, cannot be replaced or released by hand diddling alone. Self-love does not replace the good lovin' with another lovee.

Reluctant celibacy can occur through geographic isolation, being busy, or not having "stereotypical" attractive qualities, but it mainly occurs from plain not being able to find a mate. In order to mate, we have to find a mate, and there are thousands (tens of thousands? hundreds of thousands?) of men and women who live with their sexual frustration every day. This can lead to depression, anxiety, low self-esteem and anti-social behaviors, which only compound the problem. Sexual frustration is a legitimate and serious problem facing many people. Unable to express them, our sexual urges twist quickly into frustration, and in many cases it goes on longer than we feel we can cope with: that's no laughing matter.

Other reluctant celibates include couples who have been too busy to do it; partners of people who are dealing with a sexual dysfunction and cannot have sex; people in ill health who find it difficult to have sex; people who find sex painful, so don't do it but would like to if it weren't for the pain; couples separated by geography; and people who are too guilty over the death of or break-up with a spouse to face doing it with anyone else, even though they still feel sexual urges.

> *"I haven't had sex in two years. I'm a virile woman, but just can't seem to get lucky. I think my sexual motor must have shut off completely by now."*
> — Bette, 28

> *"My partner moved to Kenya six months ago, and we've stayed faithful to each other. It's not the easiest thing,*

The Case Against

Not all religions champion sexual abstinence, even though we equate sexual chastity with conservative religiosity. Throughout the ages, there have been religions that have been suspicious of abstinence and even preached against it.

The Jews and Muslims are primary frowners on sexual abstinence. They oppose celibacy because they believe strongly that couples should unite and multiply. Sex is for both procreation and pleasure.

In some branches of Judaism, sex is considered a blessing, and a duty, to be carried out on the eve of every Sabbath.

In the ancient Jewish text, the Talmud, there is a sex-positive teaching that specifies that every man can have four wives and each wife should sleep with her husband at least once a month.

being celibate, but I prefer that to cheating on her, or breaking up with her. She'll be back in three more months and I'll be busting by then, and it's corny, I know, but she's worth it to me." — Todd, 29

"It's been two months since I've had sex and that's the longest I've ever gone since I first started doing it. How do people go without it for longer than this? I'm going out of my brain." — Jeff, 23

PS: Jeff went another three months before finally getting laid.

The Chastity Belt

The chastity belt is a device of old which was originally designed for girls and boys to prevent masturbation, rather than

Chastity Guarders

In centuries past, families who did not force their daughters to wear chastity belts opted instead for "chastity guarders," who were nurses or governesses. These women held the responsibility of guarding the young girls 24/7, to protect them from any sexual advances or dalliances. An example of this is found in Shakespeare's play, Romeo and Juliet. In this play, however, the governess neglected, or failed in, her duty, since Juliet and Romeo managed to bonk secretly. Historians believe this was probably quite common so it seems teen girls have been rebelling and sneaking out to have sex for centuries.

intercourse. The medieval version of the female chastity belt consisted of a thick metal hoop which slung from the back, through the crotch, to the front, where a lock kept it securely in place. Holes were placed in the hoop to enable urination, defecation and cleaning, especially during menstruation. This hoop did not cover the entire width of the vulva area, but did prevent diddling and doing it. The boys had a sheath which covered the penis and balls.

Lock me up and throw away the key

Chastity belts have not disappeared with time. Both women and men still wear them to prevent intercourse, but they are worn as an object of sexual thrill and arousal, and are mainly popular among serious players in the B&D community.

Chastity corsets were similar devices to the chastity belt, and were believed to have been worn in the past by women in the Cheyenne Indian tribe in North America.

Girl girdles Modern female chastity belts come in a range of styles. There is everything from lockable leather underwear, to large, ornate stainless-steel locking contraptions. Most commonly, female chastity belts are like metal G-strings. The string part is leather or a chain (depending on the level of security you're after — you can, after all, knife through leather to get it off), and the belt part is, again, leather, chain or stainless steel. The front of the belt is a shield-type fitting, and can either be chain or stainless steel with holes. Once again, it depends on the level of security you want and the level of access you desire for cleaning. In every belt, there are always holes provided for cleaning and elimination of waste.

The chastity belt is thought to have been invented in Italy in the fourteenth century.

An accessory to some belts is the "thigh lock," which comprises two garter-belt-type hoops which wrap around each thigh, attach to the belt with locks, and to each other, to prevent a woman from spreading her legs further than a couple of centimeters.

Boy belts Modern male chastity belts are similar to G-strings in shape, and are also made of varying combinations of steel, chain and leather. Rather than the shield fitting in the female version, the male chastity belt has a "cock cup." The cups can come in various sizes and most men opt for a size that prevents erection. Some even have cups designed with spikes on the inside, so any partial erection that might occur is quickly punished into submission. There are holes in the cock cup, as with the female shield, to allow for urination.

Comfort

Chastity belts are not comfort items. People who wear them today like to know and feel they are wearing them. The lock-and-key celibate bondage is the paradoxical erotic appeal. The softer, looser and less secure belts are more comfortable, but they still take getting used to. Mostly, chastity belts are worn for a short time: a night as a fantasy, or a week as a sexually exciting change of pace. There have been some credible stories of people who have worn them for a few months and technically, the higher quality ones could be worn for years, although any documentation of such long-term, continued use should be viewed with skepticism.

Hand maid

Most good chastity belts have to be made to your measurements.

If they are adjustable, they can be gotten out of, with a little creative thought. Top-end belts can be made by special designers to your exact specifications, and many B&D belt-wearers like to have their belts engraved with specific art and designs.

> *"Of all sexual aberrations, chastity is the strangest."*
> —Anatole France

The appeal of wearing a chastity belt lies mainly in the feeling of being denied or possessed. Control is relinquished to the holder of the key. Most submissives get locked into their belts, and then hand the key to their dominator. The belt-wearer gets sexually excited that they cannot have sex or masturbate until their partner gives them permission, or decides they are wanted for sex. Casual belt-wearers, though, often keep their own key, go out for the night in a belt for the titillation or shock value, then unlock it once they get home.

"I knew a girl who was really into piercing, and also got into the S&M world. She wanted to try a chastity belt, but she wanted one that used her piercings. She had multiple ring-piercings in her outer and inner lips. She got a guy to pierce some more rings through the lower end of her lips, near her vaginal entrance. Then with steel string, the rings were sewn together, criss-crossed, a bit like lacing up a shoe. She could still wee, and during her period she could tug up on the laced rings to clean herself, but the rings were pulled so tight that she couldn't have sex because her hole was squeezed small from the tight sewing. She lasted a couple of weeks before getting the guy who sewed her up to split the strings open. She said it was

an alienating experience, where she felt like her genital region was somehow detached from the rest of her body, because it was 'locked' and she really couldn't use it. She said at first it was like 'out of use, out of mind,' but then like anything locked up, after awhile, she wanted to get at it, so that's why she opened herself back up. I knew her after this whole experience, so I don't know whether it's true or not, but knowing her, it probably is. I don't know anyone as adventurous as her. I hope she never does it again, though. It sounds awful compared to slinging on a regular chastity belt. And I'm not sure I think those are a good idea either." — Oliver, 27

Dirty Talk and Naughty Thoughts

passion-pleasing pillow talk and fuck-me fantasies

MOST COMMON DIRTY TALK: cock, big, pussy, cunt, God, yeah, baby, horny, suck, lick, do, don't stop, right there, wet, hard, harder, nasty, bitch, want, fuck, me, hot, you, incredible

Dirty Talk

Do people really do it? Say those nasty things out loud?

Absolutely.

Crossing the line of propriety is a sure-fire way to get horny as hell for many folks. Uttering the words that reflect our urges creates heightened arousal, both mentally and physically. Often talking dirty goes hand in hand with fantasy. Saying "fuck me, fuck me harder" can accompany a fantasy or desire for domination. Other dirty talk is designed to arouse, and often is erotic body-talk: "Bring your wet cunt over here, I want to fuck it

Pick-up Lines To Get It On
(Or Die Laughing Trying)

* Wanna play army? I'll lie down and you can blow the hell out of me.

* You've got 26 bones in your body. Want one more?

* Is that a ladder in your stocking, or the stairway to heaven?

* I'm fighting the urge to make you the happiest woman on earth tonight.

* I'd walk a million miles for one of your smiles, and even further for that thing you do with your tongue.

* If it's true we are what we eat, I could be you in the morning.

* You. Me. Whipped cream. Handcuffs. Any questions?

* (Look down at crotch.) Well, it's not going to suck itself.

* Nice outfit. It would look even better in a crumpled heap on my bedroom floor.

* Do you believe in love at first sight, or should I walk by again?

* Remember my name. You'll be screaming it later.

* Hi, I'm Mr. Right. Someone said you were looking for me.

good," or "I love your big hard cock" (use your imagination). Dirty talk can also be a means to communicate desires and timing in bed, and to raise arousal and anticipation for sex. Teasing, such as through oral or manual stimulation, bringing a partner to the brink, and then asking, "Do you want it? Do you want me?"; or a woman pulling a man up towards her, with phrases like, "Fuck me now" or "I want you inside me," are all popular forms of dirty talk.

We cross lines in the bedroom that we'd never dare to outside a sexual context. A woman in the bedroom might find it horny for her man to shout, "Fuck you're nasty, bitch, yeah," but if he growled anything like that in, say, the kitchen, he'd probably receive a walloping, and no sex, that's for sure. Tone, intent and context are everything. That said, dirty talk can be very exciting when it's illicit, secretive and outside the bedroom. At a cocktail party, the movie theatre, the markets, if you're in the mood, you can lean over and whisper something dirty and hot. This can raise arousal in the body and surge the sex hormones, which makes the anticipation for sex very exciting. Be sure you whisper this dirty talk in the ear of your partner, though. As a pick-up method, it's not a successful one.

> *"I love the lines men use to get us into bed. 'Please, I'll only put it in for a minute.' What am I, a microwave?"*
> — Beverly Mickins

🗣 *"I like talking dirty as long as it isn't explicit. I like it to stay romantic and mysterious. I love sounds in bed, but not the really dirty words."* — Pat, 23

🗣 *"The dirtier the better. And the creative stuff, too. I get tremendously turned on by my partner talking really nasty. Sometimes I like him to just talk, without even touching me, and then talk and fuck. I love it."* — Natalie, 34

🗣 *"I like talking dirty, and it took me awhile to get my girlfriend to loosen up and try it. She likes it when I say dirty things, and with some coaching she's now got a fantastic foul mouth in bed."* — Mark, 28

Role-playing

Can't imagine yourself saying such nasty things out loud? If you are motivated to learn, all it takes is practice. The most common obstacle to talking dirty is feeling self-conscious. Practice in private, so the words start to feel familiar. Some therapists say to stand in front of a mirror and say the words to yourself, but for many this is too confronting, especially for the very self-conscious types (and often we can stand there, saying dirty words to our reflections, only to wind up feeling foolish, rather than frenzied with lust).

Instead, try imagining a fantasy character, an alter ego, who finds talking dirty hot. Imagine what kinds of things this alter ego might find horny; what kinds of words and phrases? Powerful? Submissive? Really rude, or romantically inclined? Fantasize about you becoming this person. You can then do one of two things. You can jump straight into a role-play in bed with your partner, where you learn to lose your self-consciousness because you are "acting." This enables you to shelve any guilt, shame or embarrassment because you are removing your identity (or part of it) from the role you are playing. You can eventually work yourself up to having a lot of fun with your character in role-played sex.

If you're not ready to jump into a role-play quite yet, and want some more practice, hop on the Net and give your vocabulary a test drive. There are tons of talking-dirty chat rooms, where you can sign on anonymously. You can gain a sense of empowerment to talk dirty as you use the words more frequently, and you'll probably learn a few more phrases to add to your bedroom antics. (See the chapter, Spidersex.)

Talk to the hand

Masturbation is a recommended "tool" to help you learn to talk dirty. As you masturbate, talk dirty to yourself. While it may sound silly, it works because you begin to condition a sexual response in your body to the stimuli of dirty words. As your next step, you can talk dirty while engaging in mutual masturbation with your partner and then work up to doing it while you're saying it.

Telephone titillation

Phone sex is probably the most common and most popular form of talking dirty. Millions of dollars are spent annually on phone sex from calls both to 900 numbers and private ones. The types of phone sex that people engage in vary, from downright dirty, to romantic "I want to kiss you all over" types of chat. Couples who are separated for lengths of time find that phone sex gives them a sexual release and a way of still feeling sexually connected.

Those who call phone sex lines do so for sexual release, and for dirty talk, especially if their partner doesn't like it, or isn't into it. Many phone sex workers do it for the job of it, not for the love of it.

"I work as a phone sex girl. It's not bad money, and it's easy work. Plus I have a few regulars who call, which is cool, because we talk longer and I make more money. I rarely masturbate when I work. I always tell them I am, but it's fantasy, not reality. I have to keep my mind on my work, though, so I don't watch TV or read a book. What I usually do is those brainless activities, like paint my nails, bleach my upper lip, shave my legs . . . that kind of thing. It's not sexy, but, hey, the guy on the other end of the line doesn't know the difference. Every once in awhile, really rarely, I'll get into what I'm telling him, and what he's saying back, and I might have a quick wank." — Sarah, 25

Ear Me Roar

The ears, including the outer lobes and inner canal, have many nerves and are a direct port to the nervous system. Scientists call the sexual response to tickling and licking the ear combined with heavy breathing into the ear the *auriculogenital reflex* and it can be such a major turn-on that some (mainly men) can come from it.

Burning desires

If your partner is going away, and you want to send them off with a way to get off, you can make them a dirty-talk audio tape, or record a naughty mini-disc. It's also a less confronting way to talk dirty to them, if you're still practicing. You can recite or read aloud a fantasy (there are lots of erotic books and mags available with hot stories) and then tell them what you're doing to yourself, what you're wearing, what you like to do to them ... If you have to be apart, you might as well keep them company in their imagination.

Your partner doesn't have to be going away for you to do this. You can slip a homemade horny CD or tape into their car when they're not looking, and make it a prelude to what's waiting for them when they get home that night from work. It's bound to challenge their concentration levels all day!

Wanting whispers

Studies show that sex talk, both dirty talk and romantic sweet nothings, elevates the excitement level in women because it triggers mental fantasies and the feeling of being desired, which make women horny and help them reach orgasm.

One study found that women who moan out loud during sex get as turned on by their own sex sounds as by what their partner whispers or groans. Dirty talk doesn't always have to have words, or even syllables.

In fact, often we whisper subtle messages to a partner to initiate sex. We initiate sex both verbally and non-verbally. Many people are too intimidated to talk about their relationship, sex life, and satisfaction, let alone moan out loud or utter some dirty words. But whether talking for titillation, or to tackle a serious sex issue, sexual communication is critical for the health of a relationship. Couples who talk together, in bed and out of bed, from dirty talk to serious talk, are more likely to be sexually and emotionally satisfied in their relationship.

The mmmms, groans, moans and vixen vocab, the screams of ecstasy, and even those slapping, sticking and fleshy sounds of skin on skin during sex — anything our ears can hear — is erotic auditory sensation which increases our sexual response. So next time you go to initiate sex with a non-verbal touch, add a little sound to heat that dirty flirty scene.

Silence is not always golden: of people who admitted to being too embarrassed or uncomfortable to talk about sex with their partner, 40 percent were unsatisfied with their sex lives.

Desperate times call for desperate measures

Growling dirty talk is fine for enhancing sex, but if the sex is beyond salvation, snarling nasties isn't going to help the situation. If you need to give a lover the boot, mean dirty talk (i.e. "Your fucking is horrible, fuck off.") is not the solution. The "You suck shit as a lover and I'm sorry but you have to go" form below is for those cowards who just aren't any good at talking to a lover about why they don't make the grade, and are desperate for said suck-shit lover to exit stage left, never to grace your bed again.

This strategy is never advised by qualified sex therapists, and is not the way to talk about sex effectively: nothing can

---

Dear _____ ,

I regret to inform you that your audition to be my steady lover has not been successful. As you are probably aware, the audition process was rigorous, and unfortunately, you do not possess the qualities or abilities to meet the needs or requirements to be kept on past this point. I will keep your number on file, should I desperately need someone, but I suggest you audition elsewhere. So that you may find better success in your future bedroom endeavors, please allow me to offer the following reason(s) you were disqualified from the running:

(Tick those that apply.)

1. Your first name is objectionable. It's just not something I can picture myself yelling out in a fit of passion.

2. Your pinch-and-wiggle technique with my clitoris reminds me of the way a grandma squeezes a child's cheek, and that's not a turn-on.

3. You kiss like you're trying to spring-clean my mouth on spin cycle. It's dizzying, and not in a good way.

4. Your comment about being turned on when the dog watches us makes me want to yell for help and run a mile the other way.

5. Comparing my arse to your favourite porn actress's was a critical tactical error.

6. Your inadvertent admissions that you need to buy Zovirax and know when National Herpes Week is, but failure to tell me your sexual history, indicate that you may be a health hazard, or you're not the most honest of lovers.

7. Your legs are skinnier than mine. If you can fit into my pants, then you can't get into my pants.

8. You're too short. Any son that we produced would inevitably be beaten up repeatedly at school.

---

replace open, honest sexual communication, but sometimes we're desperate, or in need of a laugh to vent sexual frustration.

(In case of emergency, break book and rip out page for use.)

9. You're too tall. I'm developing a chronic neck condition from trying to kiss you.
10. They say it's not the size of the wave, but the motion of the ocean, and while your wave is average, your ocean is flat.
11. Your habit of putting your anti-snore device over your nose immediately after coming, in preparation for immediate sleep, is seriously unattractive and offputting, not to mention rude.
12. The fact that your apartment has been condemned reveals an inherent slovenliness that I fear is unbreakable, and makes me nervous about what I may catch from your sheets.
13. The phrase "my mother" has popped up far too often in conversation.
14. You still live with your parents.
15. Although I do enjoy "The X-Files," I find your fantasies about "Star Trek" characters a little disconcerting.
16. Your frequent references to your ex-girlfriend's gratitude over your sexual prowess while you were in bed with me lead me to suspect that you are too insecure to know whether or not you are good in bed.
17. Showing me your ability to touch your nose with the tip of your tongue is not a trait that works for me in foreplay.
18. Your height is out of proportion to your weight. If you should, however, happen to gain the necessary 17 vertical inches, please resubmit your application.
19. Somehow I doubt those condoms I found in your overnight bag were really necessary for a successful business trip.
20. I am out of your league; set your sights lower next time.

Sincerely, _____

🗣 *"I had a boyfriend — key word, had — who told me about the third time we had sex that he liked to talk dirty during sex. I had never really talked dirty before. I had said things like 'please' and 'oh god' and maybe the occasional 'don't stop,' but I was not a talker in bed. I told him this and we compromised that he would talk, and I would only say something if I really wanted to. It turns out he was never really interested in hearing dirty words, just hearing himself. He had an obsession with the movie* Fight Club *and would say things throughout sex like, 'I am Jack's raging hard-on' and 'I am Jack's fucking hot lover,' and scream things like, 'I am Jack's pleasure!' and 'I am Jack's meat delivery, yeah baby.' Everything was 'I am Jack's. . .' like in the movie. And some of them I couldn't even make sense of. I was incredibly patient because in a lot of other ways he was a normal, sweet boyfriend. But the time he rolled off me and said, 'I am Jack's warm afterglow,' I knew he had to go."* — Jennifer, 28

D&M (DEEP AND MEANINGFUL):
refers to long talks of the heart and mind.
Can often occur during pillow talk.

Taboos

Post-coital pillow talk ranges from "That was nice honey, sleep tight" with a grateful peck on the lips before rolling over, to hours of D&Ms. There are, however, five critical post-sex afterglow talking no-nos.

1. **Criticism of your partner's body, even innocently.** "I never noticed that stretch mark before," "It's time you waxed your back," "Have you gained weight? You seem heavier to me," "I never realized your dick was so thin" . . . All obvious no-nos.

2. **The ex.** Never bring up your past lovers when you've just bonked yourself silly with your current lover. It's obviously not cool to praise a former lover's prowess when you're in bed with your new flavor of the month, but even the slightest reference, as innocent as it may seem, can trigger jealousy and drama.

3. **Work.** Listening to the tirade of complaints about your boss and your workload stress is something we do to be supportive in a relationship, but keep it out of the bedroom, and definitely out of the afterglow of sex. It ruins the post-bonk euphoria and invites the rat race onto your cloud nine. Whining is not a warmly received encore to a show of ecstasy.

4. **Post-mortem.** "That was incredible," "You are amazing," "I love you": all acceptable post-sex post-mortems. The nitty-gritty breakdown, dissecting the play by play, though, even if it is all positive, can lead your partner to suspect that you spent more time analyzing than enjoying.

5. **Relationship matters.** Just because you're both naked and have just shared some intimacy doesn't mean it's always the appropriate time to jump into a heavy, bare-all conversation about the state of your relationship. While one might think it's the perfect time to ask, "Where are we going?" or "What are we doing?," if it's a fishing expedition for specific answers, and those don't come, it's the fastest way to have a mighty big bedroom blue. Save that conversation for another time, maybe in bed on a no-sex night, or in another room of the house.

What's the best thing you've ever heard after sex?

🗣 *"My girlfriend said to me after we had sex the first time, 'Where do you hide your red cape? Because you're superman in bed.' It made me laugh, and it also made me feel good."* — Rod, 31

🗣 *"I had a lover tell me I was yummy. It was such an out-of-character thing for him to say and it made me smile."* — Naomi, 22

PC Vocab for the New Millennium

How to speak about women and be politically correct:

* She is not a screamer or a moaner; she is vocally appreciative.
* She is not easy; she is horizontally accessible.
* She has not been around; she is a previously enjoyed companion.
* She is not horny; she is sexually focused.
* She does not have breast implants; she is medically enhanced.
* She is not a slut; she is sexually extroverted.
* She is not a two-bit whore; she is a low-cost provider.

How to speak about men and be politically correct:

* He does not have a beer gut; he has developed a liquid grain storage facility.
* He is not balding; his head is a solar panel to power a sex machine.
* He is not a cradle snatcher; he prefers generationally differential relationships.
* He is not a male chauvinist pig; he has swine empathy.
* He is not afraid of commitment; he is monogamously challenged.

Source: common Internet email forward

☜ *"A girl I was with once laughed and said,
'I'm worried about how much practice you've had,
because you're really good. We should stick to using
condoms, because you've obviously been around,
and been trained well!' I didn't know whether to be
insulted or flattered."* — Sam, 27

☜ *"I had a holiday fling with a woman who
pronounced after sex that I was the Orgasm King
of the World. What an ego boost. We had a good
laugh about it."* — Jerry, 22

☜ *"I had a four-day affair with a guy I hardly knew,
but we really connected. After we had sex the second
time, he looked at me, told me I was beautiful, and
thanked me for sharing myself with him. It was a
completely unprompted remark and I was blown
away by it. I'll never forget it, or him."* — Gail, 29

Naughty Thoughts

The mind is the body's most fertile erogenous zone. Almost everyone has sexual fantasies — young and old, male and female, prudish and promiscuous. Sometimes sexual fantasies involve things that (in real life) may seem unusual, abnormal or even illegal. When fantasies are kept as that — fantasy, not reality, they are generally harmless and serve as a private outlet for some of our sexual energy. Sexual fantasies are healthy for our sexual expression because they stimulate our sexual desire.

The average number of minutes between the times a man's thoughts turn to sex: 8.

At a pub in Paddington, Sydney, the question came up: How often do you think about sex?

🗣 *"Maybe twice a day. Is that normal or am I undersexed?"* — James, banker

🗣 *"Every hour at least, if I'm with someone. Every couple of days if I'm single, busy, and not getting any."* — Nicole, PR consultant

🗣 *"All the time. Seriously. Sex is always on my mind."* — Warren, journalist

🗣 *"Every time I see a good-looking woman."* — Tom, bar attendant

🗣 *"I think about it a lot. At least five times a day."* — Peta, waitress

🗣 *"My work right now is so boring, I must fantasize about sex at least fifteen times a day."* — Rebecca, data analyst

🗣 *"That's not a fair question. My answer doesn't count."* — Gabrielle, sexologist

Themes

There are, of course, more fantasy topics and scenarios than can be named, because fantasy is such an individual expression, however, research has shown there are some common themes among fantasizing adults. The most popular themes for sexual fantasies include:

1. Sex with someone other than your partner.
2. Threesomes.
3. Sex with a celebrity.
4. Orgies.
5. Sex with someone of another sexual orientation.
6. S&M and B&D.
7. Anal sex.
8. Forced sex.
9. Voyeurism and exhibitionism.
10. Taboo sex (animals, children, family).

Doing it fantasy-style

Some couples who wish to connect in their fantasy life as well as their real life, or who want to get to know each other's desires better, can share a fantasy together. Couples can share their top six fantasies with each other and once a month, for a year, act one out. There may need to be negotiation as quite often one partner is not interested in some of the other's fantasies. For example, a popular male fantasy is having sex with two women. If she is not into that, you may have to draw some boundaries around what you will act out as a couple. Not all fantasies are designed or desired to be acted out, so your lists should only include the ones you really, really want to try.

Proportion of women who have fantasized about a co-worker:

70 percent.

Source: Dr. John Croucher, Macquarie University

If acting out a fantasy isn't your thing, and you like your personal fantasies to stay private, thank you very much, then

In one US study, 71 percent of men and 72 percent of women reported using fantasy during foreplay to heighten arousal.

alternatively you can venture into the land of fantasy together, instead of making them reality. You can either write or tell a fantasy story together. Going through the motions of talking through a "Once Upon a Time" fantasy can be a huge turn-on. If you want to really learn what turns each other on, start a paragraph together on a piece of paper, setting up the scene, and characters. For example, a man comes to a woman's house to deliver something or fix something (pick the beginning of any porn scene to get you going). Get to a point where they have exchanged one kiss, then agree to stop writing the fantasy together, and sit in bed together, each with your own piece of paper, and write out the rest of what might happen between the two characters. When you're done, read them to each other. You'll learn a lot about your partner's desires and perceptions of erotica . . . and get hot in the process.

It is important to remember that fantasies do not always mirror our real sexual desires. If you fantasize about bondage, rape or homosexual encounters, it does not necessarily mean you want these experiences in reality. In fact, it rarely does. Fantasy is a safe way to express alternative desires that you do not want to act on in real life. In a fantasy sexual life, you can pretend to have a personality you don't, desire things you don't normally find attractive, and imagine experimentations that you're not interested in trying in reality. The function of these taboo naughty thoughts is to cross lines, test limits and awaken excitement. The thrill of fantasizing about acts and people not known to you delivers surges of hormones that bring you closer to orgasm when you are by yourself, or with a steady partner.

People sometimes worry that their partner is fantasizing about someone else when they are making love together. A great majority do, but only a minority of the time. In most healthy relationships, some fantasizing about another person, or group sex, is normal and does not at all represent a desire to hunt for pleasure elsewhere. Fantasy is imagination, not reality, and brief, sporadic fantasies about being somewhere else, or with someone else, does not mean they would prefer that to being with you.

He-man fantasies

Generally, men fantasize twice as frequently as women. While both men and women fantasize during sex, men tend to fantasize more often in non-sexual situations. Male fantasies are typically dominated by visual images, especially explicit genital images. They often involve multiple anonymous partners, are more active and aggressive, and progress quickly to explicit sexual acts.

> *"I am always at the center of my fantasy, and I'm usually surrounded by a harem of women, who are dripping with excitement to fuck me. They all want me, they like to show themselves to me, dance in front*

His Fantasy Life

* Number of men who fantasize about their wives: 9 out of 10
* Number of men who fantasize about a friend's wife: 2 out of 3
* Number of men who fantasize about their secretary: 2 in 5

Source: *What the Odds Are*

---

of me, spread their legs and masturbate in front of me, go down on me. I'm powerful and being serviced." — Jeff, 27

🗣 *"One of my fantasies is being totally dominant over a woman. She struggles to be dominant, but I win and I fantasize about taking her from behind, alternating between fucking her up her arse and pussy. I'm an arse man, so I really dig that fantasy."* — Tony, 31

🗣 *"I've got the hots for my PA. I've got a fantasy where she comes into my office, kneels down in front of me behind my desk, zips down my pants, sucks me hard, then raises her skirt, she's got no panties, she takes my hand and rubs it over her wet cunt, then sits on me, with her back facing me, and fucks me hard, while I just sit back and enjoy it, from beginning to end. Then she pulls her skirt down, smiles at me, and leaves the office."* — Bill, 33

She-beast fantasies

Female fantasies tend to focus on personal partners and people women know, or desire, and typically emphasise touching, feeling and caressing as much as intercourse. Women (straight women) do fantasize about dicks, erections, dominance and explicit acts, but most female fantasies are also generally accompanied by a sensual component, and are heavy on desire and lust, and light on violence. Rape fantasies are not uncommon, but never mean a woman wants to be raped. Rape fantasies are more commonly about wanting to feel unbridled passion and lust, and to feel dominated and out of control.

Women's fantasies are visual, but when women write out their fantasies, they tend to use many more sensual adjectives, and spend more time setting the scene and concentrating on desire and foreplay, than men.

♟ *"My favorite sexual fantasy is where I'm totally ravished by a stranger. We meet in different contexts, depending on my particular fantasy, maybe a jazz bar, maybe a pub, and he just can't control himself around me. He leads me to a dark hallway and is irrepressible. His hands and tongue are all over me, he whispers how much he wants me, how his desire for me is out of control, and we do it standing up, in this dark hallway. Afterwards, I go back to my friends in the club, and he keeps staring after me, wanting me, but I no longer want him. I got what I wanted. I once told a friend about this fantasy and she called it my 'black widow' complex. I think it's really just getting a sexual rush from desire, attention and power."* — Maria, 25

♟ *"Romance is what does it for me. My sex life with my partner is rushed at best — we have three small kids, and don't get much time for sex, and when we do, foreplay is not something we spend a lot of time on. So when I fantasize, and I do regularly while breastfeeding, doing the washing up, whenever I have a few moments alone, my erotic thoughts wander to my husband having half an hour or an hour to spend caressing me, massaging me and kissing me*

all over. I miss that, and I don't get it any more in
my real life, so I create it in my imagination."
— Christine, 34

Her Fantasy Life

The woman entered the room, and with a knowing smile teasing her full lips, she sank into the comfort of the plush chair in the corner. The handsome stranger turned, having sensed her approach. Locking his steely grey eyes on hers, he moved slowly towards her, his experienced gaze measuring her, hypnotizing her with his soft murmurs of assurance.

He sank to his knees before her and without a word, smoothly released her from her constraining attire. With a sigh of surrender, she allowed his foreign hands to unleash her bare flesh. He expertly guided her through this tender, new territory, boldly taking her to heights she had never dared to dream of, his movements deliberate, confident in his ability to satisfy her every need.

Her senses swam. She was overcome with an aching desire that had gone unfulfilled for so long. And, just as it seemed that ecstasy was within her grasp, he paused, and for one heart-stopping moment, she thought, "It's too big — it will never fit!" Then, with a sudden rush, it slid into place as if it had been made only for her.

As pleasure and contentment washed over her, she met his steady gaze, tears of gratitude shining in her eyes. And he knew it wouldn't be long before she returned. Oh, yes, this woman would want more. She would want to do it again and again and again ...

DON'T YOU JUST LOVE SHOPPING FOR SHOES?

Source: The Internet (popular email forward)

Sexy Dreams

Dream experts say that our feelings about our sexuality and sex lives are often reflected in our dreams. Specific dreams should be interpreted individually, but there are some common themes and symbols that can represent sex in our dreams.

Dreaming about sensual animals does not mean you have a deep desire to experiment with bestiality. Animals are a common reflection of our sexuality and sexual feelings in our dreams.

Top animal representations of sex in our dreams:

1. Cats.
2. Birds.
3. Horses.
4. Tigers.
5. Snakes.

Having a sensual, sexy dream in a particular setting is not only erotic (or nightmarish), but can represent hidden desires, erotic feelings, or reflect ways our sexuality feels unexpressed, trapped or unfulfilled.

Top landscape symbolisms of sex in our dreams:

1. Deserts.
2. Oceans.
3. Forests.

Out-and-out erotic dreams and nightmares can feature specific people, both familiar and strange, sensations of flying or sinking, and feelings of euphoria, calm, guilt, shame, confusion and anger. Dreams of eating, feeding another and group feasting also commonly have sexual interpretations. Dreaming of sexual intercourse or sexual play can be sexual release in your sleeping mind for your waking mind, or can have a specific interpretive meaning for you. If you regularly have sexy dreams that you can't work out the meanings of, seek out a dream interpreter, or consult a dream book. See the Carnal Knowledge chapter for recommendations for further reading.

"Afterglow"

I've broken the rules.

I've kissed and told.

I've peeped, lusted, loved, researched, questioned, interviewed, investigated, chatted, listened ... and told.

I've asked people from around the world about their desires, fantasies, best bonks, worst roots, online affairs, masturbation habits and favorite positions. I've spoken to sex workers, porn stars, virgins and celibates to get the lowdown and inside track. For a year, everywhere I went and with everyone I met, the topic of sex always came up, and I've put everything I've seen and heard in this book. Well, almost everything.

Urge is a reflection of our collective sexual urges. It reveals we are a diverse bunch: at once naughty and nice, sacred and sordid, deep and dark, moral and immoral, colorful and creative, prudish and passionate, fickle and fun, expressive and experimental, kittenish and kinky, lustful and loving.

Urge. Now you've read it, it's time to explore it, savor it, discover it, indulge it and satisfy it.

Carnal Knowledge

[*hot bedside reading and sexy net surfing*]

Recommended Bedside Reading

Most of the books listed below provided reference material for chapters in this book, and are recommended for further, more in-depth information on given topics. The bibliography provides the full publication details.

Shagging, show me how

The Illustrated Manual of Sex Therapy, 2nd edition, Helen Singer Kaplan

For Women Only, Jennifer Berman and Laura Berman

The New Our Bodies, Ourselves, Boston Women's Health Book Collective

Sex in the Time of Generation X, Gabrielle Morrissey

The New Joy of Sex, Alex Comfort

Sexual Healing, edited by Megan Gressor

The Magic of Sex, Miriam Stoppard

Sex Watching: Looking into the World of Sexual Behaviour, Milton Diamond

Titillating trivia and interesting intercourse information

Sexualia: From Prehistory to Cyberspace, Clifford Bishop and Xenia Osthelder

The Illustrated Book of Sexual Records, GL Simons

The Sex Chronicles: Strange-But-True Tales From Around the World, Lance Rancier

The Big Book of Filth, Jonathon Green

Sex Herbs, Beth Ann Petro Roybal and Gayle Skowronski

Dreams and Sexuality: Interpreting Your Sexual Dreams, Pam Spurr

Female fantasies

Women on Top, Nancy Friday

My Secret Garden, Nancy Friday

Cosmopolitan: In Your Wildest Dreams: Hot Sex Fantasies for Women by Women, Lisa Sussman

Deep Down: New Sensual Writing for Women, Laura Chester

Cosmic and spiritual sexuality

Sex and Spirit, Clifford Bishop

The Art of Sexual Ecstasy, Margo Anand

Sexual Secrets, Nik Douglas and Penny Slinger

Sexy Surfing

The sites recommended below are mainly general sexual health sites. For specific topics, keyword searches with *www.google.com* tend to be the best for less porn, more information. For specific sexual health information, do a keyword search for "family planning."

Sexuality.org

Goaskalice.com

Tantra.com

Safersex.org

Oxygen.com

Safesense.com

About.com

Sexbuzz.com

Sxetc.org

Sexualhealth.com

Bibliography

Anand, M. 1989, *The Art of Sexual Ecstasy: the path of sacred sexuality for western lovers*, J. P. Tarcher, Los Angeles.

Bechtel, S. 1993, *Practical Encyclopedia of Sex and Health*, Simon & Schuster, New York.

Berman, J. & Berman, L. 2001, *For Women Only: A Revolutionary Guide to Reclaiming Your Sex Life*, Virago Press, London.

Bishop, C. & Osthelder, X. (eds.) 2001, *Sexualia: From Prehistory to Cyberspace*, Könemann, Cologne.

Bishop, C. 2000, *Sex and Spirit: Ecstasy, Ritual and Taboo*, Duncan Baird Publishers, London.

Bullmore, A. 2001, *Cybersex: The Secret World of Internet Sex*, Carlton Books, London.

Boston Women's Health Book Collective, 1992, *The New Our Bodies, Ourselves*, Simon & Schuster, New York.

Chester, L. (ed.) 1988, *Deep Down: New Sensual Writing by Women*, Faber & Faber, London.

Comfort, A. 1994, *The New Joy of Sex: A Gourmet Guide to Lovemaking in the Nineties*, Crown Publishers, New York.

Crooks, R. & Baur, K. 2002, *Our Sexuality*, 8th edn., Wadsworth-Thomson Learning, Pacific Grove, California.

Diamond, M. 1992, *Sex Watching: Looking Into the World of Sexual Behaviour*, Prion, London.

Douglas, N. & Slinger, P. 2000, *Sexual Secrets: the Alchemy of Ecstasy*, Destiny Books, Vermont.

Friday, N. (ed.) 1999, *My Secret Garden: Women's Sexual Fantasies*, Quartet, London.

Friday, N. 1991, *Women on Top: How Real Life Has Changed Women's Sexual Fantasies*, Simon & Schuster, New York.

Goldenson, R. & Anderson, K. 1994, *The Wordsworth Dictionary of Sex*, Wordsworth Editions Ltd., Hertfordshire.

Green, J. 1999, *The Big Book of Filth*, Cassell, London.

Gressor, M. (ed.) 1997, *Sexual Healing*, Gore & Osment, Sydney.

Hatcher, R. A. & Trussell, J. 1998, *Contraceptive Technology*, 17th edn., Irvington Publishers Inc., New York.

Juan, S. 2001, *The Odd Sex: Mysteries of Our Weird and Wonderful Sex Lives Explained*, HarperCollins, Sydney.

Kaplan, H. S. 1987, *The Illustrated Manual of Sex Therapy*, 2nd edn., Brunner/Mazel, New York.

Mackay, J. 2000, *The Penguin Atlas of Human Sexual Behavior*, Penguin Reference, New York.

Morrissey, G. 1996, *Sex in the Time of Generation X*, Pan Macmillan, Sydney.

Nyström, A. 1906, *The Natural Laws of Sexual Life*, The Burton Company, Minnesota.

Rancier, L. 1997, *The Sex Chronicles: Strange-But-True Tales from Around the World*, General Publishing Group Inc., California.

Roybal, B. A. P. & Skowronski, G. 2000, *Sex Herbs: Nature's Sexual Enhancers for Men and Women*, Fusion, London.

Sex Life Survey, 20 October 2001, *The Courier-Mail*.

Sex Life Survey, 6 October 2001, *The Courier-Mail*.

Simons, G. L. 1984, *The Illustrated Book of Sexual Records*, Bell Publishing Company, New York.

Spurr, P. 2001, *Dreams and Sexuality: Interpreting Your Sexual Dreams*, Sterling Publishing Co Inc., London.

Stopes, M. C. 1926, *Sex and the Young*, Gill Publishing Co., London.

Stoppard, M. 1991, *The Magic of Sex*, Dorling Kindersley, London.

Sussman, L. 2001, *Cosmopolitan: In Your Wildest Dreams: Hot Sex Fantasies for Women by Women*, HarperCollins, London.

Sussman, L. 2000, *Cosmopolitan: Over 100 Truly Astonishing Sex Tips*, Carlton Books, London

Index

fisting 351
  male 8–9, 12
  masturbating 80, 88
  oral sex 118–119
aphrodisiacs 293–300
  foods 293–295, 301
  herbs *see* herbs, aphrodisiac
  history 293–294
  spices 294
  vitamins 300
  yohimbine 296
audio tape, dirty talk 428
auditioning for porn films 269–273

B

B&D *see* bondage and discipline
babies, effect on sex drive 128–129
basal body temperature contraceptive
  method 55
bath 83, 309
  for two 309
  masturbating in 83
benzodiazepine *see* Rohypnol
bike riding, effect on erection 201
blood pressure, effect on erection
  197–198
blueballs 8
body 1–32, 310, 392
  altering 13–14, 16–17, 26–32
  decorating 310
  female 17–32
  male 1–17
  worship 392
bondage and discipline (B&D) 239,
  344–347
  online 239
books 447–448
"box of delights" 311

breasts 30–32
  enlargement or reduction 31–32
broken penis 6
brothels 275–277
Buddhism 395–396
bulbs of clitoris 21
burlesque shows 281
butterfly vibrator 85
butyl nitrate 377

C

calendar contraceptive method 55
call girls 281
can-can shows 281
candles, sexual play with 310
castratos 312
casual sex 213–233
  at own house 231
  at partner's house 232–233
  compatibility 228–229
  "dressing to pull" 223–224
  females 219–222
  incompatibility 225–227
  males 216–219
  morning after 230–233
  pick-up techniques 213–214
  "post-mortem" 231–233
  score card 218–219
  statistics 215
  "walk of shame" 230–231
CAT *see* coital alignment technique
celibacy 58–59, 136–137, 405–422
  alternatives to intercourse
   406–410
  benefits 410–413
  chastity belt 418–422
  newfound 413–418
  reluctant 415–418

E

ears, tickling and licking 428
ecstasy (drug) 367–370
ejaculation 8–12, 88–90
    average volume 10–11
    female 88–90
    premature *see* premature
    ejaculation
email 258–259
emergency contraception 50
emoticons 243–244
enlargement 16–17, 29–32
    breasts 31–32
    clitoris 29–30
    penis 16–17
erectile problems 195–212
    alcohol, caused by 200
    alternatives to erection 211–212
    artery problems, caused by 209
    bike riding, caused by 201
    diabetes, caused by 199
    diseases, caused by 199
    hard vs. soft erection 196–197
    heart problems, caused by 198
    high blood pressure, caused by
    197–198
    hormone replacement therapy
    (HRT), treating with 211
    implants, treating with 209–210
    injection, treating with 207–208
    medical practitioner, visiting
    201–202
    medication, caused by 199
    old age, caused by 200
    poor fitness, caused by 197–198
    priapism 6, 22
    relationship problems, caused
    by 200
    smoking, caused by 198–199

    stress, caused by 201
    therapist, visiting 201–202
    vacuum devices, treating with
    210–211
    yohimbine, treating with 207
erectile tissue 21–22
    clitoris, of 21–22
erection 1–2, 5–6, 22, 211–212
    alternatives to 211–212
    clitoris, of 22
    constant *see* priapism
    penis, of 1–2, 5–6
    problems with see erectile problems
erogenous zones 1–32
    female 17–32
    male 1–17
escorts 279–281
    call girls 281
    gigolos 279–280
essential oils 305
etiquette 116, 239–241, 336–338
    Internet chat rooms, in 239–241
    post-coital 336–338
    sixty-nine, during 116
exhibitionism 356–357
experimentation 327–328, 339–359
    addiction to 357–359
    alfresco sex 353
    bondage and discipline
    (B&D) 344–347
    exhibitionism 356–357
    fetishes 351–353
    fisting 351
    masochism 341–342
    ménage à trois 349–350
    peep show 355–356
    sadism 340–341
    sadomasochism (S&M) 341–344
    swinging 347–348

riding technique 87–88
shower head, using 77–78, 83
spa, in 84
therapy, as 92
tickling technique 87
training to orgasm 174–179
vagina, substitutes for 78–80
vibrator, with *see* vibrator
webbing technique 75
medication 133–134, 199, 201–202
erectile problems, for 201–202
erection, effect on 199
low sex drive, for 133–134
meditation, masturbation as 91–92
ménage à trois 349–350
menopause 25
menstruation, oral sex during 117
methcathinone *see* speed
mini-pill, contraceptive 49
missionary position 319–320
modification of body parts *see*
alteration
mons veneris 19, 26, 29
liposuction 29
morning-after pill 50
Moulin Rouge 281
multiple orgasms 37, 185–194
female 185–190
male 190–194
maximizing 187–190
rolling orgasms 186–189
streaming orgasms 186, 188
muscles, vaginal 18, 21
music 312–314
mutual masturbation 177–179,
350–351
mystical sex *see* Tantric sex; Taoism;
Tibetan Buddhism; witchcraft

N

naked vs. dressed intercourse 330
natural contraceptive methods 55–56
Net *see* Internet
nipples 13, 30–31
female 30–31
male 13
nitrates 377
nocturnal orgasm 90–91
non-latex condoms 41
non-penetrative sex 406–409

O

occult see witchcraft
oetang piercing 13
old age, effect on erection 200
one-night stand see casual sex
online sex *see* Internet
opiates 373–374
oral sex 93–119
anus 118–119
cunnilingus see cunnilingus
fellatio see fellatio
menstruation, during 117
positions 114–115
safety tips 117
sixty-nine 115–116
talking 112–113
who goes first 112
orgasm 32–37, 90–91, 100–102,
169–194, 389–390
after intercourse 184–185
before intercourse 181
cunnilingus, during 100–102
during intercourse 181–185
faking 35–37
full-body 389–390
multiple *see* multiple orgasms

vocabulary 241–249, 434
    Internet 241–249
    politically correct 434
voyeurism 251–252, 355–356
    online 251–252
vulva 18–19, 22, 25, 27
    piercing 27

W

waxing pubic hair 26
websites on sexual health 448–449
wet dreams 90

widening penis 16–17
witchcraft 396–398
World Wide Web see Internet
worshipping the body 392

X

X-rated porn 263–264

Y

yohimbine 207, 296